IT SEEMS TO ME

It Seems to Me

1925-1935

BY HEYWOOD BROUN

HARCOURT, BRACE AND COMPANY

NEW YORK

PRINTED IN THE UNITED STATES OF AMERICA
BY QUINN & BODEN COMPANY, INC., RAHWAY, N. J.
Typography by Robert Josephy

AUTHOR'S NOTE: The pieces in this book are drawn almost entirely from newspaper columns—chiefly from *The New York World-Telegram*. They were written for quick release and a short life. No attempt has been made to revise and polish. At least two are included largely for sentimental reasons. The article entitled "The Piece That Got Me Fired" was written for *The Nation* and led to my dismissal from *The World*. "A Union of Reporters," from *The World-Telegram* of August 7, 1933, was put in the book solely because it had some effect in promoting the organization of the American Newspaper Guild, although the movement was already under way in Cleveland. I wish to thank Alexander Crosby for the work he did in looking over old scrapbooks and picking out the best he could find. The selection as it stands is largely his work. And I would like to dedicate this book, "It Seems to Me," to the Guild, which in my ripe old age enabled me to feel once again that I was really a newspaper man and not merely a columnist.

HEYWOOD BROUN

CONTENTS

from THE WORLD

SACCO AND VANZETTI   AUGUST 5, 1927   3

A CONTROVERSY   AUGUST 17, 1927   7

A SPRING SUNDAY   FEBRUARY 24, 1925   13

MARRY IN HASTE   MARCH 13, 1925   15

"WIFE OF LOT"   JUNE 5, 1925   18

BRYAN'S LAST SPEECH   AUGUST 10, 1925   21

THE WHIMMING RING   OCTOBER 7, 1925   24

A CHESTNUT TREE   JUNE 10, 1926   28

TO RESTORE ORDER   SEPTEMBER 18, 1926   32

THE MIRACLE OF DEBS   OCTOBER 23, 1926   35

MARIE OF RUMANIA   NOVEMBER 5, 1926   39

MY FIRST NUDE   NOVEMBER 29, 1926   43

A SERMON FROM SAMUEL   JANUARY 25, 1927   46

WOOING BY WIRE   FEBRUARY 8, 1927   50

EDISON'S BIRTHDAY   FEBRUARY 15, 1927   54

BETTER A MILLSTONE   MARCH 22, 1927   58

THEY BURIED THE BEARDED LADY   60

OLD CAPTAIN MIDGETT   JANUARY 27, 1928   63

WHIMS   FEBRUARY 6, 1928   67

vii

Contents

from THE NATION

THE SPORTS BAY   MARCH 14, 1928   71

THE PIECE THAT GOT ME FIRED   MAY 4, 1928   75

from THE TELEGRAM

GANDLE THE OBSCURE   FEBRUARY 19, 1929   79

CANON SHOCKS COLUMNIST   MAY 8, 1929   82

MARION THE CAT   JULY 26, 1929   86

A SHEPHERD   DECEMBER 23, 1929   89

"OH, EUCLID!"   JANUARY 10, 1930   92

LIFE AND LOWELL   JANUARY 27, 1930   95

IN THE IMAGE OF GOD   MARCH 3, 1930   98

BILL BOLITHO   JUNE 5, 1930   101

A REPLY TO MY BOSS   AUGUST 19, 1930   105

HEYWOOD COX BROUN   AUGUST 30, 1930   109

THE MAGICAL CITY   OCTOBER 31, 1930   112

"TREES," "IF," AND "INVICTUS"   DECEMBER 1, 1930   116

GABRIEL   DECEMBER 12, 1930   119

A CERTAIN CITY EDITOR   DECEMBER 15, 1930   122

from THE WORLD-TELEGRAM

THE WORLD PASSES   FEBRUARY 28, 1931   126

MORE OR LESS   MARCH 6, 1931   130

Contents

DOWN AMONG THE ANTS   MAY 2, 1931   133

THE AGITATOR   MAY 5, 1931   136

TWO-GUN CROWLEY   MAY 9, 1931   139

WALKING AROUND A GRAVE   JUNE 18, 1931   142

ACTS OF GOD   JULY 15, 1931   146

MURDER IN THE FIRST DEGREE   DECEMBER 9, 1931   148

WILLIAM NUCKLES DOAK   DECEMBER 29, 1931   152

WE THE TINDER   JANUARY 23, 1932   155

GOVERNOR ROLPH SPEAKING   APRIL 23, 1932   157

HE HAD IT ONCE   APRIL 27, 1932   161

AL'S HOUR   JULY 1, 1932   164

A PROFESSIONAL STAMPEDER   JULY 2, 1932   167

BOO!   JULY 5, 1932   170

FRAU ZETKIN   SEPTEMBER 1, 1932   173

DEAR COMRADE   NOVEMBER 11, 1932   176

APES AND ELMS   NOVEMBER 22, 1932   179

"THE CHOPINZEE"   JANUARY 10, 1933   182

BRING ON THE ARTIST   JANUARY 19, 1933   185

WHERE MINK MEETS MINK   JANUARY 27, 1933   188

THEY WILL COME BACK   FEBRUARY 27, 1933   191

THE TALE OF AN ANCIENT WRONG   APRIL 10, 1933   193

THE BURNING OF THE BOOKS   MAY 12, 1933   196

Contents

A HOUSING PROBLEM   MAY 13, 1933   198

"THE WORST IS OVER"   JUNE 8, 1933   201

AN UNDELIVERED ADDRESS   JUNE 20, 1933   204

BACK TO BELLAMY   JULY 19, 1933   207

A UNION OF REPORTERS   AUGUST 7, 1933   210

THE ARTS OF INACTIVITY   AUGUST 24, 1933   213

"I WAS NEVER MORE SERIOUS IN MY LIFE"
AUGUST 29, 1933   216

NOT BLOWN IN THE BOTTLE   SEPTEMBER 9, 1933   219

"ANY ONE AT ALL"   SEPTEMBER 11, 1933   222

TEX AND THE COOLIDGE GOLD RUSH
NOVEMBER 8, 1933   225

THE FUNERAL OF TEXAS GUINAN   NOVEMBER 13, 1933   228

A ROOM WITH A VIEW   NOVEMBER 27, 1933   231

"A FINE LESSON FOR THE WHOLE NATION"
NOVEMBER 28, 1933   234

TEMPERATURE 110   DECEMBER 5, 1933   237

PAPER WORK   JANUARY 10, 1934   240

THE TRIBUNE'S GOBLIN EDITOR   JANUARY 15, 1934   243

EMMA'S HOMECOMING   JANUARY 18, 1934   246

NOT A SURE SHOT   JANUARY 19, 1934   249

THE FIRST ROBIN   FEBRUARY 13, 1934   252

CARTER'S CRACKS UP   MARCH 10, 1934   254

THE LINDBERGH EPIC   MARCH 23, 1934   258

Contents

PASSION IN THE ANDES   APRIL 9, 1934   261

THE GRAND OLD GAL OF THE NORTH ATLANTIC
APRIL 10, 1934   265

CHUMMY CHARLIE   APRIL 28, 1934   269

AROUND THE WORLD IN FIFTY MINUTES
JUNE 5, 1934   272

THE STRIKE-BREAKER   JULY 9, 1934   275

MR. HEARST AND MR. LIPPMANN   JULY 17, 1934   278

HORSES WITH THEIR HAIR DOWN   AUGUST 6, 1934   282

I INTERVIEW A COLUMNIST   AUGUST 11, 1934   285

A MAN I LIKED   AUGUST 16, 1934   288

ALL IN A SPIRIT OF FUN   AUGUST 31, 1934   291

STAYED ON TOO LONG   SEPTEMBER 27, 1934   294

NATURE THE COPYCAT   OCTOBER 5, 1934   297

THE FIRST TRAVELER OF THE LAND
NOVEMBER 14, 1934   299

"THE WRECK OF THE *HESPERUS*"   DECEMBER 7, 1934   302

HOME GIRL MAKES GOOD   DECEMBER 13, 1934   305

THERE ISN'T ANY SANTA CLAUS   DECEMBER 15, 1934   308

ICE AND EAGLES   JANUARY 29, 1935   311

THE MAN WHO CAME BACK   FEBRUARY 12, 1935   313

A RIDE WITH ROOSEVELT   FEBRUARY 18, 1935   316

CHARLES EVANS HUGHES AS PORTIA
FEBRUARY 20, 1935   318

Contents

THE DEATH OF A HAITIAN   FEBRUARY 21, 1935   321

CHARLES A. BEARD   FEBRUARY 26, 1935   324

MR. JUSTICE HOLMES   MARCH 7, 1935   326

NEW LAMPS FOR OLD   MARCH 20, 1935   329

HARVARD INDIFFERENCE   APRIL 15, 1935   333

IT SEEMS TO ME

SACCO AND VANZETTI

When at last Judge Thayer in a tiny voice passed sentence upon Sacco and Vanzetti, a woman in the court room said with terror: "It is death condemning life!"

The men in Charlestown Prison are shining spirits, and Vanzetti has spoken with an eloquence not known elsewhere within our time. They are too bright, we shield our eyes and kill them. We are the dead, and in us there is not feeling nor imagination nor the terrible torment of lust for justice. And in the city where we sleep smug gardeners walk to keep the grass above our little houses sleek and cut whatever blade thrusts up a head above its fellows.

"The decision is unbelievably brutal," said the chairman of the Defense Committee, and he was wrong. The thing is worthy to be believed. It has happened. It will happen again, and the shame is wider than that which must rest upon Massachusetts. I have never believed that the trial of Sacco and Vanzetti was one set apart from many by reason of the passion and prejudice which encrusted all the benches. Scratch through the varnish of any judgment seat and what will you strike but hate thick-clotted from centuries of angry verdicts? Did any man ever find power within his hand except to use it as a whip?

Governor Alvan T. Fuller never had any intention in all his investigation but to put a new and higher polish upon the proceedings. The justice of the business was not his concern. He hoped to make it respectable. He called old men from high places to stand behind his chair so that he might seem to speak with all the authority of a high priest or a Pilate.

What more can these immigrants from Italy expect? It is not every prisoner who has a president of Harvard University throw on the switch for him. And Robert Grant is not only a former judge but one of the most popular dinner guests in Boston. If this is a lynching, at least the fish peddler and his friend the factory hand may take unction to their souls that they will die at the hands of men in dinner coats or academic gowns, according to the conventionalities required by the hour of execution.

Already too much has been made of the personality of Webster Thayer. To sympathizers of Sacco and Vanzetti he has seemed a man with a cloven hoof. But in no usual sense of the term is this man a villain. Although probably not a great jurist, he is without doubt as capable and conscientious as the average Massachusetts judge, and if that's enough to warm him in wet weather by all means let him stick the compliment against his ribs.

Webster Thayer has a thousand friends. He has courage, sincerity and convictions. Judge Thayer is a good man, and when he says that he made every effort to give a fair trial to the anarchists brought before him, undoubtedly he thinks it and he means it. Quite often I've heard the remark: "I wonder how that man sleeps at night?" On this point I have no first hand information, but I venture to guess that he is no more beset with uneasy dreams than most of us. He saw his duty and he thinks he did it.

And Governor Fuller, also, is not in any accepted sense of the word a miscreant. Before becoming Governor he manufactured bicycles. Nobody was cheated by his com-

4

pany. He loves his family and pays his debts. Very much he desires to be Governor again, and there is an excellent chance that this ambition will be gratified. Other governors of Massachusetts have gone far, and it is not fantastic to assume that some day he might be President. His is not a master mind, but he is a solid and substantial American, chiming in heartily with all our national ideals and aspirations.

To me the tragedy of the conviction of Sacco and Vanzetti lies in the fact that this was not a deed done by crooks and knaves. In that case we would have a campaign with the slogan "Turn the rascals out," and set up for a year or two a reform administration. Nor have I had much patience with any who would like to punish Thayer by impeachment or any other process. Unfrock him and his judicial robes would fall upon a pair of shoulders not different by the thickness of a fingernail. Men like Holmes and Brandeis do not grow on bushes. Popular government, as far as the eye can see, is always going to be administered by the Thayers and Fullers.

It has been said that the question at issue was not the guilt or innocence of Sacco and Vanzetti but whether or not they received a fair trial. I will admit that this commands my interest to some extent, but still I think it is a minor phase in the whole matter. From a Utopian point of view the trial was far from fair, but it was not more biased than a thousand which take place in this country every year. It has been pointed out that the public prosecutor neglected to call certain witnesses because their testimony would not have been favorable to his case. Are there five district attorneys, is there one, in the whole country who would do otherwise?

5

Again Professor Frankfurter has most clearly shown that the prosecution asked a trick question in regard to the pistol and made the expert seem to testify far more concretely than he was willing to commit himself. That was very wrong, but not unique. Our judicial processes are so arranged that it is to the interest of district attorneys to secure convictions rather than to ascertain justice, and if it would profit his case, there is not one who would not stoop to confuse the issue in the minds of the jurymen.

Eleven of the twelve who convicted Sacco and Vanzetti are still alive, and Governor Fuller talked to them. He reports somewhat naïvely that they all told him that they considered the trial fair. Did he expect them to report, "Why, no, Governor, we brought in a verdict of guilty just out of general depravity"?

By now there has been a long and careful sifting of the evidence in the case. It is ridiculous to say that Sacco and Vanzetti are being railroaded to the chair. The situation is much worse than that. This is a thing done cold-bloodedly and with deliberation. But care and deliberation do not guarantee justice. Even if every venerable college president in the country tottered forward to say "guilty" they could not alter facts. The tragedy of it all lies in the fact that though a Southern mountain man may move more quickly to a dirty deed of violence, his feet are set no more firmly in the path of prejudice than a Lowell ambling sedately to a hanging.

I said of Calvin Coolidge that I admired his use of "I do not choose," but he was dealing with a problem wholly personal, and had every right to withhold his reasons. For Governor Fuller I can't say the same. These are the lives of others with which he is dealing. In his fairly long statement he answers not a single point which has been made against the justice of the conviction. The deliberations of himself and his associates were secret, and seemingly it is his intention that they shall remain secret. A gentleman does not investigate and tell.

I've said these men have slept, but from now on it is our business to make them toss and turn a little, for a cry should go up from many million voices before the day set for Sacco and Vanzetti to die. We have a right to beat against tight minds with our fists and shout a word into the ears of the old men. We want to know, we will know—"Why?"

A CONTROVERSY

The World of August 12, 1927, printed the following note:

REGARDING MR. BROUN

The World has always believed in allowing the fullest possible expression of individual opinion to those of its special writers who write under their own names. Straining its interpretation of this privilege, *The World* allowed Mr. Heywood Broun to write two articles on the Sacco-Vanzetti case, in which he expressed his personal opinion with the utmost extravagance.

The World then instructed him, now that he had made his own position clear, to select other subjects for his next articles. Mr. Broun, however, continued to write on the Sacco-Vanzetti case. *The World*, thereupon, exercising its right of final decision as to what it will publish in its columns, has omitted all articles submitted by Mr. Broun.

RALPH PULITZER,
Editor, *The World*.

Mr. Ralph Pulitzer,
The World,
Pulitzer Building,
New York, N. Y.

Dear Sir:

I am inclosing herewith the statement as to my position concerning our differences over the material submitted by me for the column heretofore conducted under my name.

I would greatly appreciate your printing my inclosed statement in this column under its former caption, and, in the event that you feel that you might be waiving any legal rights which you may have by accepting this as material from me, I hereby waive any rights which may so accrue to me, it merely being my intention, should you use this material in your column, that I, of course, shall not be entitled to compensation therefor, but that you would be extending me the courtesy of giving me the same publicity which you received concerning the cause of my failure to appear as special writer in *The World*.

Should you be disinclined to print my statement in the column, I have no objections to it appearing as a communication addressed to your paper, together with the other communications which appear on the editorial page.

I assume, of course, that if any comments or corrections are made you will submit the same to me prior to printing them. I am giving no publicity to this statement at the present time but have no objection to your giving this to the other papers if you see fit.

Yours very truly,

HEYWOOD BROUN

Naturally I was interested in the column which Ralph Pulitzer wrote and which appeared in my old shop window. I was grateful to him for writing it. This seemed to me a fair and frank statement of the issue. But upon one or two points I would like the privilege of stating my own attitude. "*The World*," wrote Mr. Pulitzer, "then instructed him, now that he had made his own position clear, to select other subjects for his next articles."

My recollection is that no official notice was issued. An executive of the paper remarked rather casually that it might be better for me not to write any more about Sacco and Vanzetti. The point is not important. Even though my instructions had been definite I would still have been unable at that time to write on anything but this case. Mr. Pulitzer unintentionally does me an injustice when he suggests that I should have been satisfied to make my own position clear and then keep silent. I felt and I feel passionately about the issue. The men were not yet dead. I was not simply trying to keep my own record straight. That's not good enough.

"When Pilate saw that he could prevail nothing, but that rather a tumult was made, he took water, and washed his hands before the multitude, saying, I am innocent of the blood of this just person: see ye to it."

The judgment of the world has been that Pilate did not do enough. There is no vigor in expressing an opinion and then washing your hands.

And after all Pilate was only a sort of Governor and I'm

9

a newspaperman. *The World* would not be satisfied to declare itself upon some monstrous injustice and then depart saying, "See ye to it." If Mr. Pulitzer believes that I have any respect for the traditions of his paper, how could he expect me to behave like that?

I do respect the traditions of *The World*. It has carried on fine fights and will continue to do so. That it is in every respect superbly a liberal newspaper I cannot say. Still, it more nearly approaches this ideal than any other New York daily in its field.

The curious part about the commotion lies in the fact that fundamentally *The World* and I were on the same side. The responsible heads of the paper were disturbed, I think, not so much at my opinion as at my manners and my methods of controversy.

Mr. Pulitzer has said that I expressed my personal opinion "with the utmost extravagance." I spoke only to the limit of my belief and passion. This may be extravagance, but I see no wisdom in saving up indignation for a rainy day. It was already raining. Besides, fighters who pull their punches lose their fights.

Once there was a pitcher on the Giants who was sued for breach of promise, and fortunately this suit resulted in his love-letters being made public. The memory of one of these, I have always treasured. He wrote, "Sweetheart, they knocked me out of the box in the third inning, but it wasn't my fault. The day was cold and I couldn't sweat. Unless I can sweat I can't pitch."

I realize that I have been a special writer who sometimes embarrassed his newspaper. However, I wish to correct the impression that in the Sacco-Vanzetti case I went completely roaring mad after twice being generously afforded the privilege of vehement expression. I am sorry to say that the two subsequent columns which *The World* refused contained no fiery phrases. Although I would like it very much, I have been around long enough to realize that no columnist can possibly be accorded the right to say whatever comes into his mind. There is libel, there is obscenity, there is blasphemy; and there are policies and philosophies which his paper happens to hold especially dear. I do not anticipate that *The World* or any other newspaper would give me license to scoff at every campaign to which it committed itself. And I have not. Of course, I have always contended that in "It Seems to Me" I expressed my own opinions and did not commit the paper. This, to be sure, would not be true in the case of libel, but that has already been referred to and I did not ever involve *The World* in any suit. Ralph Pulitzer said that *The World* has always believed in "allowing the fullest possible expression of individual opinion to those of its special writers who write under their own names." And yet he also says that I was ordered not to write about the Sacco-Vanzetti case at all after I had twice gone on record. In other words, in this case the paper was prepared to censor what I might have to say even before it had been written. How full is the fullest?

There is no use in my pretending that I do not believe myself right and *The World* wrong in the present controversy. As far as Sacco and Vanzetti went, both the paper and the individual wanted an amelioration of the sentence. Nothing less than a pardon or a new trial was satisfactory to me. Apparently, *The World* believed that if life imprisonment was all that could possibly be won from Governor Fuller, that would be better than nothing. Here an interesting point in tactics arises. The editorial strategy of *The*

A Controversy

World seemingly rested upon the theory that in a desperate cause it is well to ask a little less than you hope to get. I think you should ask more.

Rigorously *The World* excluded from its editorial columns all invectives. To call names, *The World* felt, would merely stiffen the resistance of Fuller and his advisers. I did call names, and this might possibly have embarrassed *The World* in the precise sort of campaign which it deemed it wise to make. Again, *The World* undoubtedly felt anxious about the bomb outrages. With passions so high, sparks were undoubtedly to be avoided. But in spite of silly crimes of violence I felt and feel that the most tragic factor of the Sacco-Vanzetti case is the general apathy. In ten minutes' time I will guarantee to fetch from the streets of New York one hundred persons who have never heard of the case and thousands who have not the slightest idea what it is all about. This could have been a duet with the editorial page carrying the air in sweet and tenor tones while in my compartment bass rumblings were added.

By now, I am willing to admit that I am too violent, too ill-disciplined, too indiscreet to fit pleasantly into *The World's* philosophy of daily journalism. And since I cannot hit it off with *The World* I would be wise to look for work more alluring. I am still a member of Actors' Equity, the top floor is well stocked with early Brouns and I know a card-trick. In farewell to the paper I can only say that in its relations to me it was fair, generous and gallant. But that doesn't go for the Sacco-Vanzetti case.

A SPRING SUNDAY

It felt like a spring Sunday, and it looked it. Besides, the girl and the young man in the taxi just ahead were kissing. That's quite in accord with the tradition of spring—and of Sunday.

But there was a distinctive quality. As far as I could tell from the back of her head, she kissed blithely. There was gayety in the blonde bob which crinkled in the sunlight. That was the distinction. Very few people can be ardent and at the same time merry. It is a rare heroine who can say to the suitor who assails her with somber endearment, "When you call me that, smile!"

And, after all, the ability to make love frivolously is the chief characteristic which distinguishes human beings from the beasts. Nature made the animals fierce and single-minded about such things. Perhaps the same intention was decreed for us, which makes it all the more fun to dissent and digress. To me the familiar adage, "You can't cheat nature," has always been provocative of rebellion. Perhaps you can't, but anyhow it is possible to try.

And so, in addition to derision and disapproval, there was something of envy in the attitude of all those who watched the taxicab pass by. The girl and young man seemed indifferent or unaware of the commotion which they created. Quite possibly they never realized how impellingly they were thrust into the public gaze by the giddy overhead lighting of a noonday sun. At any rate, they continued to kiss.

I watched no more. I wanted to see the front of the back of that head. When my taxicab swept by I turned, and they saw me turning. The young man blushed, straightened up and scowled. But she grinned. It was a face for which I had hoped. The gayety, inherent in the swing of her head, did go all the way round.

It was a pleasant grin and the mockery of it contained practically no malice. It was a "So is your old man" sort of look. "And what are you doing with this excellent afternoon?" seemed to be her challenge.

I regret to admit that I was wholly alone in my taxicab, and that it wasn't by any means a singular coincidence. I was on my way to lunch with Aunt Caroline. It was an invitation of a week's standing. Of course, it would have been entirely reasonable for me to have accepted with the distinct proviso, "Unless there is some sudden accession of spring." And I'm not at all sure Aunt Caroline would have understood that.

So I did go to Aunt Caroline's and had lunch and discussed immoral plays, concerning which she feels very strongly. But throughout the debate I continued to think of the girl in the taxi. There was never any more than that one glance. I respected the young man's embarrassment sufficiently to turn my head front almost immediately. He was under scrutiny hardly more than ten seconds. And yet I am entirely certain he's not the young man for her. A philosophic gulf is fixed between them and she's far too good for him.

Fred (I think that would be the name) likes fun as well as the next one. On any bright afternoon he can be depended upon to crook his arm and bend his head, but within his heart he carries an invisible censor. There remains about him the buried conviction that it is wrong to kiss a girl in a taxicab. A sense of sin tempers his cheerfulness. One touch of public opinion will split all his purposes in two.

Mind you, I had not shouted, "Hey, cut that out!" or expressed any articulate disapproval. I had done no more than look at him, but that was enough. Possibly he misinterpreted my gloomy glance, or I became at that moment church and state and play jury. For him the afternoon was spoiled.

And maybe for her, but she will live to thank me. If I had not turned to look she could hardly have discovered so soon that Fred cannot, now or ever, love and grin.

MARRY IN HASTE

Of late there has been agitation for rules and regulations to make the business of getting married more difficult. I'm for making it easier. But my quarrel is less with laws than social custom.

All those who are asked to give advice, and many others, are forever saying "Go slow" and "Think it over." Of course, a certain number of hasty marriages crash on the rocks, but few seem to take account of the fact that there are also tragedies arising out of excessive caution. My guess is that these are more numerous. In any wholly logical debate on the theme: "Resolved, that it is better not to marry," the affirmative side should be the favorite.

Marriage must always remain among the extra hazardous risks. The best chance is to take a short, sharp sprint before jumping. Walking up on the bar never makes it any less dangerous. I think that the value of reasonableness in the matter is vastly exaggerated. People who play hunches do much better than those who figure out the chances.

There is a notion that two people who have known each other for years and share a community of interests can embark upon the adventure with a certain assurance of success. I don't think so. A lot of money might be made in laying odds against just such marriages. The only real argument for marriage is that it remains the best method for getting acquainted.

I don't even hold with any of the radical theories about the value of trial marriages. I have known people who lived with entire happiness in sin and promptly went to smash as soon as they undertook the extra responsibility of legal union.

Most of the generalizations are untrue and the rules are no good. But a hunch is a hint from the lower caverns of the mind and should not be dismissed lightly. In a sense the term "hasty marriage" is inaccurate. A young man meets a young woman and he, or she, suggests the next day, or the next week, "Let's get married." If they obey the impulse and drive to Greenwich all their friends, parents and guardians will exclaim, "Wasn't that foolish for Joe and Hilda to take such a grave step without mature consideration. They shouldn't have been so hasty."

Hasty! Not at all. As a matter of fact Joe was twenty-six when he went to Greenwich and Hilda was two years older. At the age of seven Joe's romantic pattern was finished and sealed. Circumstances of his early environment made him the sort of person who could find happiness in marriage only with a slender young woman, having blue eyes and a particular shade of brown hair. And the precise shape of her hands was also ordained nineteen years before he went to Greenwich.

Hilda's romantic image was red hair, a particular conformation of the shoulders and a certain drawling quality of voice. And these obligations were set in her mind at the age of eight. Neither one could have given you any accurate picture of his precise romantic requirements. They called it "Love at first sight," which is not as sentimental or impossible as it sounds. But that doesn't mean that it was in any true sense of the word "hasty." Joe had waited nineteen years and Hilda twenty before finding a mate to meet specifications.

I'm not saying that they wouldn't be better off if Joe was earning $10,000 a year instead of $4,000, and it may be that the difference in religious faith made certain difficulties. Still, Joe might have waited ten years more and married a girl with square hands instead of long ones. Every consideration of good sense might have pointed to this particular experiment, but it would have been doomed at the start. Indeed, it would have been doomed way back in the years before, when Joe had just turned seven.

"But," said Hilda's mother, "what I said to her was, 'How on earth can you tell that you love this young man? You've only known him a week. That isn't what I call love. I call it infatuation. There's got to be more than that before you get married.'"

If Hilda had asked me, I would have told her that there isn't any more.

And I don't for the life of me understand why people speak so contemptuously of what they call "calf love." It is among the truest and most profound of all the human passions and if everybody married his or her first love, I think it might be elegant.

"WIFE OF LOT"

In Sunday School I often found myself on the side of the Old Testament villains and against some of the Old Testament heroes. Esau is inevitably a more attractive man than Jacob, and among the women Vashti is finer grained than Esther. But in examining over Genesis in preparation for the great trial, I find still another Biblical character who seems to me deserving honor not yet accorded to her in any generous measure.

She is a woman without a name and nothing which she said in life has been recorded. Yet her fame should endure. That she was kinswoman to Eve is evident enough, for in her, too, there blazed the spirit of research. Indeed, if it had not been for Eve and this other, science might not have come into this world ever. But for them, these mothers of science (it never seems to have had a father of any great significance), Dayton's ball park might have gone on to the end of time without echoing to the eloquence of any ideal more lofty than the familiar "Kill the umpire!"

Like Mr. Scopes, she was a person of an inquiring mind. She had to know in spite of penalties. The one vital incident in her life is related in a single sentence: "But his wife looked back from behind him, and she became a pillar of salt."

18

"Wife of Lot"

Generally it is assumed that this was a doom, a punishment visited upon the wife of Lot because she turned to watch the fire and brimstone as it rained from the skies upon Sodom and upon Gomorrah. It is true that the commandment, "Look not behind thee," had been imposed upon Lot, but it is not altogether clear that this prohibition was also issued to the wife of Lot. However, the point is not important. I believe she would have looked in any case and I am not at all prepared to admit that her end was of a sort to make mankind shudder and draw back in the future from other courageous investigation.

It is at least debatable as to whether this was not canonization rather than punishment which fell upon her. The estate of being a white and shining column in this flat country of the plains may have been by a great margin more desirable than the station—"Wife of Lot." It is not easy for any woman to lose her identity in the shadow of a great man and it is worse when she has to play a supporting rôle to a husband of distinctly minor quality. Lot does not seem to have been a very prepossessing person. When the mob besieged his house in Sodom he was overready to suggest a cowardly compromise. You may remember that he offered to turn his daughters over to the ruffians. Later, when informed of the impending destruction of his home city, he quailed before the advice that he should flee to the mountains and suggested that he be allowed to escape to Zoar, because that was a city and, as he meachingly added, "Is it not a little one?" From town to suburb was about the most to which Lot could nerve himself. He had not the hardihood to dare the mountains.

Subsequently, to be sure, he did make the trip and again it was great fear that moved him. Under the rigors of primitive life in a cave he seemed to have gone pretty much to pieces, and the Bible records that he became drunken and degenerate.

It was not, then, altogether tragic to leave off being the wife of Lot and become instead a towering white shaft of cleanly salt. Even in life she may well have been a little contemptuous of this man of hers. We know that "she looked back from behind him." Evidently, in his terror at the destruction which rained from the heavens, Lot was going as fast as his legs would carry him towards safety. If he had ever known of "Women and children first" he forgot it in his fright.

But she asked no favors of him. Nor for that matter of anyone. Her desire to know the nature of this fiery phenomenon was more passionate than any terror. I hope we may assume that when she looked back she had opportunity to see clearly and to record in her mind the facts concerning the mighty convulsion. This I think is so, for symbolically her fate conforms to this conception. The achievement of knowledge is a crystallization.

The seed of Lot was preserved in the world by incestuous sin, following the flight from Sodom, but I will not grant that the wife of Lot ceased ever as a continuing influence upon the life and thought of mankind. She brought to life a savor. It endures.

After the fire and the brimstone peace came again to the plains where once the city stood. Under stars and moon the pillar of salt gleamed bright. And over it blew the mountain breeze. From behind a star Prometheus looked down and bowed low. He called her name. I don't know what that is, but I am quite certain it was something other than "Wife of Lot."

BRYAN'S LAST SPEECH

It was a mistake, I think, for newspapers to let the last speech of William Jennings Bryan pass unchallenged. Among other things this was a doubtful compliment to Mr. Bryan. Liking him not at all, I am still prepared to admit that he was a hard fighter, and since the conviction of survival was strong within him he probably would have preferred to have the controversy continued. Death disturbed the issue in no way.

In fact, Mr. Bryan's own philosophy was not the issue. He merely happened to be the most articulate and conspicuous person within a large group. I have always felt that the metropolitan press minimized the numerical strength of the people for whom Mr. Bryan spoke. There was a tendency to talk as if the particular sort of fundamentalism which came to the surface in Dayton was peculiar to the little towns of America. To be sure, these semi-rural communities comprised a very large proportion of our country, but over and above that is the fact that precisely the same mentality abounds within our largest cities.

To a conspicuous degree William Jennings Bryan was lazy-minded. This quality was partially concealed by the terrific physical and emotional energy of the man, but the inertia of his thinking rises up from every line of that last speech which he never delivered. In this sense death betrayed him. The value of his personal performance might have given spirit to that which lies supinely on the paper.

During the Scopes trial the story goes about that Mr.

Bryan had worked prodigiously upon a speech which was to be the master effort of his career. It was said that he had spent from three to four months in preparing this address. As to the time which he actually took in composition there can be no check-up. It is a long speech but is very largely a patchwork of remembered phrases. There was a purpose, though probably unconscious, in Mr. Bryan's bitter battle against those who approached problems through the faculty of reasoning. Something of jealousy was in this bitter hostility, for Mr. Bryan could not reason.

I am not generalizing in speaking of the address to the jury as a lazy speech. As it happens, I read the article which Mr. Bryan wrote for the *Forum* a few weeks before the trial, and into the address designed for twelve men of Dayton he incorporated word for word and paragraph for paragraph that earlier article. In other words, nothing that happened in Dayton registered at all in Mr. Bryan's consciousness. The material which he prepared before hearing the case sufficed him without the change of a comma, even after testimony had been taken.

Possibly it may be said that he had studied the subject of evolution so carefully before going to Tennessee that it was impossible for him to encounter new material. The only answer to that is that on the witness stand Mr. Bryan admitted how slight had been his researches. An active-minded man would not have fallen back so readily upon so familiar a phrase in his repertoire as the line about the age of the rocks and the Rock of Ages.

It was the Commoner's conception that faith had brought about the solidification of his thinking, but he overlooked another factor. The profession of lecturing trained Mr. Bryan into the habit of grooved reflection. The stress of travel from point to point and the strain imposed by large audiences make it impossible for a lecturer to proceed except over roads to which he has become accustomed. He cleaves to familiar things and avoids all which is strange and novel. In course of time this affects his psychological processes even at such times as he is not upon the platform. He has become a disc whose whole mental surface is scarred with recorded impressions. There's no room for more. The man is marred by finality.

One thing which I found annoying in most of the stories of the Scopes trial was the manner in which the reporters invariably referred to Mr. Bryan's "simple faith" and likewise to the "simple faith of the mountain folk." Familiar and traditional this faith may be, but it is anything but simple. The emotional cleavage between modernists and fundamentalists is ridiculously twisted about. The overtone is of a conflict between a theology of the quiet-minded and something new and ornate which has been raised up against it. Now, this is not at all in accord with the facts. The objection against the liberals in the various evangelical denominations is that they are arguing and working for the curtailment rather than for the elaboration of creeds. Dr. Fosdick, for instance, preaches a faith far more simple than that outlined by Mr. Bryan.

This does not inevitably prove that Dr. Fosdick is right and that William Jennings Bryan was wrong, but at least it should remove from the modernists the reproach that they are seeking to impose upon the world new-fangled and complicated articles of faith.

Indeed, the misconception touches many things in addition to religious belief. There is a tendency to confuse simplicity and ignorance. Widely it is felt that education consists of weighting a knapsack for the back of a man. Knowledge is thought of as a burden, which must make the way of life more difficult than it appears to untutored or primitive man.

But here, again, facts do not uphold this curious fallacy. The universe of a savage is far more elaborately and fearsomely organized than the universe as seen by a modern scientist. Darwin, for instance, did not throw the world into chaos, but brought order out of confusion. As the world progresses and man takes hold of truths, he is able with each step forward to cast aside ten fables as soon as his fingers close upon a fact. Wisdom consists of crystallization. The true business of education is to cut away the weeds and let reality flourish in light and air.

THE WHIMMING RING

It was not a wishing ring which the Prince gave to the Princess upon a certain Christmas, but a whimming ring and that is quite different, the copy desk or proofroom of *The World* to the contrary. Incidentally, the young man and the young woman might as well have names by now. She was the Princess Fair A Day and he was William.

When he gave her the ring, Prince William told her plainly enough that it was no such magic instrument as the lamp of Aladdin. Indeed, he was skeptical that there ever had been such a lamp.

"How is it possible," he asked, "that one should ever have

the power to gain all things whatsoever within the dream of desire? There are hopes too mighty and too terrible to be granted. And other things so misty that not even a genie might lay hold of them."

The scope of the whimming ring, he said, was less than this. If Fair A Day wanted a new red dress that she could get by turning the gold circlet upon her finger. It would be, he thought, a process easier than touring about the stores or even telephoning to the merchants of the town. The red dress fetched by the slave of the ring would not necessarily be the best and most glorious of all red dresses possible, but it would be a good red dress. Approximately it would fit and excellently it would wear. Precious stones, flowers, perfumes, objects of ivory, laces, sweetmeats, all these were to be had for the turning of the whimming ring.

But it happened, on this Christmas, Fair A Day desired none of these things. All her longing was given over to the loss of a Prince. Ten years ago he went away to die in the wars. This was the Prince Rubin of the Rubies, for so the little islands of his kingdom were called. Fair A Day had seen him just twice, and once was the night before the march. They stood in the red garden beyond the gates of his palace. And he sang her a ruddy little song. Rubin was taller than Fair A Day. Taller than William. Perhaps he was fairer.

He sang high and low in the moonlight. His voice rippled and clung to some notes. As he sang she was just a shade critical. It would be simpler, she thought, if he sang without the sob and she gravely suspected that he tackled tones a bit above his range. Assuredly, he was of the minstrels who listened to their own notes and liked them mightily.

All that she knew, at least dimly, in the red garden when

he said his farewell. Already the troops of the Rubies were on the march. They sang his song lustily down the road and faintly as they ferried to the mainland. He stood too stalwart; a moon half an inch less broad and a shade off the hue of pure gold would have been better. And there can be in a royal garden roses too many. The thing was theater and an edge of realism was needed to cut the heart from out her. Two days later Rubin died upon the field and then her unshed tears were loosed. For five years she wept whenever roses bloomed and sobs shook her in theaters and cafés at such times as violins played the marching song of the Ruby Islanders. After six years she no longer cried, but she told herself and her friends, "I am mournful always at the sound of that merry tune." And before she set foot in any garden it was her custom to say, "I cannot walk very far if you have roses. For me they are too painful."

In the seventh year after the death of Rubin, Princess Fair A Day married Prince William with great pomp. Bugles blew and she threw back her head and said, "I must forget." Whether or not she tried, I do not know, but it was at her own command that rose bushes grew beneath the palace window.

And now ten years were gone. The Princess sat alone in a room and moonlight came through the window. A beam set the whimming ring to gleaming. It must have been a still night, for the sound of music drifted over the high walls of the palace. The big orchestra at the Café Frenzy was swinging away at the marching song of the Ruby Islanders, and that was no great coincidence, for the tune endured as the favorite of all fox trots and this was a gala night.

Already the Princess had turned the ring several times to ask for favors and receive them. On the table before her lay a red dress, an ivory fan and a five-pound box of candy. The genie of the whimming ring came without any disturbing clap of thunder and he left behind him scarcely more smoke than a flash-light photograph.

Asking was easy and yet the Princess hesitated and did not turn the ring though a wish pounded within her. She feared to cross the limits of the spell set around her finger. It would embarrass her, it would shame the little genie if he were compelled to say, "That I cannot do, Your Majesty." He was not the slave of her wishes, but only the servant of her whims.

Still, she did cross over to the door and locked it so that no one but the genie and one other could enter. She tried to rest but could not still the throbbing of the great wish. How could one turn a ring of gold and gain a miracle? A genie scarcely three feet high, was he a messenger fit to hurl against the hard fact of death? Could he fetch and carry back a hero gone so many years?

The violins wailed into the refrain and one note lingered. Fair A Day spun the ring around upon her finger. Like a kitten leaping from a table, the soft feet of the genie squished upon thick carpet.

"There is something I want," she said and paused.

"Your whim is my command," answered the little man.

She looked at him bleakly. "It is not a whim," whispered Fair A Day. "This is a mighty wish. My heart bleeds for this."

"All I can do is whims," said the knee-high genie and he rapped his head upon the soft carpet three times in apology for the imperfection of his power.

And still the Princess spoke. "I want you to bring to this room now a man who has been dead ten years. I want him

to stand before me as he stood in a red garden long ago.
I want him to come to me singing. I want him in the flesh
and body that he wore."

"And the man?" said the genie.

"Prince Rubin of the Rubies."

A happy smile swept the face of the genie. "Oh, yes, indeed!" he said. "That I can do. I am the slave of your
whims."

Her sudden loud cry caught him half in misty outline as
he began to fade upon the progress of his mission.

"A whim?" demanded the Princess.

"A whim," said the genie very firmly for a man of his
size.

"Then," said Fair A Day, sadly, "let the dead Prince
sleep. Bring me violets for my ball gown."

A CHESTNUT TREE

Real estate agents in New York City overlook some very
important factors when they list a house. The man comes
round with a printed paper and asks questions. He wants
to know the number of rooms. Whether you've got hardwood floors. The size of the lot and mortgages. Very carefully he notes the condition of the furnace and the plumbing. But not one to whom I've talked has ever asked, "How
many trees have you got?"

And this seems to me vital. Many people buy a house
just to get the trees which are thrown in with the deal. I've

got three and a large part of the overhang from a tree next door. This trespasser, from a strictly material standpoint, is a finer tree than any which I possess, but I prefer my own horse chestnut just the same. It's a one-man tree and would never think of dividing its loyalty between two houses.

I'm not quite sure that it is a horse chestnut. The case is circumstantial. Two years ago it behaved like a chestnut and burst out into big white blossoms in the spring. Nothing of the sort has occurred since. Possibly this was just an experiment. Maybe it's elm that got bored and turned giddy for one season to see what it would be like.

I'm rather afraid this was a last fling. Nothing came of the white blossoms and the tree's failure to achieve economic independence seems to have broken its spirit. This year it barely managed to bring out a few leaves. A good many of the branches have quit cold. Kind words, possibly, would have made all the difference in the world, but this was my first year with the tree and I took the white blossoms casually instead of going out to the backyard every day and saying, "Well, well, that certainly is extraordinary."

At the present time I give the tree a good deal of attention in a rough sort of way. When I'm in earshot I make a point of invariably referring to it as a chestnut in order to resolve its doubts, and I exercise it regularly. Inertia may be one of the things which ails it. Once upon a time that tree could see all the way to the Hudson and across into Jersey. When storms came roaring over the Palisades the old chestnut bickered around with the wind and arched its back and touched its toes. That's the stuff to keep the sap moving.

But then the city came in and walled the tree around with shelter. A huge apartment house blocks off the gales from the Drive. And on the 86th Street side two other monster buildings stand guard and take the buffets from the north wind. In storm time the tree can hear the thunder and see the lightning, and high above its head awnings tug at their fastenings, shutters flap like the wings of racing buzzards, and there's a loud whistling in the chimney-pots. But the chestnut sits on the side lines, for the gale hardly ever swirls all the way down to the bottom of the canyon.

The tree is protected and it never asked to be. That theory about a chestnut's place is in the home makes no appeal to any tree of proper spirit.

"Damn all this damn censorship," I think the tree would like to say, and then continue, "If you stand to the wind and keep your chin up a storm may break your backbone. And scare you, too. There were times in the old days when I could feel the rumpus all through my rigging. And I used to think my last hour had come. My roots ached after a big battle.

"But after the thing was over I liked it. I could sort of stretch myself and say, 'I'm still here.' And there was a sort of kick in knowing that you'd been through it all and come out with everything but a few leaves and little branches. Facts, like a big storm, can kill you. There's no sense in denying that. But there's also such a thing as dry rot. That'll get you too when you have to live a sheltered life with brick walls all around you."

And so it has been my custom to go out and try to act like a cyclone to the chestnut. I grab a branch and endeavor to shake the whole structure. Feinting with my left, I swing the right and all the time I use my fighting face. I'm afraid it's no go. The tree seems to be aware of the fact that I am no tornado. It does no more than creak a little with petulance. There's none of the wild, free action which a tree takes on during a truly proper storm.

City life has got that chestnut. If I were philanthropically inclined and able to buy up and tear down all the neighboring buildings, I would be doing the chestnut no great favor. It's not the tree it used to be. There's a good deal of sentimentality in all its moaning and reminiscing of the days when it was way uptown and bucked the unchecked breezes. Any fair-sized flurry would tear the old fellow limb from limb. He's wholly out of training and wouldn't remember any more the difficult technique of yielding just so much to every gust and slipping back and weaving in and out among the air currents.

One good wallop of the wind would snap him right in two. And maybe that's the way he wants to go, instead of dying as he is by inches and coming back each season with a few leaves less and having every year still one more branch go numb and useless.

Still, I can't allow myself to go on in such speculation. I have my own troubles. Sooner than let the tragedy of that tree completely break my heart, I'll take an ax the next time I go out for exercise and cut him down and end things for him.

I mentioned two more trees, but there's not much to be said for them. They have little personality and no history. They're strictly city bred, that slim type of sapling which springs up in vacant lots and smells so strong in summer. Never having known any other existence except backyard life, they make no complaint. That's just as well. I'd like to hear them kicking. Those trees I could break between thumb and forefinger. Or, maybe, thumb and a couple of other fingers. And, anyhow, you can't see them except from the kitchen door. They don't add particularly to the attractiveness of the premises.

The chestnut lives more intimately with the house. He's tall enough to look in the pantry window and command a fair view of the other two back windows as well. As far as I know, there was never any famous person lived in this house, nor has any notable crime been committed here as yet. The succession of householders has been wholly middleclass. But we bourgeois have tragedy and comedy and farce in our lives. It may be that the chestnut could hand out anecdotes if you pumped him.

Fortunately, I can look at him square and fearless. He's got nothing on me. Well, at least, I don't think he has.

TO RESTORE ORDER

They ought to land the marines in Florida. Within a year a single county has established a record of sixty-three lashings by masked outlaws. And very likely there were more which never came to be reported. Among those who were whipped two died. Both men and women were victims of the hooded gangs, and most of those dragged out upon the roads at night were accused of "laxity of morals."

By now the governor of the State of Florida has spoken and has revealed the fact that he is not competent to deal with the situation. After warning the sheriff that such pranks should cease, Governor Martin went on to say, "I also told him that for white women to be taken out and beaten by white men was inconceivable, and that it was going to stop in Putnam County if it took all the resources of my office to do so."

And so we have the not very inspiring spectacle of the executive of a large state meeting the threat of lawlessness with a timid plea to the boys to be more discriminating in picking their shots. I am not reading too much into the Governor's statement, I think, in saying that his message may well be construed by the lashers as a mild request that they return to the more traditional Southern practice of hounding Negroes.

It would be unjust, though, to suggest that only in the fair Southland do fools sit in the high places. Here in our own dear Empire State sat a parson no farther away than Beacon who preached a sermon to assembled Kluxers and tastefully captioned it "Kooties of the Kommonwealth." This was in an edifice dedicated to Christ, a name as yet not meddled with in Klannish spelling.

And in our own state, too, Major General Edwards held forth, but he is a Massachusetts man and not our own. The General is worried over "the insidious poison" being spread among our youth—"the most idealistic of any youth in the world." And the General was frank enough to be specific as to the nature of the poison which might impair American ideals.

"I speak," he said, "of this internationalism, this brotherly love, this 'no more war,' 'outlaw war,' 'peace and freedom' and 'industrial democracy.' "

According to the General all these horrid phrases are being "disseminated through 1611 publications circulated in the United States, only seventy-seven of which are printed in this country and in the English language."

"The rest," he added, "are printed in foreign languages or brought into this country to influence those of foreign birth who do not understand our system or our methods."

Somebody really ought to tell the General that not all the phrases to which he objects were made abroad. While he was at the front and unable to keep up with developments behind the fighting line good citizens were informed, and through official channels, that the current conflict was a war to end war. "No more war," was used quite freely then —or possibly the prevalent spirit might be more accurately expressed with "Just one more war and we'll all go home."

And about this "brotherly love" to which the General takes exception: It isn't, as he believes, a nasty notion devised by the Communists and paid for with Russian gold. Truly, General, it is much older than that. Get your pastor to tell you about it.

Nor is "peace and freedom" an ideal manufactured solely beyond the borders of this country. Just how much is actually made here I couldn't say, but there has been talk of these commodities for many years. Once they were highly treasured up New England way where Edwards comes from. Even if the General had his way and peace and freedom became contraband at all our boundary lines, I doubt if it would be possible to enforce the embargo. There has not yet been any government powerful enough to prevent some little freedom from being bootlegged in.

One thing was lacking in the General's speech as reported in the newspapers. Although he mentioned the phrases which seemed to him poisonous to the most idealistic youth in the world, he suggested no alternate set of slogans. If it is ever permitted for another to do a General's thinking for him, I suggest that he advocate the dissemination of such

34

patriotic phrases as: "Another little war wouldn't do us any harm," "Treat 'em rough" and "Victory without peace."

It is a curious thing how certain combinations of words can't stand wind and weather, while others take on dignity after the storms have beaten against them. At the same time it was said, the phrase of which I am thinking seemed to most Americans unhappy. The man who wrote it down was himself a little troubled and not altogether certain that he had intended to say just what he did. Already, though, reproach has left the words which once were scorned, and in a hundred years what will you wager that the motto best preserved out of all which were flung about during the war won't be "Too proud to fight"?

THE MIRACLE OF DEBS

Eugene V. Debs is dead and everybody says that he was a good man. He was no better and no worse when he served a sentence at Atlanta.

I imagine that now it would be difficult to find many to defend the jailing of Debs. But at the time of the trial he received little support outside the radical ranks.

The problem involved was not simple. I hated the thing they did to Debs even at the time, and I was not then a pacifist. Yet I realize that almost nobody means precisely what he says when he makes the declaration, "I'm in favor of free speech." I think I mean it, but it is not difficult for me to imagine situations in which I would be gravely tempted to enforce silence on anyone who seemed to be dangerous to the cause I favored.

Free speech is about as good a cause as the world has ever known. But, like the poor, it is always with us and gets shoved aside in favor of things which seem at some given moment more vital. They never are more vital. Not when you look back at them from a distance. When the necessity of free speech is most important we shut it off. Everybody favors free speech in the slack moments when no axes are being ground.

It would have been better for America to have lost the war than to lose free speech. I think so, but I imagine it is a minority opinion. However, a majority right now can be drummed up to support the contention that it was wrong to put Debs in prison. That won't keep the country from sending some other Debs to jail in some other day when panic psychology prevails.

You see, there was another aspect to the Debs case, a point of view which really begs the question. It was foolish to send him to jail. His opposition to the war was not effective. A wise dictator, someone like Shaw's Julius Caesar, for instance, would have given Debs better treatment than he got from our democracy.

Eugene Debs was a beloved figure and a tragic one. All his life he led lost causes. He captured the intense loyalty of a small section of our people, but I think that he affected the general thought of his time to a slight degree. Very few recognized him for what he was. It became the habit to speak of him as a man molded after the manner of Lenin or Trotzky. And that was a grotesque misconception. People were constantly overlooking the fact that Debs was a

Hoosier, a native product in every strand of him. He was a sort of Whitcomb Riley turned politically minded.

It does not seem to me that he was a great man. At least he was not a great intellect. But Woodward has argued persuasively that neither was George Washington. In summing up the Father of His Country, this most recent biographer says in effect that all Washington had was character. By any test such as that Debs was great. Certainly he had character. There was more of goodness in him than bubbled up in any other American of his day. He had some humor, or otherwise a religion might have been built up about him, for he was thoroughly Messianic. And it was a strange quirk which set this gentle, sentimental Middle-Westerner in the leadership of a party often fierce and militant.

Though not a Christian by any precise standard, Debs was the Christian-Socialist type. That, I'm afraid, is outmoded. He did feel that wrongs could be righted by touching the compassion of the world. Perhaps they can. It has not happened yet. Of cold, logical Marxianism, Debs possessed very little. He was never the brains of his party. I never met him, but I read many of his speeches, and most of them seemed to be second-rate utterances. But when his great moment came a miracle occurred. Debs made a speech to the judge and jury at Columbus after his conviction, and to me it seems one of the most beautiful and moving passages in the English language. He was for that one afternoon touched with inspiration. If anybody told me that tongues of fire danced upon his shoulders as he spoke, I would believe it.

Whenever I write anything about churches, ministers write in and say: "But of course you have no faith in miracles and the supernatural." And that is a long way off the target. For better or worse I can't stand out for a minute against mysticism. I think there are very few ministers ready to believe in as many miracles as I accept, because I cannot help myself. The speech which Debs made is to me a thing miraculous, because in it he displayed a gift for singing prose which was never with him on any other day of his life. And if you ask me, I'll also have to admit that I don't see how Lincoln came to the Gettysburg Address by any pathway which can be charted. There was in that nothing to suggest the utterance of a man who had been a small time politician and who might reasonably be expected to have formed his habits of speech in the rough and tumble school of give and take political debate in which his formative years were spent.

Something was in Debs, seemingly, that did not come out unless you saw him. I'm told that even those speeches of his which seemed to any reader indifferent stuff, took on vitality from his presence. A hard-bitten Socialist told me once, "Gene Debs is the only one who can get away with the sentimental flummery that's been tied onto Socialism in this country. Pretty nearly always it gives me a swift pain to go around to meetings and have people call me 'comrade.' That's a lot of bunk. But the funny part of it is that when Debs says 'comrade' it's all right. He means it. That old man with the burning eyes actually believes that there can be such a thing as the brotherhood of man. And that's not the funniest part of it. As long as he's around I believe it myself."

With the death of Debs, American Socialism is almost sure to grow more scientific, more bitter, possibly more effective. The party is not likely to forget that in Russia it was force which won the day, and not persuasion.

I've said that it did not seem to me that Debs was a great man in life, but he will come to greatness by and by. There are in him the seeds of symbolism. He was a sentimental Socialist, and that line has dwindled all over the world. Radicals talk now in terms of men and guns and power, and unless you get in at the beginning of the meeting and orient yourself, this could just as well be Security Leaguers or any other junkers in session.

The Debs idea will not die. To be sure, it was not his first at all. He carried on an older tradition. It will come to pass. There can be a brotherhood of man.

MARIE OF RUMANIA

"It was," wrote Her Majesty the Queen of Rumania in yesterday's *World*, "rush, rush, rush."

By a curious coincidence I made precisely the same observation in the story of my visit to America about two weeks ago. However, I realize that practically all plagiarism is unconscious or accidental.

Public opinion in this country runs like a shower bath. We have no temperatures between hot and cold. And because some seem to have steamed in a rather excessive manner toward the royal visitor others have turned icy. Various reasons have been ventured in explanation of the visit of Marie of Rumania, but it does not seem to me that any of them is discreditable. If it be so that the Queen is here in lieu of a debt commission, I fail to see why that is not a perfectly legitimate mission. And if she merely came for the ride, that too affords no ground for criticism.

Nor need there be any reason whatsoever given to appease the spiteful. Tradition ought to work both ways and it is no more than just that a queen should have the privilege of looking at a few cats.

American institutions need not totter at one touch of cordiality toward a queen. And on the other hand those of us—the majority, of course—who have no patience with the "king business" can hardly hope to upset any thrones merely by making faces at the lady from Rumania.

From some quarters has come sharp and angry protest because at one or two receptions American kings and captains of finance bent over the hand of Marie and kissed it. There is nothing essentially servile in that. It is no more than a gesture of politeness. Nobody is much harmed and every gentleman in the group who followed the custom is entitled to go home, or elsewhere, and kiss whomsoever he pleases with a clear conscience.

To say that you do not hold at all with monarchies, even the most limited, is one thing, but to deny that there is any romantic appeal in kings and queens and princes is quite another. Titles ran through all the fairy stories which I heard in the beginning. At that time I felt it would be fine to meet a real live prince, and later I did so. Nor was my childish estimate all wrong. It was fine. This particular prince gave poker parties and always drew to inside straights. My impression is that he disappointed no one except H. 3rd, who asked with a certain petulance, "Where's your black velvet suit?"

Royalty ought to dress up to the requirements set by the men who drew the pictures for the fairy tale books. Marie's pearls and diamonds are not one stone too many. Once or twice, as I remember, I've seen her picture in the daily papers or perhaps it was some rotogravure section and she lived up admirably to my notion of what a queen should look like. She has given an admirable performance and there are not half a dozen actresses in America who could fill the rôle as well.

In a little while all the kings and queens of the world will depart from off their thrones. There will be no princes left, but pretenders sitting in Paris cafés and crying over cognac. And that will be a pity. England, when it goes permanently Labor, may be more wise and kind. A liberal land might well support a king and queen, or maybe two of each in reasonable magnificence. They animate first nights at the theater to a considerable degree. And kings, I think, are preferable to mayors for throwing out the ball at the beginning of the season. But most of all they have a right to live and reign in moderation, because they do amuse the children.

At one great reception for Marie there stood at the foot of her throne-like chair a zealous hostess who whispered to each guest as he approached, "You mustn't touch the Queen."

"Ah, yes," said one veteran bridge player when he received the admonition, "I know that rule. I'd have to play her."

Many features of the Russian Revolution were excellent, but some of the by-products disturbed me. I do not even now care much about being waited upon by grand dukes, and my favorite restaurant was ruined for me because they got a duchess for the kitchen. The head waiter had been a colonel of crack cavalry and each time it became necessary to tip him I had the uneasy feeling that I was slipping something to General Pershing. At the hat check window stood a cossack a little less than seven feet in height, and when I left my overcoat with him I knew that I could never get it back except by his great grace and mercy.

I am not one to row in restaurants and complain about the steak or potatoes. What they bring I take, and generally it is good enough to be received with gratitude. If not, what of it? There will be other days and other steaks. Still, I like to reserve for myself the right upon some one occasion not yet out of the box to raise a great commotion and swank and storm and swear. I never could do that with colonels and grand dukes about. My ancestors were peasants and when even a second lieutenant swung up the street they called him "Herr" and gave him all the sidewalk he might require. And of course if a real live duke ever came to town these forbears of mine spent all the day upon their hands and knees. Perhaps that is giving them a little too much. Mostly they were on their bellies.

There is something in heredity. It cannot be denied. Accordingly I go no more to the restaurant where the grand dukes wait. Never, under the most flagrant provocation, could I nerve myself to say, "Cyril, these eggs are not so good." And certainly I'd be abashed to accuse anyone ranking as high as colonel of gypping me about a supper check.

Of course it may be that not all the waiters at the place actually were grand dukes, and I never went out to the kitchen and asked the grand duchess at the stove to show me her credentials. It was enough that the suspicion had been put into my mind. Once a member of the party with which I sat did summon up courage to ask the bus boy if he were really closely related to the late Czar. He made no answer, but he looked so wistful that it was quite evident his pride had been hurt and it became necessary for us to tip him double.

You see, the trouble with me is that I inherited an insufficient amount of vengeful feeling. Kings, princes, dukes and even local squires rode their horses so that they stepped upon the toes of my ancestors, who did nothing about it except to apologize. I would, then, have joined most eagerly in pulling down the Bastille, but if anybody had caught me at it and given me a sharp look I'm rather afraid I would have put it back again.

MY FIRST NUDE

My first nude sold the other day for a price which was not made public, but which is reported to have been 25 cents. Personally, I felt that it was a $3 picture; but a creative artist may be too indulgent with himself and since 25 cents was the best offer I let it go.

In this case the profit was not great, although I do believe in quick and frequent sales. My biggest money-maker is "Tempest on a Wooded Coast." This has never fetched more than $2.35 but I have sold it four times already. There is a point in almost every party at my house in which somebody gets the notion that he wants to buy "Tempest on a Wooded Coast" and pay cash. But it seems to be the sort of picture men forget. When the purchaser goes he always leaves the painting behind him although it is quite dry. Whether this is second thought or inadvertence, I don't profess to know. I merely stick it back upon the shelf and wait for another buyer to come along.

The purchase of paintings for speculation is not the noblest of all motives, though there is nothing snide in it, and I have always wondered why the dealers did not seek to encourage this sort of patronage through publicity. Many a true story could be told.

There is the familiar anecdote about Van Gogh, who took a still life of some sabots to his butcher in Paris and let him have it for 5 francs. And as the artist was coming from the shop a beggar in dire need accosted him and got the money. This same picture sold at auction later for $20,000, and by now is worth even more.

Then there was Rousseau, the postal clerk in Paris who drew as kindergarten children do and showed his brilliant pictures around to friends, who promptly had a good laugh at these crudities. Indeed, it is said that once, when Rousseau was taken into court because of indorsing someone's note, his lawyer produced some of the pictures and showed them to the judge in an effort to prove that his client was not wholly adult-minded. And he won the case. It may have been one of this very lot which sold at an auction of John Quinn's collection for $50,000.

The chances of any casual visitor's picking up a potential Van Gogh or Rousseau in some little gallery are somewhat slight, but people will buy lots in Florida and stock in oil wells. And though the certificates are often pretty, few of them may be classed as works of art.

A dealer told me just the other day that he'd had a happy afternoon because he sold a picture to a customer who bought it for the very simple reason that he liked it. This, so the dealer said, is very rare. According to his theory, people buy pictures from a snobbish desire to be regarded as patrons of the arts or from the hope that the thing they buy will appreciate in value. "Snobbish" was his word, but I wouldn't call it quite that. To me it is more reasonable for a wealthy man to make a display by collecting pictures than by assembling leather books, horses or assorted shirt studs.

The graphic arts languish in America because not 1 percent of the present population ever buys a painting for any reason whatsoever. And yet for prints in tacky gilt frames there is always a ready market.

I have my doubts as to whether picture dealers rank among the smartest men in this community. Possibly they are adept enough in making a bargain once a customer has come prepared to buy, but certainly they do not pull them in. The average man of middling means has not the slightest notion of how to buy a painting, even if he happens to think he'd like one. Most of the galleries I know are forbidding and aloof and the stranger within the gates is made to feel as if he ought to have a letter from his pastor, and excellent social references as well, before he even ventures to ask anybody in the shop how much some certain picture costs.

A large department store, which will not be nameless, called Macy's, undertook some time ago to maintain a department devoted to the paintings of young and little known Americans. My impression is that the store has not kept up this innovation, though to my mind the idea was excellent. The hope of the American painter should be in getting his pictures into department stores, butchers', druggists' or delicatessen shops. Here people would come and buy who never by any chance venture inside a gallery.

A SERMON FROM SAMUEL

There is, we are told by many, a fundamentalist conflict between science and religion, and yet the creed of every scientist and seeker after truth is stated eloquently in the Bible out of the mouth of one of the greatest heroes of the Old Testament. Look into the seventeenth chapter of the First Book of Samuel and read the two paragraphs which describe the preparations of David for his battle against Goliath. Here you will read:

"And Saul armed David with his armor, and he put an helmet of brass upon his head; also he armed him with a coat of mail. And David girded his sword upon his armor, and he assayed to go; for he had not proved it. And David said unto Saul, I cannot go with these; for I have not proved them. And David put them off him."

As you know, David killed Goliath with a pebble of his own choosing. He knew the heft of that rock, for he thumbed it over and tested it before he took it into battle. In a fight for life David was not disposed to depend on hearsay and hand-me-downs.

Now the armor of the King undoubtedly looked good. It is fair to assume that it was highly polished and blinked at the sun. And the helmet was all gold and glittering. But the man who was to meet Goliath had to be sure. The big Philistine was a pretty fine old skeptic on his own account and not one to bow down and surrender to the first brass hat who challenged him. David, in borrowed metal, would very probably have been no more than a hickory nut in the hands of the giant.

Pictorially, the gear was an excellent suggestion. Upon the fine young body of the boy this armor of the King set well. And, for many, the gift of Saul would have had great psychic significance. It would be a charm and a talisman. Very likely there was magic in it. More than that, the armor held the weight of authority. Saul recommended it. But, even with all this, something vital was missing in the accouterments. Nothing out of David's own experience sanctioned it.

As guardian of his father's sheep he had killed a lion and a bear. Against those savage beasts he went unhampered by any such trappings. And the methods which worked in animal experimentation should, in the light of reason, be efficacious against Philistines.

Throughout the story David is pictured as moving with the utmost confidence.

"The Lord has delivered me out of the paw of the lion, and out of the paw of the bear," he said. "He will deliver me out of the hand of this Philistine."

David was then a mystic, but not to excess. There was no disposition on his part to say, "Let God do it," and take no pains on his own account. Had he felt that he was no more than a pawn in the proceedings he would hardly have bothered his head to put off the armor once Saul had strapped it on. God could help a man in mail as easily as one who went naked into battle.

And when David went from Saul on his way to the front he "chose him five smooth stones out of the brook." Nothing was left to chance in this. It was an enlightened faith which animated David. You may be sure he took the stones best fitted for his purpose, and did not say, like our own Fundamentalists, "It is enough for me to lean upon the Rock of Ages."

God was not vexed at these precautions. He does not frown on those who tincture faith with ruddy drops of hearty reason. This has been so from the beginning. The first inhalation Adam knew was the breath of God, but into this ancestor lungs were created, and from that time on it became the business of the man to do his breathing for himself.

It may be that there were smiles in heaven at the extent and precision of David, scientist, who was about to risk his life for the glory of his God. After all, there is no getting away from the fact that David did take "five smooth stones." Had he been addicted to a lean-back, lazy faith, one would have sufficed. And some who do negate all power and virtue of the human will would face Goliath with no rock at all, feeling that man is a poor thing and wholly powerless to help himself. David was not like that. He felt it entirely possible that he might miss with his first shot, and after that he was prepared to go on firing and firing with all the strength of soul and shoulders until the time came for him to meet his God. I doubt if he thought of himself as a miserable sinner, or cared to acknowledge that there was no health in him.

"And David put his hand in his bag, and took thence a stone, and slang it, and smote the Philistine in his forehead, that the stone sunk into his forehead; and he fell upon his face to the earth."

For this victory David did give thanks to God, but first he ran and cut off Goliath's head to round out the accomplishment and make it certain. The comment of the chronicler misses, to my mind, some of the significance of the event.

"So David prevailed over the Philistine with a sling and with a stone, and smote the Philistine, and slew him; but there was no sword in the hand of David."

If I read the intention of this comment aright, the chronicler means to imply that it was the greater miracle that David succeeded in his mission without the use of a sword. That interpretation of the incident does not appeal to me. Had David come to grips with Goliath, I think the result might well have been quite different. In swordplay he could not match the giant. Goliath killed hundreds of godly folk who attempted to stand up to him toe to toe and exchange blows. That was not the way to conquer him. Granted that the scheme of God was made manifest in the final result, I still maintain that David was chosen champion of Israel not only because he possessed faith but also in reward for the undoubted fact that he used his intelligence in the solution of the problem. I hold with none of the theologians who seem to maintain that God is contemptuous of the wisdom of man and that he honors those who proceed quite aimlessly about the business of kingdom coming.

But to abandon the theological aspects of the incident, it seems to me there is an excellent moral in David's decision to wear nothing which he could not prove. Most of us prance into battle quite readily in any shining raiment which is tossed to us. Helmets which look enough like gold are pulled down over our ears, so that even the possibility of proof is shut out from the mind of man. And so we move heavily and clumsily weighted down with beliefs and suppositions and theories which simply are not so. Never mind what King or Kleagle has handed out this stuff. Let's put it off until we know.

49

WOOING BY WIRE

They say a corporation has no soul, but I say look at the Western Union. Last Christmas the company sent me a folder showing how I could wire Christmas greetings simply by mentioning a number at any branch office. The wording of the good cheer was already prepared by a company official called, I suppose, Assistant Supervisor of Sentiment.

And now Valentine's Day approaches. I make this statement not on my own authority, but through the assurance of the Western Union. In this bitter world, sweating and striving in the struggle for existence, I might easily forget February 14. I'm a business man, and my days and nights are often given over to concern and wonder as to whether I have any money in the bank. I make big deals by day and dream of them by night. My spirits are apt to rise and fall with American Sumatra Tobacco. Often I wake in a cold sweat after some nightmare in which I have watched our entire currant crop destroyed by the boll weevil.

And in this harsh world it is well that there should be some organization not limited and bound by thought of profit and loss. It was with a distinct thrill, then, that I opened the envelope yesterday morning and perceived in the very center of the little folder a great red heart inscribed, "For my valentine," and underneath it, "Western Union." I never knew they cared.

My assumption had been that our relations were purely professional and perfunctory. The last time I entered one of the branch offices the young woman in charge did not so much as wink at me. She seemed entirely cool and distant as she asked: "And so you want it to go collect?" It's true I heard from the back of the room a distinctly rhythmic pulsation, but I never took it for heart throbs. I thought it was merely the clatter of telegraph keys.

And so once again Valentine's Day approaches. In all truth I will confess I probably should not have remembered save for the fact that the Western Union nudged me.

"In the old days," says the folder, "Valentine sentiments were framed in lacy frills and furbelows, and then dropped to rest in the depths of a mail box; there was no better way.

"Today the distinctive valentine is a telegraph billet-doux that speeds swiftly and true as Cupid's dart. It is then delivered on a special blank—in a special envelope."

Some might object that the Western Union in taking over the functions of Eros is too meddlesome, but this is decidedly captious, for a large range of choice is left to anyone who wishes to lay his heart by wire at any feet. Nor do I understand that the company places any limit upon the number or destination of protestations of complete affection which any individual may send. If you choose to be poetic the Western Union will serve as your bard. And if you bridle at this form of expression the list of numbered messages also contains sentiments expressed in good, bluff, manly fashion. Consider, for instance, Number 6:

I lost my heart around somewhere;
Just give me yours, and I'll call it square.

You don't like that, eh? You say that you are no great mush like the Western Union Telegraph Company? All right, be patient and look at Number 11:

No fuss or feathers, no Cupids or hearts. Just a warm
friendly greeting on Valentine's Day.

The latter message I would call a good business man's valentine but for the fact that it goes six words over the traditional ten. Still, in the end this might be much cheaper than some of the other messages on the company's list. I don't see how it would be possible to take anybody into court on the basis of "Just a warm friendly greeting." Not always is the Western Union so careful to keep passion and definite commitment out of the telegrams it recommends to its clients. There's dynamite in Number 2:

I like you, I love you, I want you all the time, so please wire me back that you'll be my valentine.

Here the company has been guilty of a slight oversight. Nowhere in the folder is there any list of suggestions for the use of those who contemplate answers to the form valentines. Such a list would have taken very little space. It might simply read:

1. Yes.

2. No.

Still, to me the "I like you, I love you" valentine is the most appealing of the whole Western Union dozen. I rather suspect that there's a tender little story behind it. The Assistant Supervisor of Sentiment for the Eastern Division is still a young man. He was, as I have already intimated, chosen for his sensitivity and his sympathy for the love problems of others. Very probably he ran an "Advice to the Lovelorn" column before his services were snapped up by the great corporation. Obviously, the Western Union possesses a soul, but just as obviously life in its service cannot be continually a round of romance. It has its stocks and bonds and wire troubles. As Valentine's Day, 1927, approached the Assistant Supervisor of Sentiment was worried.

"Am I growing hard?" he said to himself. "Can not it be that the life has got me?"

Sitting at his great flat-topped desk he summoned Miss Higgins, and undertook to dictate to her a line of valentine verse for the spring rush. "When I have been here twenty-five years will I, too, be as efficient as Miss Higgins?" The Assistant Supervisor thought to himself, "I wonder where she gets shoes as common sense as that." There seemed to be no snap or fire in the telegrams which he devised. Wearily he said: "That'll be all, Miss Higgins," and, then, as a new thought struck him, "Will you please ask Miss Sylvia Darcy to step in."

He heard the rustle and the crinkle of her as she approached. Looking up was too dangerous. "Miss Darcy, will you take a letter," he said, in the same firm tone that had been suggested in the course he once took in "How to get ahead in business." Sharply he rapped his right forefinger on the glass-top desk. That was also in the course.

"I like you," he began, and then hesitated. "Business is business" was the phrase which pounded in his head, but up behind it came another rider with a different and a louder clatter, drowning out the slogan to which he clung. Everything seemed to go black before his eyes. He was only whispering when he said, "I love you, I want you all the time." They are to be married in May, and that's how Number 2 on the Western Union's list of valentine suggestions came to be written.

Has the legal department of the company ever considered the possibility of having to defend a suit brought by someone who was induced to marry on account of one of its recommended valentines? There is at least the possibility that one might woo by Western Union and repent by Postal.

EDISON'S BIRTHDAY

I get to thinking, often, that it would be fun to be a famous man—and then, once every year, Thomas A. Edison has a birthday party.

His eightieth, which he celebrated last Friday, did not sound enticing. A great deal of the time was given over to posing for newspaper photographers. Some of my best friends are newspaper photographers. I might even say some of the best newspaper photographers are my friends. And yet I feel that when one or two are gathered together for professional purposes you have a nuisance, and that a dozen or more constitute a plague.

And, of course, there were also reporters. Naturally, I'm not going to turn traitor to my own guild and say anything against reporters. They are, as Mr. Joel used to say on the menu of his restaurant, "the most lovable folk in the world."

Still, I can think of more pleasurable pastimes than playing ring-around-a-rosie with a mass of correspondents and answering their questions.

Naturally, I am speaking only by surmise and not out of experience. No reporter has ever asked me any question except "Have you got a match?" or something of that sort. But I am just as competent to answer some of the questions flung at Mr. Edison as he is himself.

"Is there a God?" was one of the queries written down and handed to "the sage of Menlo Park"—or to be more precise, "the white-haired sage of Menlo Park." Possibly the

54

theory was that Mr. Edison had in his head an answer to this question because he puts things into test tubes and holds them up to the light. Many experiments have been made by Edison in search after knowledge of various kinds, but this particular problem still seems to lie a little beyond his finger-tips. At any rate he wrote, "I do not know—do you?" This seems to me an excellent answer, as good as can be expected from anyone, even from a man who has come to be called by us a sage.

And there was another question which went, "Where does one go when he dies?" Edison did make some attempt to answer this, but he was not altogether direct in his reply. "The human body," he wrote, "consists of millions of living entities which leave the body when it dies." This, naturally, did not satisfy the reporter who was after a story. Every city editor would want something more definite than that about life after death. It is newspaper practice to get the name, the street and number whenever possible.

And so the reporter wrote out another slip and on it asked, "What becomes of them?"

"Nobody knows," replied Mr. Edison, which leaves the newspapers with another mystery on their hands to add to the Elwell case and the disappearance of Dorothy Arnold. I doubt whether the best digger on any staff will be able to find out, even though they detach him from all other service and put him on this one assignment for a year.

After photography and hard questions there was a short ride in a Ford car, and a luncheon with speeches and the reading of two poems. It does not sound to me like much of a birthday. The thing is killing my ambition. I may change my mind and decide not to be famous after all. My present

intention is not to have a single photographer at my eightieth birthday party and no reporter at all except myself.

Although he has no particular talent for fashioning birthday parties, there is ample evidence that Mr. Edison is a
happy man. When the great ones of the world give inter-
views and say that in the whole field of human activity they
have found work the most fun, I generally do not believe
them. This time I am convinced. It was a description of his
desk and the pigeon-holes in it which dispelled my doubts.
I read: "The holes are labeled 'Disc records,' 'Amberola,'
'Diamond points,' 'New things.'" Any man who can keep
a cubbyhole for "new things" when he is eighty is handling
the problem of life with satisfaction to himself. It might
even be in time that Thomas Edison will reach into dark
recesses of this compartment and drag out the definite answers to those two queries of the reporters which he could
not solve. Possibly all he needs is a little more time.

Newspaper reporters have a habit of bestowing the title
of "sage" somewhat too readily. They speak of sages almost
as often as dramatic critics and book reviewers refer to
"genius." Because Mr. Edison is a great inventor we on the
newspapers want to know what he thinks of prohibition and
the policy of the United States in Nicaragua. You know he
could be a great inventor and be wholly uninformed and
inept on both these topics.

Some might be inclined to make a point and to say that
Thomas A. Edison is not precisely a great scientist. He is
a great inventor, and a distinction can be set up. This is a
little too hairline for me, but at least it is reasonable to question whether he is in any sense a philosopher. He is, of
course, a man who has profoundly reshaped the world in
which he lives. It is hard to think of anyone who has so

radically altered the material substance of tangible things in the daily habits of the average citizen. Columbus, coming home with a brand new continent swinging at his belt, didn't begin to make the same alterations in the daily routing of Paul and Paula.

In a sense, Edison has put new territory into the hands of humankind. The actual borders of our existence are not truly more wide when some explorer announces, "I have found the North Pole." No new meadow is opened to our footstep if he says, "I've found the South Pole." It was a more accessible blackness which Edison opened up for his fellows. He has murdered sleep, or at any rate he's sent it reeling. It used to be an immoral thing to sit up late because tallow was costly and inefficient. Candlelight was bad for the eyes, and so we got into the habit of thinking that anything more than a pinch of it was bad for the soul.

Mr. Edison harnessed electricity in such a way that no more than a light touch upon a button divides sleeping from waking. Obviously, he has increased the span of life, for he has put billions of waking hours into the hands of men. The dreams he has slain if placed end to end would reach from here to heaven's gate and back again.

In performing this feat, Thomas Edison has performed a service and also assumed a responsibility. What waking dreams, I wonder, has he given to replace those he killed? In making life longer I wonder whether he made it any thicker. Of late years Edison has begun to talk a little of his inventions in terms of end results, but these were only slightly on his mind in the moments when he was driving fiercely forward to discovery. It was the joy itself and not the game which commanded his interest and enthusiasm. I'll wager he did not pause once while pursuing the invention of motion picture devices to say, "And if I get it this will mean bathing beauties, 'Came the dawn,' and custard pies." It was not his job to reason what was to come of it all.

An inventor very possibly can't ever be a philosopher. The function is so different. Plato would be inclined to pause again and again in any given job to say, "Yes, but what essential thing will come out of this?"

BETTER A MILLSTONE

"Thank God," so the phrase goes, "I have a sense of humor."

This I have never included in any prayer acknowledging Divine favors. It were better to have a millstone hung around the neck. Humor is the coward's livery, and there is great wisdom in the popular challenge, "Laugh that off." For generally we laugh at the things which we are afraid to face and fight. If the story of Peter in the high priest's house were more detailed, we should probably find that some funny remark accompanied his denial of association with Christ. Peter made a joke of the charge, and there was superb irony in the crowing of the cock, for that sound came hard on the heels of the apostate's cackle.

Hell is paved not with good intentions but with wisecracks. None of the vital men and women who have ever lived could see a joke. They were too intent upon the sight of things at which one cannot and should not smile.

Humor is grit in the evolutionary process. "Does it matter?" is the underlying mood in almost every expression of humor. And, of course, it does matter.

"Oh, he takes himself too seriously," is the standardized reproach set up to tangle the feet of all marching men.

The heart's breath which is needed to keep on going when the taste of blood is in the mouth can easily be dissipated in a laugh. Of course, there are situations in which humor eases tension. People can and do forget their troubles when the clowns perform. But I can't see that this is signal service. Troubles are not solved by the simple process of forgetting them. I've never seen one laid except by those who had the nerve to keep on boring in and swinging, and the man said to be worth while who can smile when everything goes dead wrong is a quitter who is just about ready to heave in a sponge and make a jest of all his tribulations.

It is possible to name one or two great ones of the world who employed humor, but I think it may still be maintained that they used it without actually having it. Lincoln told stories to political audiences and even to the members of his cabinet, but I think it would be excessive to think of him as a humorous man, and certainly most of the fun of Mark Twain was wholly alien to his underlying spirit.

When the sense of humor is very strongly developed something else must be atrophied. People who laugh a great deal are not truly quick but are actually unimaginative. No man who uses his eyes to observe all the things which lie within his range of vision can possibly avoid the conclusion, "What is there to laugh at?"

Instead of a national Laugh Week there ought to be an annual period set aside to be known as "Keep-Off-That-Silly-Grin Month."

Of course, this is too sweeping. I should and probably

will come back to note exceptions. Obviously, the sort of wit which bites your hand off does not belong in the class of merriment which dissipates fighting energy.

THEY BURIED THE BEARDED LADY

There was a funeral on Thursday in Drummond, Okla., for Mme. Sidonia Barsey, "the bearded lady." The author of the brief dispatch wrote under the seeming impression that she was the last and only representative of her profession. There must be, here and there, other bearded ladies, but Mme. Barsey may well have been the best known of all. "She had excited the wonder of countless thousands in the side shows of circuses."

No explanation was given of the manner in which she came to die in this tiny place, for "Drummond is a town of 200 inhabitants, south of Enid." To me Enid conveys no more than Drummond, but, since the local correspondent uses it as a point of orientation, this may be a settlement large enough to afford hospitality to a passing circus.

Still, there was no mention in the story of other show folk. Mme. Barsey seems to have died a lonely freak, surrounded by the drab normality of a little town. Possibly Drummond served her as a retreat. The wonder of countless thousands may come in time to throb unpleasantly.

But from this point of view a small town seems a poor place for privacy. Any sensitive person, stricken with beard or other blemish, would more readily find solace in a city.

They Buried the Bearded Lady

The healing compassion of indifference is known only in the haunts of the many. The beard of Mme. Barsey was "iron gray and heavy." In Drummond, Okla., that could hardly have failed to excite comment and attention. A stroll along Broadway might have been accomplished with far less tribulation than a walk down Main Street.

"It is," the cynical New Yorker would say to himself, "only a false beard, and if I turn about I shall find an advertising display. Why should I buy another safety razor?"

But in saying this the cynical New Yorker would be less than truthful. Of course, as a matter of fact, he isn't really cynical. Here we are crowded so close that we must in sheer self-protection overlook the beams and motes in the eyes of brothers.

Once I saw a two-headed calf led down Broadway and nobody followed after it. Maybe Broadway was under the delusion that all calves are so. Even so, if ever I grow an eye in the middle of my forehead, I shall live close to crowds, for there I may hope to find a curiosity more kindly than that which grows wild in the open spaces.

To be sure, I may be all wrong in assuming that Mme. Barsey disliked excited wonder. After all, she had lived with it at her elbow for many seasons. In the beginning she traded off embarrassment for bread and butter. But bearded ladies do not live by bread alone. For nineteen years Mme. Barsey went up and down the countryside bowing to those who passed her chair upon a high platform and selling her own photographs. She came, I suppose, to think of herself as an artist, and in conversation with others of the tent colony she spoke of these appearances as "my work."

In her heart she believed that the secret of her success was personality. It is worth noting that she allowed the beard to go gray and made no attempt to retouch it. Still she can hardly have escaped the afflicting thought, some time or other before the nineteen years were done, that there was no future in this job of hers. She had gone as far as possible.

Perhaps in her spare time she was writing a book. Certainly she was equipped to reveal a highly specialized point of view. How does life seem to a bearded lady? Would it be a bitter book, I wonder, or did she feel that all was right with the world?

And what did she think of the modern girl with her addiction to cigarets and knickerbockers? Mme. Barsey, I feel sure, was impatient at all the newer rowdiness of women. That attitude would inevitably be forced upon her by circumstances. After all, her post with the circus depended, among other things, upon the fact that she was a lady.

They buried her in Drummond and a pastor of the Congregational Church offered a prayer and gave a short sermon. Unfortunately, nothing of his discourse was reported in the news dispatches. I am eager to know what he said. It was a difficult but a stimulating opportunity. The church was crowded. Many more than Drummond's 200 edged their way in. Any funeral is an event in rural Oklahoma, and this was a service to commemorate the death of a bearded lady.

I hope that with his first words the young preacher stilled the ribald hum in the church. Mme. Barsey was, in this world, a freak and she was not yet free from her stigma of strangeness. Farmer boys grinned across the aisles at their fellows. "A majority of the spectators," says the news dispatch, "attended only to get a last look at the bearded lady."

It was the very necessary task of the preacher to bring home to the shuffling crowd the fact that a share in the dignity of mortality must no longer be denied to the person of whom he spoke. She who had lived a bearded lady became in death a woman and no longer an exile.

OLD CAPTAIN MIDGETT

It seemed a silly storm, an undergraduate commotion. Gales are like that. The first page made it prankish with all the reports of signs blown down and windows broken and pictures of solid citizens chasing after hats.

I would have had no respect for the demonstration if I had not found, tucked off in a corner, the story of Captain Midgett. There was not much to draw attention in that direction. The head read simply, "Captain L. Bannister Midgett." It was a page of social notes and obits. The name was humorous, and I expected to find the usual formal paragraph about the death of one who had served his bank long and well. Instead I read:

"NORFOLK, Va., January 25.—As the terrific gale that swept the coast last night was howling over the Bodie Island, N. C., Coast Guard Station, Captain L. Bannister Midgett, probably the greatest life saver along the coast, died while seated in a chair in the station. Captain Midgett was seventy years old, and he had passed fifty years saving men and women from sinking ships. He took part in rescuing crews from almost one hundred vessels. He was known as the 'Hatteras Lion.' "

And after that I could see that there was some pattern

and some purpose in the tempest. Nature is a great sentimentalist. The Captain as he appears to me was tall, white-
haired and bearded. He walked with a limp, because of a
leg he broke while beaching his lifeboat in a heavy surf.

Even before supper the wind was high enough to indicate a full attendance down at the Coast Guard station.
"Why, Captain, you are surely not going down there tonight," one of the women folk objected, when old man
Midgett took his coat from the hook inside the door. Maybe
the Hatteras Lion growled at his granddaughter or possibly
he merely grunted.

They saw him turn at the gate and head for the sea with
his beard whipping in the salt spray like a banner. All the
boys would be there. This was no night to be missed by a
a man who had been in at the death of a hundred ships.
You couldn't exactly say that the old man was honing for
trouble, but there is a thrill in wrecks that can't be had by
sitting home and playing checkers. And, after all, these two,
the sea and the captain, had fought so many battles that
some sort of admiration would hold them.

Midgett never used harsh words or called the ocean an
old devil. Surely you couldn't lodge any charge of treachery
against the sea on this occasion. The storm came openly and
yelling. He knew it would be worse before it grew any
better. The game leg never twinged for anything less than
seventy miles an hour. "A right smart blow," he said to himself when he got to the road which skirts the beach and
found that the cross-fire made it necessary to tack the last
hundred yards up to the station. Later he found it necessary
to moderate his estimate. One of the youngsters provoked
him.

Bill Turpening came in wet and dripping from a patrol

which took him all the way down to the bones of the *Mary Ellis.*

"Mr. Midgett," he said, "you've been on this island man and boy for quite a spell but I guess you never saw it blow any harder."

"Captain to you," answered the Hatteras Lion, "and don't talk silly."

Bill shut his mouth at that, but old man Midgett had been touched in a sensitive spot. After seventy years a man gets choosy about storms. "Big" comes to be a word he rarely uses, and "biggest" is left for boys to play with.

"Now in '78 that was a real rip snorter," said the Captain. "And that was January, just about this time, if I remember."

He looked about for confirmation but they were all settled down to listen. And they hadn't been there. These were striplings.

"Ice come flying through the air and cut you. It was like a crazy man throwing knives."

"Never saw it blow any harder!" muttered old man Midgett under his breath and snorted. "Why, if any of you'd been alive in '82, they could maybe talk about storms. Blew the roof right off the station."

Everybody nodded in agreement, and after a bit they got the door fastened back again. A gust that screamed rattled all the windows and the Hatteras Lion shook his head as if it were a challenge.

"They don't have any storms like we used to have. What do the scientific fellows say about that? Getting soft. Everybody. Everything. Girls painting their faces and drinking gin."

That reminded somebody of something, and they passed the bottle to the Captain.

"Hell's bells, no," said Midgett. "That's what I call mocking God's blessings. We're all warm and comfortable in here with a stove. Put another log on, Charlie. Save that till you need it. This night ain't over yet. That mate from the schooner in '93, ice on him six inches thick. Had to thaw him from inside and out."

"Well, Captain," said Bill, hoping to find him mollified by now, "what was the toughest storm you ever been through?"

"Don't know as I could say. 'Seventy-eight was a good one, I'm not denying that. But I hadn't seen so many then. You've got to live with storms and get the feel of them before you talk about 'em. Get out in the boat and they're all bad. Maybe some that ain't so bad are the worst ones. Let 'em come big enough and you just got to stand by and respect 'em. I wouldn't like to say which was the biggest. I haven't seen 'em all yet."

"And how many wrecks have you seen, Captain?"

"Never kept count. Used to be nights when they kept you too busy. Toted that gun eight miles, we did, in '91. Bad winter, '91. Sailing vessels mostly. Not so many now. Just as well. Couldn't get the crews for 'em today. I don't know. Reverend Jones may have the right idea. This jazz doesn't do good. The Lord never intended people to go hopping up and down."

Still Captain Midgett listened appreciatively and not to the wild music flying around the station. The night was scored for bagpipes and bass drums.

" 'For those in peril on the sea,' " muttered the old man. "We couldn't help. Just have to sit," and he seemed to sigh and sink deeper in his chair.

The wind was rising. Bill Turpening was tempted to talk

66

again and suggest that maybe before the night was out this would be the biggest even in Captain Midgett's memory. But the best the gale could do, with all its fury, was to lull the Hatteras Lion into a doze. More was coming. Suddenly the storm seemed to reach down and take the station by the throat. In from two window sashes came flying glass that splintered on the floor.

Captain Midgett didn't stir. Bill shook his head. He knew when he was beaten.

"Guess the old man's right," he said. "They've got to come bigger than this to make him notice. Just look at the way he's sleeping through the racket. He's got 'em licked."

WHIMS

Bruce Barton in a recent syndicated editorial speaks ill of whims. "Convictions," he writes, "are splendid when they relate to important matters; they are a public nuisance when they provoke a row over a petty detail."

I think Mr. Barton is ever so wrong, nor is his case strengthened by the examples he offers. He speaks of a friend of his with a taste for eggs boiled two and one-half minutes. Against three-minute eggs and two-minute eggs he made constant protest. And Mr. Barton says that thirty seconds make very little difference. Here is rank heresy. No one but a man insensitive to eggs could utter such a sentiment. Let Mr. Barton stand silent in his room some morning and toll off thirty seconds. He will find it a period of existence at which no connoisseur of time or cookery can afford to sneeze. Save in Chicago three heavyweight boxing championships could pass in thirty seconds. Thousands of touchdowns have been made with no longer than that to go. Salvation itself has been gained in shorter compass.

And remember all the time the water was boiling. Thirty seconds make a lot of difference to an egg, no matter how it affects Mr. Barton. Let him, indeed, put his finger in a kettle and decide after that whether half a minute is an inconsiderable interval.

A chef of genius should never attempt even the simplest dish without a stop-watch. And eggs are not a simple dish. To a man who really cares the precise extent of coagulation is a matter of the greatest moment. A three-minute egg is nothing like a two-minute egg. The difference is deeper than a grave and wider than any church door. As a matter of fact, both varieties are inferior. An egg should be boiled four and one-half minutes if it is to be encountered in its finest estate. Then only does it appear half-yielding and half-resisting, like a poet being interviewed about his private life.

Broad is the theme of the egg and its nature, but the question of whims is even more extensive. Bruce Barton speaks of convictions as if they came into life full grown. Nothing like it. Every conviction was a whim at birth. If I remember what was taught to me in school, Christopher Columbus proved the world was round by making an egg stand on one end. I don't quite understand the pertinence of this, and maybe I've grown muddled about the whole business and the egg incident referred to something else. Anyhow, the scheme of Columbus must have been modest in the beginning. The eyes of Isabella were bright, or maybe it was her jewels. Out of little things like that could come caravels and a new continent.

Orville Wright as a little boy had a kite and fussed over it so much that everybody said, "Oh, don't be silly. What difference does it make if the thing stays up a minute or ten seconds?" And today Ruth Elder is a star in vaudeville.

The tax on tea was tiny. No more was required of William Tell than that he should take off his hat to somebody. India had a mutiny because of grease in cartridges, and the fact that it is possible to rhyme Maine and Spain induced America to intervene in Cuba. This last is perhaps a little beside the point, but let it go. What I am trying to say is that a conviction about a seeming trifle may be momentous. Of course, it may be a nuisance. But that is just as true about a conviction relating to a matter called important.

I happen to know a woman who chooses to retain her own name though married. Very many have said, "What does it matter?" The woman in question has several answers to that, but the best one is, "It matters to me." And in the technique of maintaining her point I believe she takes a position which is unassailable. Never does she allow any person, however casual the contact, to call her "Mrs. Howard Browne" without correcting him. It is a nuisance. She knows that. Some near and dear to her have suggested, "Oh, can't you let it pass just once?" And she can't, nor can anybody with a cause afford to make exceptions. Let just a little water trickle through a dike and presently you've got the ocean.

I'm surprised at Bruce Barton, for he knows his Bible well. The heresy which he promotes was rebuked most strikingly in the New Testament. When they asked Peter if he knew the Nazarene he pretended not to be a follower. Quite properly Peter might have said that his testimony at the moment was of no particular consequence. To stand there and declare his faith could constitute a nuisance. In days before one was allowed to bow down in the house of Rimmon. It won't do. When a man has a conviction, great or small, about eggs or eternity, he must wear it always in plain sight, pulled down tight upon his forehead. I don't think a man should check even a tiny conviction in any corridor. When it comes time to go out into the world again there is too much danger that it will be missing. And often they will hand you the wrong one.

Worst of all is Mr. Barton's complaint that people afflicted by loyalty to little purposes come to be nuisances. Whenever in history did a conviction roost on top of the world without its toll of turmoil? William Lloyd Garrison, who freed the slaves, was probably the most unmitigated nuisance America has ever seen. He talked of nothing else, and always in a loud voice. It was his purpose to be heard. Nobody expects to find comfort and companionability in reformers. Of course, Mr. Barton may say that I have distorted his contention. He spoke of cranks and I've referred to prophets. But there is no lantern by which the crank may be distinguished from the reformer when the night is dark. Just as every conviction begins as a whim so does every emancipator serve his apprenticeship as a crank. A fanatic is a great leader who is just entering the room.

I can remember back to the day when woman suffrage seemed to most people in America just about as important as two-minute eggs. Most of the credit for success goes now to the placid and patient people in the movement who frowned upon disorder. But it was the rowdy women who put it over. Centuries of persuasion would never have accomplished as much as was gained by those who kicked and screamed and picketed. Of course they were nuisances. No body politic is in a healthy state till it begins to itch.

Maybe they will never raise a monument to Bruce Barton's friend who fought to get his eggs boiled two minutes and thirty seconds, but he is a cousin, possibly distant, of all the men and women who have nagged the world a little closer to the heart's desire. Consider the egg agitator: suppose he said, "This is three minutes. That's only thirty seconds wrong—what of it?" Well, the next day they might slip him a four-minute egg, and later one done six or even seven. Before he knew it he would be accepting any hard-boiled thing and saying meekly, "Better not make a fuss."

THE SPORTS BAY

"Gifts of gold and jewels for the cover of the 'Golden Book' of the Cathedral of St. John the Divine were asked by Bishop William T. Manning at the luncheon of the women's division. The gold will be melted down and used for the cover of the huge book which is to preserve forever the name of every person who has contributed to the building fund. The precious stones will be used to decorate the cover."

If I said that this marked once again the exceeding vulgarity of the little bishop I might be misunderstood since popular usage has done so much to limit "vulgarity" to something said in a burlesque show. Possibly it would be better and kinder to speak of the man's immaturity. Throughout the campaign the drive for Cathedral moneys has been conducted with all the dignity and decorum of a children's pageant. I can see no earthly reason why the names of donors should be preserved. The bishop cannot find scriptural sanction for that. According to the accounts in the newspapers Dr. Manning "suggested that many women possessed precious heirlooms, wedding rings, and jewels, which they would not share with another human being, but would gladly give to the Cathedral."

But it would seem to me that if a ring were to be stripped from some left finger not so much as a digit of the right hand should be aware of this; much less should that hand grip a pen to celebrate the deed in a golden book. Also I am somewhat scandalized to learn that the good bishop can speak so casually of the removal of wedding rings. It was my former impression that he wanted them fastened into the bone by iron rivets.

However, the whole problem goes a little deeper than mere criticism of certain mummeries and shows, which have attended the building of St. John the Divine. There is no indication that Dr. Manning has ever paused for so much as a moment to ponder whether or not there was any reasonable and decent need whatsoever for a huge and costly church building. Like a child with blocks, he rears up a structure for the sake of the game and takes no account of the purpose. If there lived today some great architect, skilled in Gothic intricacies, the building might serve an esthetic purpose no matter how reckless the waste of the treasure. But there is no arresting beauty in this building. Nothing of the new liveliness and pace of modern architecture is in it.

At the very best it is no more than a competent echo of an age which has gone by. Surely no travelers will come from the edges of the world to view the pile on Morningside. The same thing has been done too often in the past and with more genius and gusto.

Probably it is only just to admit the entire sincerity of Bishop Manning's purpose. His is a medieval mind and nothing has happened through the centuries to move him from the old belief that God is served and pleased by treats and parties. Do not blame me for the blasphemy if I suggest that in our own day the custom of currying favor by spendthriftiness has passed into other relations than those which exist between God and man.

There is nothing agnostical or even modernistic in holding that in the eyes of a cosmic Creator the completed cathedral will seem no more than a broken bit of shell upon the sand. Even with the best intentions in the world Bishop Manning cannot raise any towers as high as the Andes. It is doubtful if he can even build extensively enough to call down a confusion of tongues upon himself and his followers.

But most of all I am puzzled about the great book with its binding of gold and jewels. Is this, by any chance, intended somewhat to lighten the burdens of St. Peter and his clerks? By some coincidence, which may be Satan's doing, this latest call for treasure to ornament an eternal address book comes at the moment when the bread-line in New York grows longer and begins to curl around the corner on the cold nights. Down in Second Avenue a hospital must close because the trustees no longer feel competent to shoulder an annual deficit of $30,000. The poor cry out for bread, and gravely Bishop Manning lays another stone upon the house of God.

The Sports Bay

It is an essential article of faith that man should love his God and love his neighbor, but surely there is no implication that the manifestation of devotion should take the self-same form. God would not be mocked if William Manning melted down gold to make a hospital rather than a belated Gothic edifice. Cool reason must suggest that in the completed structure there will be rather more elbowroom for Episcopalians than they can conveniently utilize. Of course, it was said in the beginning that this was to be a house of faith for all people but that notion seemed loosely rooted when Dr. Manning found it necessary to refuse a contribution sent by Dr. Guthrie. To be sure the money came from an Episcopal clergyman but it is only fair to admit that he saw many things not precisely eye to eye with Bishop Manning.

Still, I think Dr. Guthrie might have been irritated with some little reason, for the bishop had no trouble at all in accepting funds raised by Tex Rickard. If there was any gap between the philosophy of the promoter and the preacher it was bridged without great difficulty. Indeed at the moment Dr. Manning seems almost as enthusiastic about sports as is the matchmaker of Madison Square Garden. And that shows a generous spirit, for Mr. Rickard has drawn down much more in dividends earned by his fighters. Still a few of the jabs and uppercuts have landed for the glory of the Cathedral.

There is to be a sports bay in the edifice of St. John the Divine. Horsemen, golfers, boxers have all been recruited to pay tithes so that one window may display man drawing closer to the infinite through muscular prowess. And in the "Golden Book" it is not too much to hope that we may find some such entry as "Benny Leonard vs. Kid Mulligan—Leonard the winner by a knockout in the third round."

Unfortunately, the professional baseball people have done very little. At last accounts the big leagues had contributed no more than $100 to the fund for the bay. Unless something is done about this quickly the stained-glass sporting section will be less than adequate. Surely there is need of a panel showing an umpire with upraised finger and Babe Ruth half turned about scowling and caught by the artist at the very moment his lips frame the phrase "You robber!"

THE PIECE THAT GOT ME FIRED

There ought to be a place in New York City for a liberal newspaper. No daily has ventured into the vast territory which lies between the radical press and the New York *World*. The radicals themselves are meagerly served in English-language papers. There will be no argument, I think, that *The World* comes closest to being an American *Manchester Guardian*, but it is at best on the outer rim of the target. Possibly the contention may be raised that there are not enough liberals in New York to support a daily paper. It seems to me the try is worth making. Liberals need not be born. They can be trained by care and kindness.

The word "liberal" itself has fallen into disrepute. To a radical it is a label for a man who professes friendship and then rushes away for his thirty pieces of silver as soon as the crisis comes. In the eyes of the conservatives a liberal is

75

a dirty Red who probably bought his dinner coat with Russian gold. Neither interpretation is accurate and it should not be impossible to expose the fallacy of such reasoning. First of all, there must be a tradition and that takes time. There was the possibility of an enduring association of political liberals when Theodore Roosevelt started the Progressive Party. The leadership was not ideal and many of the followers who clustered around the Colonel were about as liberal as Frank A. Munsey. Still it was effective leadership and we have none now.

Lacking a political haven, the liberal of America might still be rallied into the support of some powerful daily paper content to run the risk of expressing minority thought. This discussion is confined to the New York field. Perhaps in some other city such a paper does exist. I do not know its name, though possibly the Baltimore *Sun* lives up to the requirements. *The World* does not because it switches front so frequently. Nobody has a right to demand that an editor shall never change his mind. New facts on any given situation may require a complete right-about-face. But *The World* on numerous occasions has been able to take two, three, or even four different stands with precisely the same material in hand. So constant were the shifts during the Sacco-Vanzetti case that the paper seemed like an old car going up a hill. In regard to Nicaragua *The World* has thundered on Thursdays and whispered on Monday mornings. Again and again the paper has managed to get a perfect full-Nelson on some public problem only to let its opponent slip away because its fingers were too feeble.

It does not seem to me that the paper possesses either courage or tenacity. Of the honest intentions of all its executives I have not the slightest doubt. I think the fault lies in a certain squeamishness. That there should be some reaction from the flagrant pornography of the tabloids is no more than reasonable, but this development in journalism cannot be met with prudishness. To be specific I cite a *World* editorial on the recent squabble about the proposed birth-control exhibit at the Parents' Exposition in Grand Central Palace. In the beginning Mrs. Sanger's organization was promised a place and this promise was later rescinded at the demand of the Board of Education. The advice of *The World* to the birth controllers was that they should go quietly and make no commotion. "Now it is quite obvious," said *The World*, "that a building swarming with children is no place for a birth-control exhibit."

It may be obvious to *The World*, but I must insist that the reasons for exclusion are not so evident to me. I should think that a building swarming with children ought to be a very logical place for a birth-control exhibit. The fact of the matter is that in the mind of *The World* there is something dirty about birth control. In a quiet way the paper may even approve of the movement, but it is not the sort of thing one likes to talk about in print. Some of the readers would be shocked, and *The World* lives in deadly terror of shocking any reader. As a matter of fact, Mrs. Sanger and her associates intended nothing more dreadful than an exhibit of charts showing population curves and such statistical material. It is the term "birth control" which frightened the newspaper. Not so long ago a Sunday editor insisted on editing a contribution to one of the newspaper columns. Somebody had written in to say that before the triumphs of Lindbergh most Americans had regarded all Scandinavians as dull-witted. "Heywood," said the responsible editor, "don't you realize that our Swedish readers would be offended?"

During the war *The World* was active in attacking hyphenated loyalty, but to the paper's credit it should be remarked that it indulged in far less red-baiting than any of its rivals. Now that hostilities have ended, *The World* cannot get over a certain group consciousness. It has, in addition to "Swedish readers," "Methodist readers," "Baptist readers," "Italian readers," and, perhaps above all, "Catholic readers." When somebody gets angry and sends me a scurrilous postal card he almost always attacks *The World* on the ground that it is under Jewish influence and therefore Bolshevist. This, of course, is ridiculously wide of the mark. *The World* of today has few roots in the Jewish community. Very probably it does command a considerable circulation among the young intellectual group of the East Side, but *The Times* is very obviously the Bible of the arrived and successful Jewish citizen of New York. As a matter of fact, it is my experience that there is very little clannishness among the Jews of New York. There is less standardization than in any other group. Save for downright abuse there is no resentment.

The Irish are quite a different proposition. Admitting the danger of generalities I would contend that the Irish are the cry-babies of the Western world. Even the mildest quip will set them off into resolutions and protests. And still more precarious is the position of the New York newspaperman who ventures any criticism of the Catholic Church. There is not a single New York editor who does not live in mortal terror of the power of this group. It is not a case of numbers but of organization. Of course if anybody dared nothing in the world would happen. If the church can bluff its way into a preferred position the fault lies not with the Catholics but with the editors. But New York will never know a truly liberal paper until one is founded which has no allegiance with and no timidity about any group, racial, religious or national. Perhaps the first thing needed for a liberal paper is capital, but even more important is courage.

GANDLE THE OBSCURE

Fame has jogged on by and left me jilted. A chance has gone to ride, even as far as posterity perhaps, by clinging to another's coat-tails.

Deems Taylor's announcement that he has dropped the tragic fantasy which was to have been his second opera for the Metropolitan finds me the pitiful protagonist. It was my novel "Gandle Follows His Nose" upon which Mr. Taylor planned to found his musical drama. In the beginning this was supposed to be a secret, but I never did keep it well, and at this late date I see no reason why I should not rend my clothing in the market place.

If Bunny could have gone on in this new form he would have been a sort of Cinderella man. The book in which he lived and died fell like a pin in some great foundry. Indeed, the publisher had predicted as much, for he wrote me when he received the manuscript that it was a puny and feeble work and that it might be better for me to destroy it. "Our reputation can stand it," he added, "but I don't know whether yours can."

Tersely I telegraphed, "Go to press!"

And throughout the years I had saved up Mr. Liveright's bleak letter, purposing to wave it in his face on the great night when the violins began to sob and Bunny, clad in purple tights, bowed to the diamond horseshoe.

And I would be sitting somewhere in back because Mack's tailcoat does not fit me so very well. After Taylor and the conductor and all the singers had taken the requisite number of bows I felt that there might be a shout for "Broun!" In fact, I knew it, for I planned to start it. Now I shall never know just what one does when roses are thrust upon him suddenly.

Nor will I get the cigaret case. In the beginning it was to have been gold. When Deems told me that he planned to make an opera out of "Gandle" I was delighted, and when he added, "Now, as to the financial part of it"—I stopped him with a lordly gesture.

"This is sheer luck for me," I said, "so don't let's mention money. I will be perfectly satisfied if I get a gold cigaret case out of this."

"A gold cigaret case!" answered Deems, incredulous. "I guess you have some misconception as to the rewards of music."

But, anyhow, I won't get the silver-plated case.

This opera was in no sense planned as a collaboration. Deems Taylor simply took the book to use as much or as little as he liked and in his own words. In hope of unearned prestige I sold Bunny down the river, and perhaps my present frustration is a punishment quite justified.

Some little time after the first conference Deems read me his scenario of the operatic version. Still in conciliatory mood, I said, "I think that's very good," though at every change, however minor, the wounds of Bunny bled afresh, while I had slight twinges in the shoulder. Gandle did not rise up from his grave with that same body which he had worn in life. Already I could see that my beautiful hero was in a fair way of becoming merely the shell for an operatic tenor.

"Nobody can remember who first called him Bunny. That name he seems almost to have brought with him into the world. It was coined out of his skin, white as a rabbit, and there was a twitch to his nose, and his eyes swept right and left. But his shock of hair was black as a dragon's belly."

Now nobody in the Metropolitan would ever look like that, and Agatha was "the fairest and most virtuous lady in all the world," which is asking too much of any soprano.

Moreover, there was Yom to think of. Genielike, it was his custom to sit on a mountain and rest his feet upon some lower hill across the valley. At Mr. Kahn's place they would have been compelled to make him a bass-baritone perched precariously on stilts. And the elephants and the mighty armies of King Helgas, winding up the mountain road toward Kadia, would all of them have been minified.

Still I did hope to hear the music for the moment when the bugles blew and the elephants all trumpeted because the way was steep.

It was then that Gandle's voice rose high as he cried out, "It is no use. We have no chance. Let's go and fight them in the pass." And that time, even though the others ran away, he did turn back the host of Helgas.

Yes, I still think my Gandle was quite a fellow, and probably he is better off up in the mountains with an arrow through his heart than strutting around before the boxholders and bickering out an aria with the first flute making pace.

"Danger had come a second time as if it were a season." Bunny could not turn back Helgas again, and when they tossed his body to one side so that no passing elephant might slip and stumble he opened his eyes and said, "I am still here."

In a measure Gandle spoke the truth. Lacking orchestral accompaniment, his survival is meager. Few read the book when it first appeared, and there now remains just one devoted follower. Every year along about this time I take the little novel down and read it through. And then, with an egotism pardonable when one remembers that he and I are quite alone, I say to myself, "I must have been damned good when I wrote that."

So here's to you, Bunny, and here's to me. To hell with the fiddles!

CANON SHOCKS COLUMNIST

For the first time in some ten or twenty years I have been definitely shocked by a piece of writing about sex. Undoubtedly the three paragraphs are not obscene in the eyes of the law, for I draw the quotation from a widely circulated bulletin published by the International Reform Federation. Moreover, the author is Canon William Sheafe Chase, clergyman and a lifelong crusader for censorship of plays and books.

Indeed, I beg you to be indulgent with the Canon and not judge him too harshly. It is well known that denunciation of things held to be pornographic will often inflame a reformer to a point where he quite unconsciously violates good taste.

Speaking of Mary Ware Dennett's "The Sex Side of Life," Canon Chase writes:

"The pamphlet does not correctly speak of sex desires as a longing for motherhood and fatherhood but as an opportunity for 'an unsurpassed joy' and 'the very greatest pleasure in all human experience.' Why did Mrs. Dennett misstate this to her children?

"Ask a mother how it compares with the pleasure of nursing her own baby, and she will tell you the pamphlet is criminally deceiving the young she is trying to teach.

"Ask a fine athlete how the act compares with the joy of winning an athletic contest, and he will say that the writer of such advice to the young is not only incorrect but must be abnormal."

Now, I ask you to compare this statement of the good Canon with what Mary Ware Dennett has to say on the same subject. And remember that the Canon's bulletin is freely circulated, while Mrs. Dennett has been sentenced to spend three hundred days in jail.

"The sex attraction is the deepest feeling that human beings know," writes Mrs. Dennett on page 9 of her pamphlet. "It is far more than a mere sensation of the body. It takes in the emotions and the mind and the soul, and that is why so much of our happiness is dependent upon it."

And may I ask you on this evidence which seems to you the clean, the healthy and the normal mind?

The Dennett case went deep into the roots of communal

psychology. The defendant was convicted because she dared to say that love was beautiful. Some reformers hold that this is true but that the fact should be kept quiet in the presence of adolescents. Canon Chase, somewhat more logically, holds that it shouldn't be said because it isn't true. At least, he holds that love is not to be compared to the ecstasy of winning your "Y" in the hammer throw.

This, of course, is a pretty broad subject, and I do not see how it can be decided in a debate between Canon Chase and me. In the first place, I do not know whether he qualifies as an expert witness, for in the record books there is no mention of the races he has run. However, I contend that if Mrs. Dennett errs she has erred in company with Shakespeare, Milton, Wagner, Shelley, and the author of "The Song of Solomon." Respectfully I urge Canon Chase to turn to that part of his Bible and decide for himself whether the Scriptural poet is talking of lacrosse.

Even if it so happens that the Brooklyn pastor cannot qualify as one fitted to give expert testimony I must admit the same about myself. I hold no medals. But years ago I got a pewter mug for winning the tennis championship of the North Entry of Thayer Hall. And, in spite of that vivid and joyful recollection, I still will cast my vote to string along with Shakespeare and with Shelley.

If Canon Chase is right, then Romeo was a fool and Juliet no better than abnormal. And Ruth, who gleaned, should have tended her sheaves and left Boaz alone. And Father Adam, who could not possibly have been corrupted by Mrs. Dennett (known to the press as "the old gentlewoman"), seems to have given up Eden because of the love of woman. But in those days there was no intercollegiate football and the A.A.U. was not yet founded.

If Canon Chase is right all lyric poetry had better be burned by the public hangman and there will hardly be an opera left fit for performance before any who can't abide misstatements.

Gone, too, will be the old verities celebrated in the legends. The prince in the story did not wake the sleeping princess, but rather, left her to sweet slumber's anesthesia and went upon his way to pitch horseshoes at a neighboring palace. And wasn't Ulysses naïve to fill the sailors' ears with wax lest they hear the song of sirens? Had Canon Chase been on that bridge he would have summoned all hands aft to play deck shuffleboard.

And yet the question raised by Canon Chase is not one to be lightly dismissed. If love is but a minor thing, then the world has been wrong-headed from the very beginning. Of course, Canon Chase may say that he has no desire to minimize that love which is of the spirit. It seems to me that soul and body are subtly interwoven. What God hath joined together let no dogmatic parson put asunder.

Canon William Sheafe Chase is not the first pessimist to insist that nature has tricked us all into a sorry mess and that sex is a fundamental blunder of creation. In that case Hamlet was quite right in urging a nunnery upon Ophelia, but the Canon is almost the first critic to insist that the melancholy Dane was altogether normal.

But is it really true that Nurmi knows more of the joy of life than Bobby Burns or any of the Bonnie Prince Charlies? History would be the poorer if Canon Chase is sound in his contention. I'd hate to hear that Antony actually asked for waivers on Cleopatra and finally traded her for a left-hand pitcher and a utility infielder from the Three I League.

MARION THE CAT

Marion, the cat, has come back, and I don't know exactly what to think about it. Since she is about to give hostages to fortune, I can't say exactly that I am glad, and yet she arouses my admiration.

Not because she is going to have kittens. In the feline world such accomplishments are both common and casual, but I must say that she does know her way around the big city. One week ago I appealed to a soft-hearted female and said, "Take that damn cat away from here or I will do her violence."

As a matter of fact, I didn't really intend to do anything more to the cat than tell her, "Won't you please get out of here?" However, my display of masterful truthlessness was sufficient to impress the soft-hearted female, and she went away with Marion in her arms.

But there was no convincing the cat that she was going to a better place than she had ever known. Halfway down the block she scratched Lady Bountiful with great severity and ran into a family hotel. The door man was not inclined to let a passing stranger, even though she happened to be one of neat appearance, conduct a cat hunt through his corridors. Marion was missing, and I practically dismissed her from my mind. No guilt lay upon my conscience. It was not my fault if she were wandering through the corridors of a family hotel without a reservation. And this same hotel is several blocks removed from my penthouse apartment.

Marion the Cat

How she found her way back I shall never know. But beyond a doubt it is the same cat. To identify her by expectancy would be risking much on circumstantial evidence, but there can't be an unlimited number of female cats with green paint on the right foreleg and two and one-half inches hacked off the tail. Nor do I believe that there are many who mew in this same insistent and annoying manner.

How did she get up here again? This is the tenth floor, and there is always somebody in attendance at the downstairs entrance. It is not likely that Marion rang the bell and said to the elevator man, "I want to go to Broun's apartment." She couldn't have done that, because she doesn't know my name. In fact, there is no definite evidence that she is aware of the fact that I write a newspaper column.

Nevertheless, she seems to have some intuitive realization of this circumstance. In her mind she is entitled to salmon and cream for life because I once wrote a column around her. It seems to be her notion that the kittens will be welcomed into the home as additional sources of copy. But there is a flaw in this facile and feline reasoning. She has forgotten the law of diminishing returns or unearned increment, or whatever it is called. It sounds airtight to say if one cat yields two columns six kittens are good for twelve. But that is putting the job of column conducting upon much too mechanical a basis.

It is entirely possible that I shall never write another cat column in my life. If the kittens want support and publicity they must earn it by indulging in provocative pranks of one sort or another. They must be as lively as Marmon Motors, or I shall pass them by and tell why I gave up Standard Brands and decided to support the sagging motors.

And maybe there won't be six kittens. I could do with

less. The contingency opens up other mathematical and horrifying speculations. Cats, I understand, marry young and are prolific. Allow each of the six a half dozen offspring of her own and the net result is thirty-six, which is excessive for any parlor, bedroom, and bath.

To be sure, a few in all the lot may be male, but there is small comfort in that, because one never knows about cats until they make some such palpable demonstration of their feminism. There's no telling in advance which side they are on. And even the most swaggering and Don Juanish may cause the householder to worry lest this pet, too, is about to become a mother.

In fact, I am told by a discouraged fancier that all cats turn out to be female if you give them shelter long enough. This wars against my conception of biology, but with luck running as it has done recently I expect far less than a fifty-fifty break in the matter of the sexes.

There are, I believe, institutions and establishments which take in cats given over to the traditional frailty of their breed. I could send Marion away, but since she has fought her way back from the gutter to this lone and lofty roof it would argue in me a lack of decent sentimentality.

She is a nuisance. My impending responsibility for new arrivals fills me with terror, and yet if a cat selects this single apartment out of all New York as just the proper influence for impressionable kittens I must admit that the compliment is gratefully received. A cat is nobody's fool, and if Marion feels that this place has prospects and that I am a promising young author you can't expect me to set her straight.

A SHEPHERD

The host of heaven and the angel of the Lord had filled the sky with radiance. Now, the glory of God was gone, and the shepherds and the sheep stood under dim starlight. The men were shaken by the wonders they had seen and heard, and, like the animals, they huddled close.

"Let us now," said the eldest one of the shepherds, "go even unto Bethlehem and see this thing which has come to pass, which the Lord hath made known unto us."

The City of David lay behind a far, high hill, upon the crest of which there danced a star. The men made haste to be away, but as they broke out of the circle there was one called Amos who remained. He dug his crook into the turf and clung to it.

"Come," cried the eldest of the shepherds, but Amos shook his head. They marveled, and called out: "It is true. It was an angel. You heard the tidings. A Saviour is born."

"I heard," said Amos. "I will abide."

The eldest walked back from the road to the little knoll on which Amos stood.

"You do not understand," the old man told him. "We have a sign from God. An angel has commanded us. We go to worship the Saviour, who is even now born in Bethlehem. God has made his will manifest."

"It is not in my heart," replied Amos.

And now the eldest of the shepherds was angry.

"With your eyes," he cried out, "you have seen the host of heaven in these dark hills. And you heard, for it was like the thunder when 'Glory to God in the Highest' came ringing to us out of the night."

And again Amos said, "It is not in my heart."

Another then broke in: "Because the hills still stand and the sky has not fallen it is not enough for Amos. He must have something louder than the voice of God."

Amos held more tightly to his crook and answered, "I have need of a whisper."

They laughed at him and said, "What should this voice say in your ears?"

He was silent, and they pressed about him and shouted mockingly: "Tell us now. What says the God of Amos, the little shepherd of a hundred sheep?"

Meekness fell away from him. He took his hands from off the crook and raised them high.

"I, too, am a God," said Amos in a loud, strange voice, "and to my hundred I am a savior."

And when the din of the angry shepherds about him slackened Amos pointed to his hundred.

"See my flock," he said. "See the fright of them. The fear of the bright angel and of the voices is still upon them. God is busy in Bethlehem. He has no time for a hundred sheep. They are my sheep. I will abide."

This the others did not take so much amiss, for they saw that there was a terror in all the flocks, and they, too, knew the ways of sheep. And before the shepherds went away on the road to Bethlehem toward the bright star each one talked to Amos and told him what he should do for the care of the several flocks. And yet one or two turned back a moment to taunt Amos before they reached the dip in the road which led to the City of David. It was said, "We shall see new glories at the throne of God, and you, Amos—you will see sheep."

Amos paid no heed, for he thought to himself, "One shepherd the less will not matter at the throne of God." Nor did he have time to be troubled that he was not to see the Child who was come to save the world. There was much to be done among the flocks, and Amos walked between the sheep and made under his tongue a clucking noise, which was a way he had, and to his hundred and to the others it was a sound finer and more friendly than the voice of the bright angel. Presently the animals ceased to tremble and began to graze as the sun came up over the hill where the star had been.

"For sheep," said Amos to himself, "the angels shine too much. A shepherd is better."

With the morning the others came up the road from Bethlehem, and they told Amos of the manger and of the wise men who had mingled there with shepherds. And they described to him the gifts—gold, frankincense and myrrh. And when they were done they said, "And did you see wonders here in the fields with the sheep?"

Amos told them, "Now my hundred are one hundred and one," and he showed them a lamb which had been born just before the dawn.

"Was there for this a great voice out of heaven?" asked the eldest of the shepherds.

Amos shook his head and smiled, and there was in his face that which seemed to the shepherds a wonder even in a night of wonders.

"To my heart," he said, "there came a whisper."

"OH, EUCLID!"

New York has just lived through the most extraordinary riot in its history. It was necessary to call out the police reserves because a mob of 3,500 people fought to get into the Museum of Natural History to hear about the Einstein theory.

In days gone by people have rioted about bread and beer, but this time collars were torn and heads bashed for the sake of science. One can imagine Patrolman Hogan engulfed in the milling throng and see the bluecoat as he cries out, "So it's relativity you want, and I'm the boy to give it to you"—wham!

Quite possibly a nest of mathematical speakeasies will grow up in the neighborhood of the museum—places where one raps three times at the door and says, "I'm a friend of Charlie Duckworth's." Once inside, the patron will be able to get stellar space and ether at seventy cents a throw.

My feeling is that if the populace of New York is hungry for higher mathematics it should be served. Evidently the theatrical managers have guessed wrong. They have gone along in the same old way, giving people plays about sex and crooks and money, with never a word about parallel lines and their sweet rendezvous at infinity.

Triangles we have had, but not the right kind. There was a husband, a wife and a lover, but no hypotenuse on which to build a square. And the public has stayed away from the playhouses in droves. To gain admission to the museum they riot.

"Oh, Euclid!"

Since managers boast that they give the public what it wants, some effort should be made immediately to present a drama dealing with plane or solid geometry. Why have the Shuberts been so inactive while this Einstein racket was gathering momentum? Fortunately, I am in a position to offer producers just the entertainment which is needed to appease the mathematical mob. I have just finished a musical revue which is to be called "I Love My Einstein, but, Oh, Euclid!"

The first scene should be sufficient to make it a smash hit. As soon as the curtain rises twenty chorus girls walk slowly across the stage in full view of the audience. They wear, among other things, pink tights. There is no song or dance, and not a word is spoken. But if proper type casting has taken place the effect should be enormously exciting.

I think that by the time the fifth girl in the line has passed by a buzz of comment will come from spectators in the front rows. One first nighter, after gazing long and hard at the girls in tights, will be unable to restrain himself any longer. His happy shout, "A straight line is the shortest distance between two points!" will ring through the house. From the lobby the news will pass out along Broadway. There will be dancing in the streets, and somebody will wake Mayor Walker to tell him the good news. A Fifth Avenue mob in front of the Plaza will kill a man who maintains that light travels in curved lines.

After the first scene it will be unnecessary for the chorus to appear any more. The rest of my comedy concerns the more intimate life of Euclid. Indeed, it deals with his momentous discovery that the square on the hypotenuse of a right-angle triangle equals the sum of the squares on the two other sides.

"Oh, Euclid!"

The scene is Alexandria, where the great Greek scholar went to teach. Alexandria being in Egypt will make it possible to introduce the character of Cleopatra. I rather think there will be a river song. It seems that the Nile has been doing nothing through all the centuries except just roll along. This extraordinary fact will be mentioned in a song called "Old Gal River." Maybe it will be necessary to bring the chorus back.

The first act is outside the home of Euclid. Although it is after 3 in the morning, all the lights in his apartment are going full tilt. He is working on the sum of the squares on the two other sides. The poor man can't seem to strike a balance. He is just a nickel out of the way. You may be sure nobody in all Alexandria will get much sleep this night.

A wanton passes under the window and speaks to a soldier. He rebukes her by pointing to the shade behind which the sage is working. She blushes and goes home, resolved to study plane geometry and be a better girl.

"I wonder whether he'll ever get it," remarks a traveling man from Jericho.

"I'll lay you two to one against it," says a gambler from Judea, who is under the impression that Euclid has been fixed and that the proposition is in the bag.

A dog barks, and in the distance sleigh bells are heard. Just as a big clock strikes 4 to a waltz tune Euclid's window flies open. "Eureka!" he cries, stealing another man's stuff, and to the accompaniment of four Hawaiians strumming "Old Gal River" he demonstrates from the second floor on a small blackboard that the square on the hypotenuse is equal to the sum of the squares on the two other sides. It turns out that the particular hypotenuse he picked happened to have an inferiority complex.

94

But Freud doesn't come in until the next act. He and Pythagoras and Einstein and Thomas A. Edison are discovered in a speakeasy splitting an atom. Whenever anybody draws a geometrical figure on a piece of paper Dr. Freud starts to hum "Mighty lak a—" But the rest of the crowd knows Freud and always stops him before he can go on. The Shuberts need have no fear. "Oh, Euclid!" is a clean show.

LIFE AND LOWELL

Harvard University has discharged twenty scrubwomen rather than raise their wages from thirty-five to thirty-seven cents an hour. The scrubwomen themselves asked for no increase in salary, but it so happens that the State of Massachusetts has a minimum wage law which provides boards to set certain standards of pay for women and minors in certain industries.

When the board called the university's attention to the fact that it was underpaying its scrubwomen Harvard's answer was to discharge them. The university has announced that it will replace them with men who may perhaps be able to do a greater amount of work, and there is no minimum wage for men. Possibly ten men will be able to do the work of twenty middle-aged and elderly women.

This will result in a considerable saving to the university. Had it paid the women a legal living wage the sum would have amounted to almost $600 a year. Equipment for the scrub football team hardly costs that much in a season.

But the most interesting element in the problem is not the bare economic details but the human phase. A. Lawrence Lowell, president of Harvard, has passed upon the issue, and his attitude is interesting. William M. Duvall, a young Methodist clergyman in East Cambridge, was disturbed by the plight of one of his parishioners. Mrs. Emma Trafton had been employed by Harvard for thirteen years. She was discharged without notice on November 1. The college was kinder to Mrs. Katherine Donahue, who had worked for Harvard for thirty-three years. She was not discharged until the Saturday before Christmas. Mr. Duvall wrote to Mr. Lowell and received the following reply:

"I have inquired into the discharge of Mrs. Emma Trafton from the Widener Library, and I find that the Minimum Wage Board has been complaining of our employing women for these purposes at less than thirty-seven cents an hour, and hence the university has felt constrained to replace them with men. Some of them—I hope many of them—will be able to be employed at some other work in the university."

In other words, the reward of thirty-three years of work for Harvard University is the pious hope of the president that possibly something will turn up.

We used to have a song about how the football team was sweeping down the field and that we would do or die with the Crimson until the last chalk line was passed. The precise phrasing escapes me, but the words were to that effect. Well, Mrs. Katherine Donahue has had thirty-three years of sweeping. One might suppose at the end of that time she would have passed the last chalk line and landed in some haven of honor or security.

But it seems not. She carries with her into a bleak and cheerless world merely the tepid hope of a Lowell. Just try to warm your toes with that!

Thirty-three years is a long time to work for a college, whether the job be scrubbing or teaching. In my opinion, Mrs. Donahue has done rather more to tidy up the place than even A. Lawrence Lowell himself. She left no dark and clotted stains behind her.

It is said unofficially that some of the women had grown too old and too feeble to do their work with competence. One never does grow younger in scrubbing 'round under the book shelves for thirty-three years. In old Gore Hall and later in the new Widener Library Mrs. Donahue may have paused now and then for a second to look up at the battalions of books. They reached from floor to ceiling. In them was the stuff to make one free. But they were not for the likes of her. This was fodder for the Lodges and the Lowells and the Cabots.

And yet I would not say that the education of A. Lawrence Lowell had been altogether successful. He has failed to learn that there are things which men and colleges may not do with honor.

Myself, I did not frequent much the premises kept neat by Mrs. Donahue. My four years brought me no degree. No, not even a note from President Lowell. Accordingly, I cannot say that as an alumnus I demand humanity from Lowell and from Harvard.

But I will demand it just the same. This is no private fight. "I hope," says A. Lawrence Lowell. And I say "hope" be damned! Unless Harvard takes immediate steps to fix a pension system for its veteran employees it will forfeit any right to stand as a leader in enlightenment. A university is a living organism, and when the heart has ceased to beat death and corruption of the flesh set in.

"The veterans of industry are entitled to a pension as well as the veterans of war." I quote from a leaflet issued on this case by the Harvard University Socialist Club. And the story was first called to public attention by Gardner Jackson, who has written about it in the current *Nation*.

Already, I am told, certain prominent alumni of the university have taken steps to right the wrong. That's good. It's up to Harvard to choose between life and Lowell.

IN THE IMAGE OF GOD

The text for my sermon is to be found in the twenty-sixth verse of the first chapter of Genesis: "And God said, Let us make man in our image, after our likeness: and let them have dominion"—

And if I were a clergyman I would preach a great many sermons on this text and similar ones, because the churches are too much inclined to cast man down rather than raise him up. It was the serpent which crawled upon his belly. Adam came in this world standing on his own two feet, and that's where he belongs.

He need not sit in shamefaced silence and let anybody tell him that he is puny and a miserable sinner. Man is a first class job. Indeed, the first chapter of Genesis ends with the statement, "And God saw every thing that he had made, and, behold, it was very good."

It is not my notion that man represents the ultimate and crowning achievement of creation. Give him a few more million years and he can add cubits to his stature and raise the roof of his head to make room for bigger and better cranial convolutions. But he will do until the superman arrives.

Often parsons exhort us to look at the sun and other bodies and realize our own insignificance. The sun is pretty bright and pretty big, but man can put his hand out and catch all its essential properties in a lamp of violet rays. It does not seem to me that man need take back talk from any of the planets. Mere size should not make him craven. He has outstayed the mammoth and is well on his way to conquer those even vaster forces of sea and sky.

Now and then the earth does rise up to smite him. The greatest disaster of our time was the Japanese earthquake, and it moved thousands of editorial writers and other preachers to musing on the mightiness of nature and the puniness of man.

But it seems to me that this was by no means the only possible interpretation of the event. Far from scoring against man and his mightiness, the episode furnished still one more proof of human tenacity. Thousands died in Tokio, but millions lived. Across that plain where the city lies the earthquakes roll like sluggish waves. Each year hundreds or more tug at the roots of Tokio. When bamboo quivers there it is not the wind.

So it has gone on for centuries. This is, perhaps, the mightiest yet of all recorded assaults, and man remains. In a thousand years nature has not been able to shake him off.

Though the ground has rocked and swayed beneath him like a broncho, the little Japanese sits tight. And across the world of water from his fellow men there should come a mighty and defiant shout, "Ride him, cowboy!"

The boxing writers have named Johnny Risko the rubber man because he springs up again when borne down by blows. But this is not a unique distinction. There's a lot of gutta-percha even in the worst of us. It seems to me that resiliency is an almost universal trait in human kind. Within a year the tea houses stood in the streets where the dead did lie. Geishas sang once more of Johnkeen. "Yokohama, Nagasaki, Kobe, maru hoi!" And when any Babylon falls don't be surprised to see it bounce.

Who says that man is puny? He falls asleep and dies awhile and then he is up again. The stream of life force has not been dammed in our time and will not till the earth crumbles. Even then I rather expect that it will change to the car ahead and still continue. After the wave and the hurricane and the earthquake life crawls out from under the débris and starts on another lap.

One of the most fascinating things in "The Green Pastures" is the scene in which the ark comes finally to rest upon its mountain top. Up comes the sun, and up rise men and elephants. Noah opens the back door, and you hear the beasts rush out in search of life and lampposts. I am not one who can accept the fact that this particular flood was factually true, but it is authentic in a more important sense. It is spiritually true. Man does come through catastrophes and fill the ranks again.

What permanent victory has nature ever won from us? Neither ice nor fires nor floods have checked the succession of human kind. Other species have given up the fight, but man is the finest animal of the lot. The sun cannot drive him from the tropics, and beyond the Arctic in barren lands, where even the microbe cannot live, he sets his foot down and sends back pictures for Sunday rotogravure sections.

To be sure, our perch upon the earth is precarious. Only the crust has been completely won. Flame and water menace from beneath, and above are mighty bodies capable of flipping the whole globe into the dust bin. But they haven't done it yet. Nature has the weight and nature has the punch, but whom did she ever lick? Man has staggered and bled and reeled from hammer blows, but he hasn't been counted out as yet.

Until the final ten has been tolled who dares to say that he is puny?

BILL BOLITHO

Bolitho's dead at Avignon. There has passed, I think, the most brilliant journalist of our time. This is not the overstatement of one who mourns a friend. While he flourished I expressed the opinion that Bolitho's best was far and away beyond the topmost reach of any newspaper competitor.

It was pleasant to praise him because he lent some of his glory and achievement to all the rest. I think that there is no reporter or critic or columnist who does not smart under the popular and snobbish assumption that anybody who sets his stuff down day by day is of necessity a hack. All men live under the hope that one day they may touch greatness, and it is essential for them to feel that when they drive home the thrust the medium in which they live and labor shall be sufficient for their purpose.

It is not inevitable that today's strip of news print should be no more than tattered scraps in tomorrow's dust bin. The man who writes well enough and thinks through the thing before him can win his immortality, even though his piece appears obscurely in a Wall Street edition. Most of us on papers, for all our swagger, are at least five and a half times too humble. We are apt to say, "Oh, I'm just a newspaperman." When called upon to justify ourselves we smirk and behave as if the thing we did were really of but small importance.

We know better than that. There is no reason why a first rate man on any newspaper should yield precedence to every novelist and minor poet and little essayist. In city rooms I've known the whole crowd to gape at some member of the staff in considerable awe and whisper behind his back, "He's written a book."

There's no special magic in getting between boards. Last year's novel is just as dead as last year's paper. Indeed, I know few sights more horrible than second-hand book stalls on which dead volumes are exposed to wind and weather, completely dead and lacking only decent burial.

Bolitho, to be sure, had his fling in bound sheets, but much of his finest appeared in the *New York World*. And these essays will still remain, though he is dead at Avignon.

From the standpoint of the old-fashioned school Bolitho could hardly be called a newspaperman at all, let alone a leader in the first rank. There still endure graybeards who detest frills and shake their heads to say that news is all and that anything else which creeps into a paper is so much folly.

But these graybeards employ a tight and tenuous definition of news. They mean no more than the report of the thing which has happened. They feel that it is the part of newspapermen to behave like members of the Light Brigade and refuse to reason why.

Such a definition would have excluded William Bolitho almost completely. He was far more interested in the explanation than in the event. Many had better eyes to see and ears to hear but less of analytical power. Sometimes, like an overeager shortstop who throws before the ball is in his hands, Bolitho began to interpret episodes which were still in motion. It is hard for any interpreter to remain patient until the play has been completed.

Yet news must be a deeper and a more significant thing than a mere recital of names, addresses and the doctor's diagnosis. Causes, however far beneath the surface they may lie, are distinctly within the province of journalism. That is, if journalism is to be a kingdom and not a little parish.

For instance, I mean just this: Some little time ago a group of Jewish internes were cruelly hazed in a public hospital. Naturally, all the papers reported the facts of this incident. There they stopped, and I say they stopped because they did not have a sufficiently keen vision to see the whole way to the uttermost boundaries of journalistic territory. It is not enough to discuss the symptom. The disease itself must be investigated. It was the function of papers then, and it is the function of papers now, to get at the root of conditions which underlie strife and prejudice and turmoil. The story of Gastonia should not have ended just because the strike ceased.

It was as the leader of journalistic exploration, deep into

the human heart and mind, that Bolitho made his mark. If the standard which he set can even be approximated it may well be that seekers after education will not turn to some five-foot shelf or scrapbook, but find their road to knowledge in the living, daily record of things which lie about them. Indeed, I would call a man well read if he could hold the dinner table spellbound with an accurate discussion of the dispatches from Russia. That would mean much more than if he lived up to the advertisements by giving the date of Walt Whitman's birth and a few lines from his best-known poems.

Indeed, for this opinion I can cite distinguished authority. Dr. Nicholas Murray Butler in his commencement address at Columbia talked on "The Insulated Life" and said, "A liberal education is not to be confused with mere attendance at school or college or with the possession of a certificate to that effect." And later he added, "A liberal education is that which is worthy of a free man and which fits a man for intellectual and spiritual freedom."

It seems to me that no man can know life sufficiently to understand freedom until he has gone down into it—until, like a dog on a spring day, he has actually nozzled his way beneath the surface. William Bolitho had been newsboy, day laborer, student, soldier, writer, before he died. The last time I saw him he told me of his days as a mason's helper on a construction job in Cape Town.

Naturally it has been said that this brilliant journalist of 39 had much of his finest potentialities still ahead of him. That's true, but still he had been all the way around the track before he died at Avignon.

A REPLY TO MY BOSS

Any working newspaperman is naturally pleased when the editor finds it necessary to sit down and write a piece.

My gratification was double because in this case it gave me one more day of vacation. But, naturally, I am grieved to find Roy W. Howard enmeshed in error. He objects to my running for Congress on the Socialist ticket in the Seventeenth District, New York, for four reasons:

1. No Scripps-Howard feature writer has ever gone to Congress.

2. The odds seem to be overwhelmingly against my election.

3. The profession of journalism is more important than that of politics.

4. Independence of thought precludes party membership.

One and two seem to square off pretty well from Mr. Howard's point of view, although I want to say a little more about the second later. In saying that journalism is more important than politics and that Broun could be "more constructive in a column than in Congress" Mr. Howard raises an issue which does not exist. The two things are not mutually exclusive. During the campaign this column will appear as usual. I don't expect to see it any better or any worse. When and if elected I should most certainly have daily opinions and the desire to see them in newsprint. There is no reason why a man or a woman could not be both columnist and Congressman. If Mr. Howard disagrees I suggest that he secure an option on the newspaper services of Mrs. Ruth Pratt to be exercised immediately after election day.

The real sticking point is party affiliation. I am quite sure that the fact of its being Socialist does not enter into the problem. Surely it would be far more embarrassing for a liberal newspaper to have its columnist affiliated with the Tammany machine or the Republican organization of Sam Koenig than to be serving under the leadership of Norman Thomas.

Indeed, *The Telegram* supported Thomas for mayor, and I trust that it will also indorse him this year in his fight for Congress. But I don't know. Right here comes the weakness of an individual or an organization construing independence as meaning a permanent place on the sidelines. In order to have any coherence of policy it is necessary to make something more than annual alliances. At times the Scripps-Howard independence becomes little more than erratic whimsy. A liberal, for instance, may be pardoned if he rubs his eyes and asks querulously, "What is this liberal independence?" when he observes *The Telegram* supporting in one national election a LaFollette and the next time around a Hoover. As the rowing experts say, the boat doesn't seem to run well between strokes.

I think it not in the least inconsistent for Mr. Howard to stop well short of complete acceptance of the Socialist program and, nevertheless, support Thomas for mayor, as was the case last year. It would be silly for a passenger to say, "I can't get on that Van Cortlandt Park express, because I want to go only as far as 72nd Street." Surely Thomas and the rest of us are going in the direction toward which the Scripps-Howard papers are heading. Why shouldn't they get on board? We'll let them off when they think they've reached their destination.

Independent liberals always get beaten in American elections because they reserve their commitments until a month or so before election. Sam Koenig and John F. Curry work three hundred and sixty-five days a year. Organization can't be beaten without organization. The Socialist Party offers the only existing machinery by which the Republican-Democratic alliance can be overthrown. It is hopeless to try to cleanse these parties from within. That's been tried. Mrs. Pratt herself made a gallant effort to free the local Republican organization of Koenigism. She failed. My newspaper friends tell me that after election day she will be out of office. Sam won't.

My newspaper friends did not tell me that I would be elected. Herbert Bayard Swope, who used to be a newspaperman, said that I had a good chance. The rest were less encouraging. They felt that an enthusiastic Curry would do more for his candidate than a perfunctory Koenig. The Republican and Democratic organizations are not parties so much as marching clubs. For them this is no more than a drill or, more exactly, a game. When the final whistle has blown the Tammany crowd huddles and gives three long cheers for Koenig and the Republicans do as much for Curry. The whole fight is carried on in a spirit of good, clean fun. Anybody caught slugging will be immediately sent to the locker room.

Mr. Howard knows this as well as and better than I do. He has fought the fight against Ewald and Vitale and Vause. And yet he says that I should stay on the sidelines with him and the rest of the Scripps-Howard executives joining in the long-drawn independent-liberal cheer of "Hold 'em, forces of reform and decency!" With all due respect for the cheering section the man who gets down onto the field and tries to spill a few of the trick plays is doing a great deal more. I'm going to do all I can.

Since when did it become a reproach to tackle a job with the odds vastly against you? It is not impossible to win. Twenty-one thousand votes out of the sixty thousand which Mr. Howard has mentioned would be enough. There should be that many people who are sick of Hoover's fake prosperity and Tammany's very real prosperity for Tammany officials. This could be Jim Dandy all over again even though I admit a certain slackness in any metaphor which links me to a race horse. And maybe the name isn't altogether suitable, either. But let it go.

In fact, I am afraid that it will be necessary for me to avoid any great insistence on the campaign in this column. Columnar modesty is against an overexploitation of the first person singular. Fair play forbids my using weapons against my opponents which they do not possess. If I attacked Brodsky in this column he would have every right to demand an equal amount of space for reply. I would have to print it. And as he is an amateur at the business maybe he wouldn't write a good column. That has been known to happen even in the case of regulars. And surely everybody can see how palpably improper it would be for me to solicit campaign contributions, through the medium of this column, to be sent to Morris L. Ernst, 285 Madison Avenue.

But I am tired of hearing all this talk about how the honest average citizen should get into politics and not leave it to the machine professionals. I am tired of hearing this, because I am average and honest, and yet when I do get in my own boss tells me that this is no business for me. It's everybody's business and nobody's business.

But I am even more tired of standing with well-meaning liberals weaving a daisy chain of good intentions. I want to break that chain and enlist for duration. Here goes!

HEYWOOD COX BROUN

I had not intended to write anything about the death of my father, but I must. If I include many other fathers in this brief column, it may be possible to escape the charge of bad taste. But this has always been, by intent and instinct, a personal record. There is such a thing as leaning over too far.

On the day my father died I sat down and marked time by writing a column about the sea and cats and preoccupations which may move men to achieve a literary style. It was warmed-over stuff from half and three-quarters remembered columns written years ago.

But in any such painful effort to gain detachment from the thing actually in your mind there must be a very palpable insincerity. That I came to realize. And the acuteness of the realization was accented by the paragraphs in the newspapers which marked the passing of a man of 80.

And at this point it is fair enough to generalize. Save in the case of the very great, and perhaps not even then, the news notes must inevitably be inadequate. The reporter ascertains when this man was born and where, with what business activities he was affiliated, the list of his clubs and the names of surviving relatives. Of this one it is said that for forty years he was engaged in the cotton market. Of another it may be related that he helped to found an athletic club or was a dignitary in some fraternal organization. And through any such wide-meshed set of facts the real man must slip through.

Every individual is more than his job, his social activities and his span of years. It is a pity that when each one of us dies the essence may not survive, whether the person be notable or not.

In the heart of everyone there is the desire to know what will be said about him in the papers. I remember a story of two years ago about a dying newspaperman who called his wife to his bedside when his end was near and with his remaining store of strength and voice dictated to her what he would like to have printed about himself. As he wrote it the paragraphs appeared humble and modest enough. But at least the dying man was assured that the facts were straight.

What I have in mind are things less tangible. Somebody called me on the telephone the afternoon of my father's death to ask for some little information about him. I failed, because there was much I forgot in the matter of mere material detail and even more I left out because it hardly fell within the tradition of what constitutes a conventional obituary.

Later it seemed to me unsatisfactory that a man of long life should have his existence summed up to some extent as "the father of the newspaper columnist." Such a report shifts the emphasis. It makes the wrong man seem the debtor.

And yet there are practical difficulties in presenting any

true and live picture within the confines of limited news-paper space. Once there was written a complete portrait of my father, but by a man who never knew him. And this adequate portrait required the full generosity of a two-volume novel. If you play the game of identifying your friends with famous folk of fiction I can explain my father to you by saying that he was to the life Thackeray's Colonel Newcome with just a dash of Major Pendennis.

The reporter at the other end of the telephone would have been surprised if, instead of saying that Heywood Cox Broun was the founder of a printing business and a member of the Racquet and Tennis Club, I had said, "The most important thing to mention is that Mr. Broun was just about the most charming man anybody had ever known."

And yet this report would have been more accurate and vital.

I have always been interested in problems of heredity and the curious manner in which people are conditioned by ricochet rather than direct fire. For instance, there is the fact that my father was an ardent National Guardsman and at one time among the four or five crack rifle shots in the entire country. When I was a child the house was filled with gold and silver medals as tokens of this prowess. And I, his son, am a fanatical pacifist and have never so much as fired a gun in my life.

Yet there is consistency in this. We were always told, as children, never to point a gun at anybody—not even a cap pistol—and it is not altogether strange that I grew up with a feeling that there is something almost inherently evil in firearms.

When I went to tell him that I was running for Congress on the Socialist ticket he was a little surprised and yet not displeased, though I was turning on a road which ran almost at right angles from his highway. We kept close through many episodes in which I followed philosophies quite foreign to his own. We kept close because of his wisdom. All he ever wanted to know was whether I believed honestly and sincerely in the path which I had chosen. If I could convince him of that the thing I did was all right, whether or not he grasped the detail of my emotion or my reasoning.

And in some respects I have tried to follow more closely the tradition which he set. I take pride in the fact that my father was a gay man. That he liked to give and receive parties. For many years after he was well past 70 we kept, with all the ardor of a religious rite, a cocktail hour.

I have always felt that truly kindly people, like my father, must be men who have themselves a flair for fun. Only from the exuberant is it possible to get an enlivening return in the execution of the commandment "Love thy neighbor as thyself." Nor could his tombstone have a better inscription than this: "He took and gave much joy in life."

THE MAGICAL CITY

Here's a letter from Miss V. M., all the way from Fargo, N. D., and she says: "Can you tell someone who's never been in New York, and maybe never will be, how to be a New Yorker? I work out here in an office from 9 to 5, and I don't get much chance to read, but I do get *The American*

Mercury and *The New Yorker*. And the radio at night makes me feel more in touch with the East. I listen, and I'm trying to develop a classical taste in music. Recently I ordered a dress from a New York store that I saw in an advertisement and a set of bridge cards from a shop on Fifth Avenue. That made me feel pretty good because they came from New York. Maybe you would be kind enough to tell me if I'm on the right track to becoming a New Yorker. This place where I live—this Fargo—is just a small town. Tell me what New York's like, and forgive me if I don't sign my name, because I don't want everybody in Fargo to know my secret ambition."

Well, Miss V. M., there are a hundred thousand others who feel just the way you do. There always have been. Probably you know the story of the prodigal son, and I guess there was also a prodigal daughter. Everybody thinks that over the rim of the horizon, beyond the hills, there must be some place which is different—a town where life isn't made up of washing the dishes after supper and getting up at 8 o'clock in the morning to go to work. I suppose people in France feel that way about Paris, and years ago there were boys and girls who said, "If I could only get away from this one-horse town and go to Babylon or Carthage or Rome!"

Don't expect me to run down New York and say that it's all a sham and a delusion. I can't do that in honesty. This is my home. I was born here—or near enough. As a matter of fact, I was born in Brooklyn, but at the age of 1 year and 6 months I persuaded my parents to take me to New York proper, and I've been here ever since. I think it's a good thing to be a New Yorker—when you are in New

York—but in Fargo I'd be a Fargoian or a Fargoite, or whatever you call it.

You say, Miss V. M., that maybe you never will be a New Yorker, but that you'd like to be. Well, this is a free city. Come if you must. But don't expect too much. I know it's easy to think of Manhattan as the magical city where all the buildings are a thousand feet tall and the men six or seven. And the women beautiful in proportion. And the streets, I hear, are paved with gold. But don't forget, Miss V. M., that life can be just as humdrum in this magical city as in Dubuque or Fargo. New York isn't made up entirely of opera singers and motion picture actresses and novelists. Plenty of us get up at night and go to work and watch the clock till 5 and then come home. We wash dishes here, too, just the same as in Kansas City.

The truth of it all is that people are much alike wherever you find them. And so are cities. The same talking pictures are shown from coast to coast at the same time, and the same comic strips and the same performers on the radio. There's hardly a nickel's worth of difference. We speak the same language and share the same emotions and have the same joys. I started to say we breathe the same air—but, of course, we don't. You have better air out in Fargo. You don't have to take a peck of coal dust in along with each breath.

It's a curious thing how Americans beyond the borders of New York regard this particular city. They think of it either as a Utopia or—an inferno. And it isn't either. We are not different in any essential way—neither more kind nor more cruel. I've read a lot of syndicate stuff about the magic island of Manhattan, and it's all based on the same fallacy. Journalists here send out "New York letters" to people

throughout the country. They have to write about something, and so they make up this picture of a city in
which everybody talks like George Jean Nathan or H. L.
Mencken.

Some people think New York is gayer and happier and
more glamorous than any other place on the map. And there
is also a very widespread school of thought that believes
that New York, and more particularly Manhattan, is an
evil and a vicious settlement. Particularly in recent years a
great deal has been said about New York's not being American at all but a "foreign city."

You may hear it said out where the West begins, "Oh,
they are all Jews there in New York." I remember in George
Kaufman's play, "June Moon," one of the characters remarked, "I understand there are four million Jews in New
York alone." And one of the players answered, "What do
you mean—alone?"

There are millions of Jews in New York but it's silly to
make a reproach of that. The Jews are not newcomers to
America. It was a Jew—Haim Solomon—who saved the
American Revolution by raising money for the Continental
Congress. Jews were in New York way back when it was
New Amsterdam, in the days of Peter Stuyvesant. Some
American Jewish families are among our oldest settlers.
Decidedly they belong.

But why and where did this talk arise about "foreigners"
and 100 percent Americans? That's new; it isn't in accord
with our traditions.

And in recent years, I hear, a certain number say about
Americans who are foreign born or of foreign extraction,
"Why don't they go back where they came from?" Yes,
but I want to know what are they going to take with them?

Are these "foreigners" to take with them the railroad tracks which they laid across the plains when every foot of the way was a fight with savage Indians? Are they to take with them the roads they laid in the heat of the day? Are they to take the buildings they reared and the bridges they built? And I want to know whether they are to take with them—back where they came from—the bones of their honored dead, who have fought in every American war, shoulder to shoulder with the native born, in every conflict from Yorktown to Château-Thierry?

"TREES," "IF," AND "INVICTUS"

Sitting idly by the radio last night, twirling the dials, I happened upon an hour devoted to celebrating the methods of a famous tree surgery house. And, inevitably, the period was introduced by a rendition of Joyce Kilmer's well-known poem.

I wouldn't be the one to evaluate Kilmer's precise position in the world of poetry, but "Trees" (if I have the name right) is one of the most annoying pieces of verse within my knowledge. The other one is Kipling's "If," with third place reserved for Henley's "Invictus."

"Trees" maddens me, because it contains the most insincere line ever written by mortal man. Surely the Kilmer tongue must have been not far from the Kilmer cheek when he wrote, "Poems are made by fools like me."

I mean that Joyce Kilmer must have felt as he was writing his poem, "This is pretty good stuff." It did turn out to be his most popular poem, but, good or bad, successful or unsuccessful, the motivating force in any kind of composition is the feeling that, on the whole, you are a somewhat superior person, with information or fireworks worth showing to the assembled community.

Kilmer, as a professional poet, never thought for a moment that poets were fools or insignificant puddlers in the pool of ultimate values. He thought well of himself and of the art in which he dabbled. He was indulging in a wholly spurious humility.

As a matter of fact, his major contention is at least subject to debate. I'm not willing to grant that even the worst tree is a production which dwarfs the best poem. I've seen scraggly pines which were not fit to be mentioned in the same breath with "An Ode to a Grecian Urn." The poem has and will last longer, and its foliage offers more refreshment.

I might as well admit that much of nature worship leaves me outside and agnostic. I can take my mountains and my sunsets like a gentleman or leave them alone. Not every peak is impressive, and the clouds sometimes marshal themselves into colors and combinations which are distinctly ham. It wouldn't be at all a bad arrangement to have no sunset permitted without the personal approval of Turner.

My swiftest pain comes from such articulate folk as are fond of saying that they prefer trees to people. It is one of the counts which I hold against Gene Tunney. I met him at a luncheon shortly after he had won the heavyweight championship. I tried to draw him out and get some expression of the elation which I supposed he would feel at being a current hero and idol.

In particular, I wanted to know if he didn't get a kick out of being recognized by taxi drivers. This has always seemed to me one of the most exciting forms of tribute. One of the proudest moments of my life occurred just two nights ago, when a driver who was hitherto a stranger to me turned from the wheel and said, "Heywood, I caught you on the radio last night, and you were all right."

In justice to Mr. Tunney, it must be pointed out that my elation over the incident came from the fact that it was unusual and surprising. If a taxi driver recognizes a newspaper columnist that's news as far as the columnist is concerned. In the case of a heavyweight champion his most casual excursion is certain to attract a crowd.

But reluctant idols develop clay feet sooner than the rest. It was fun to watch Jack Dempsey and notice the way in which he reveled at having stragglers come to heel to call him, "Hey, Champ!"

Once or twice I have complained in this column of the growing avidity of autograph hounds. The present eagerness of the collectors is so great that they buttonhole even the most unlikely subjects. I'm afraid that this was an insincerity on my part. As one distinctly subject to flattery, I am pleased to be asked, "Won't you sign my album and add a few sentiments?" It makes me feel like the Button Gwinnet of my time.

But Tunney told me that all these raids into his privacy were a bore and an annoyance. Striking a somewhat theatrical attitude he exclaimed: "I want to get away from it all! I want to get into the solitudes of the great north woods. The more I see of people the better I like trees."

And from that moment I set down the handsome young heavyweight as a phony. It is reasonable enough that everybody should have his pet tree, but a passion for an entire forest seems to me excessive. After you've seen a hundred oaks you've practically seen them all. A sapling in a front yard is more impressive than ten square miles of timberland.

And a city tree which maintains life and welfare within a well entirely surrounded by skyscrapers is indubitably more gallant than even a redwood which merely happens to be one of the gang in a grove.

GABRIEL

I find my mind goes back to Gabriel.

Naturally, everybody feels bad when a good actor dies, and Wesley Hill was such a special kind of good actor. He had been on the stage for forty years, but I never saw him until "The Green Pastures" was produced. As a matter of fact, most of his early career was with medicine shows and traveling "Uncle Tom" troupes. I believe he had only a few previous Broadway appearances.

Of all the angels in the play Gabriel was the darkest. In fact, it would be pretty hard to be much darker than Wesley Hill. Nobody will be able to come along in the patronizing way of the Nordic to say, "Oh, yes, he was quite good, but that was on account of his white blood."

I don't think I ever saw any actor enjoy a rôle so much. He moved around the stage of the Mansfield like a child in a pageant. He was terribly glad to be playing Gabriel. That's why he was such a good Gabriel.

After all, one expects angels to be joyous.

To me heaven seems a much more attractive place ever since I saw "The Green Pastures" and Wesley Hill. Very few writers have been able to present an acceptable abode for the blessed. Any fool can do a hell.

The trouble with heaven in literature is that the fabricator practically always leaves humor out of it. There's too much jasper and not enough jokes.

But here at last was a twinkling angel. The spheres rolled in their courses, and so did his eyes.

It must have been difficult for him of an evening to take off his wings of gold and his green robe and go home to Harlem. For a little space in a theater every night he stood as a symbol of power. After all, he carried, slung around his neck, the trumpet, and he only needed to blow a few notes upon it to send the world crashing and blazing into empty space.

It has been remarked that after an actor plays Lincoln or Napoleon for a while he begins to act like the character. He carries the delusions of grandeur with him even into the Lambs Club. But Wesley Hill was never an angel except in the best sense of the word.

I met him at a Harlem fish fry which was given in honor of the author, the producer and Richard Harrison, who plays the Lord. The Lord and Gabriel were great friends both on and off.

Gabriel, as I knew him, was a person of infinite jest. He could make the daily transition from heaven to Harlem without loss of dignity or kindliness. In his rôle there was that gorgeous combination of a humor approaching even the farcical and an ability to turn it off, to hold up his hand, as it were, to say, "Not funny any more."

. To him and to Harrison fell the greatest and the most dangerous moment in "The Green Pastures." I have said several times that Marc Connelly put the play to the test in almost the first few minutes of the second scene. The fish fry is funny and meant to be, although even before the entrance of the Lord I have always been a little annoyed at such patrons as put their heads back and howl as if they were viewing sheer extravaganza. It wasn't as funny as all that. After all, it is a humorous heaven and not a clownish one.

And then comes the moment when nobody must laugh if the audience is going to prove worthy of its chance to collaborate in a great play. It is a startling line which was committed to the Angel Gabriel. In fact, it is to me almost the finest single line in modern drama—"Gangway for the Lord God Jehovah!"

It may be that the audience fails upon occasion. I have never seen it do so. Always there came a great silence, and, better than that, a rigidity. It was as if Gabriel had actually put his lips to the trumpet. We were all called to judgment.

Much has been said and written about Richard Harrison and the impressive simplicity and dignity of his entrance. Not half enough has been said. The evolution of a veteran elocutionist into a wholly convincing and natural actor has always seemed to me an authentic miracle of the theater.

But now that Gabriel is gone I am reminded of how much he contributed to that particular scene. If he had read the line of introduction wrong by so much as half a tone the Lord could hardly command the rapt attention which the situation requires. David Garrick couldn't.

Gabriel was eternally right. The chief comedian of "The Green Pastures" came to be for that moment the everlasting straight man.

And so I hope that somewhere in space and time a trumpet blows for him and that along the Milky Way and back of the furthest stars a voice in all ways adequate cries out, "Gangway for Gabriel!"

A CERTAIN CITY EDITOR

It is a curious trail of fame which will continue now that Charles E. Chapin has died in Sing Sing. As long as newspapers exist reporters will regale one another with Chapin anecdotes. And it may be that a good story is as enduring a monument as any granite.

In the Chapin legend—and he became a mythical figure even before he entered the prison silences—a curious duality exists. Some of the stories concern the manner in which Chapin scored off one of his hirelings, while the others celebrate with equal avidity the manner in which a hireling scored off him.

The most famous of the tales has Irvin Cobb as its hero. It was Mr. Cobb who remarked, upon hearing that his city editor was ill, "Nothing trivial, I hope."

The second most famous anecdote I believe to be an invention. It is, of course, the story of the reporter who called back to say: "When I told him you wanted a statement about the divorce, Mr. Chapin, he took me by the scruff of the neck and threw me downstairs. He's a big, powerful fellow, and he shouted after me, 'If you ever come back I'll break your jaw!'"

To which, according to the legend, Mr. Chapin said from his end of the line, "You go back and tell that big bum he can't intimidate me."

Less familiar is the story of the involuntary pallbearer, related to me by the late Shep Friedman, who was the victim in the case. Mr. Friedman reported three-quarters of an hour late and realized that nothing but an ingenious lie could save his job. It was suicide, of course, to plead delay in the subway or anything of the sort, for Chapin would merely refer to the Interborough reports and publicly expose the falsity of any such claim.

Shep Friedman was more imaginative than that. He said:

"Mr. Chapin, I'm terribly sorry to be late, but a very curious thing happened as I was leaving my apartment. A poor fellow across the hall died two nights ago, and today the undertaker came for him. But he had only two assistants with him. He thought there'd be somebody in the family to help, but there wasn't. And so he asked me to help him carry the coffin down to the hearse. I never knew the dead man. I don't even know his name, but he lived right across the hall, and so, naturally, I couldn't refuse."

Chapin received the story graciously and attempted no cross-examination, but half an hour later he beckoned the reporter over to his desk.

"Shep," he said, "I think we have a first page human interest story here."

"What story?" Friedman wanted to know.

"Why, the story of the involuntary pallbearer," answered

the city editor. "Get his name and all the details and give me six hundred words."

Friedman found the later stages of invention much more difficult than the early ones, but he went through with the lie. When the yarn had been finished he appealed to the make-up man to keep it out. "It never happened," he explained. Naturally, Chapin had no intention of printing any such bare-faced fabrication, and he had also issued his secret orders to the make-up man, but as each edition of the paper came up from the composing room he would roar with indignation and say: "What's become of that story of the involuntary pallbearer? I want that for page one!"

But when that day was done he dropped the matter and never mentioned it again. He was satisfied with a typically Chapinesque revenge.

And there was the reporter who came to work one day before the regular pay week began.

"My check is for only six days instead of seven," he told the city editor. "If they don't add it on I'll never make up for that extra work I did."

"That'll be all right," said Chapin. "I'll keep it in mind. When I fire you I'll fire you one day early."

Even in prison Chapin did not depart wholly from his anecdotage. Stories clustered around him during the trial and after. There seems to be authentication for the fable that when he was in peril of a possible first degree verdict he took occasion to rebuke the reporters in court and say, "Not one of you has written a good story on this case yet."

The verdict was that Chapin was suffering from a mental collapse when he shot his wife, and he received a sentence of twenty years. It seems likely that the judgment was just, for in prison his nature changed entirely.

Still, he had not become all sweetness and light immediately. He retained some trace of the detached and objective attitude which made him such a superb news man. Only a few summers ago a newspaper woman went to see Warden Lawes on some matter in behalf of the League for the Abolition of Capital Punishment. At the end of the conference the warden suggested that she call on Chapin. The editor was courteous to the reporter and wanted to know her mission. When she told him his face clouded. "I never heard anything so silly," he exclaimed. "How do you think we're going to keep people from killing one another without capital punishment?"

For a time he edited the prison paper and that inspired a fiction writer, whose name I have forgotten, to do a piece for *Collier's* about the city editor who had found complete contentment. It was the story of a prison newspaper executive who had come at last to a place where there was no rival to scoop him.

But it was in his flower beds and bird houses that Chapin found at last the peace which passes understanding. He said to the newspaper woman whom he rebuked for her views about capital punishment, "We have a lot of men here who are considered hard and desperate, but I can tell you that in all the years I've had that bird house in the yard not one of them has ever hurt a single bird."

Whether the man still retained any of his old executive arrogance or not I do not know, but it was almost unheard of for an inmate to be anything but careful in stepping around Charlie Chapin's flower beds.

I have never heard of a more curious career which seemed almost to bridge the gap between Simon Legree and St. Francis. Maybe he always did like roses better than reporters.

THE WORLD PASSES

I sat and watched a paper die. We waited in the home of a man who once had run it. A flash came over the phone. *The World* was ended.

F. P. A. looked eagerly at a bowl of fruit upon the table and said, "Mr. Swope, where have you been buying your apples?"

The World fired me, and *The Telegram* gave me a job. Now, *The Telegram* owns *The World*. This is a fantastic set of chances almost like those which might appear in somebody's dream of revenge. But I never thought much of revenge. I wouldn't give a nickel for this one. If I could, by raising my hand, bring dead papers back to life I'd do so.

Sometimes in this column I have opposed the theories of those who would break up mergers, end chain stores and try the trick of unscrambling large-scale production. I've said that this could not be done—that it wasn't even expedient. In the long run the happiness of all of us depends upon increased efficiency and a shorter sum of toil. That's true. I still believe it. I wouldn't weep about a shoe factory or a branch line railroad shutting down.

But newspapers are different. I am a newspaperman. There are many things to be said for this new combination. It is my sincere belief that the Scripps-Howard chain is qualified by its record and its potentialities to carry on the Pulitzer tradition of liberal journalism. In fact, I'll go further and say that, as far as my personal experience goes, *The Tele-*

gram has been more alert and valiant in its independent attitude than *The World* papers.

Yet I hope, at least, that this may be the end of mergers. The economic pressure for consolidation still continues. A newspaper is, among other things, a business. And, even so, it must be more than that. A lawyer at the hearing before Surrogate Foley expressed amazement that a paper which had lost almost $2,000,000 within a year could command any of that intangible value known as "good will." He was reasoning from the basis upon which fish are canned and wire wheels turned out.

A newspaper is a rule unto itself. It has a soul for salvation or damnation. I was pleased to hear much said about intangibles in all the accounts of the preliminary negotiations leading up to the present merger. I was glad that for once the emphasis was taken away from mere machinery. The fact of presses and linotype equipment was never stressed in the proceedings. This didn't count. The intangibles of a newspaper are the men and women who make it.

First in America, and now in a frenzied form in Russia, there grows a cult which bows and bangs its head upon the floor in worship of the machine. In some calculations man is no more than a device to pull upon a gadget. But here, at last, there was talk of millions, and checks in huge amounts were passed—not for apparatus, moving belts and intricate mechanism. This was a deal for a name and for some of the people who contributed to the making of the name.

Since my feeling is strong that a newspaper can neither rise nor fall beyond or below its staff, I was stirred by the notion—the dream—that *World* men might take over *The World*. I realize, as they do now, the difficulties which lay in the path of any such plan. I'll readily admit that 1,000 to 1 would be a generous price against any such undertaking. But we are, or ought to be, lovers of long shots. There's nothing particularly stirring when the favorite coasts home in front. Although the newspaper crowd didn't put their project over, it isn't fair to call this miss plain failure.

For almost the first time in my life I watched reporters animated by a group consciousness. Newspapermen are blandly and, I think, blindly individualistic. Once I was president of a press writers' union. There were four members. The three others were the secretary, the vice-president and the treasurer. The treasurer never had much responsibility. Nobody would join us, because the average reporter carried in his knapsack the baton of a managing editor, or even the dim hope of being some day a dramatic critic. What did he want with organization? He stood on two feet —a single unit.

But for a time down in *The World* office there was the excitement, the hip-hip-hooray—call it even the hysteria—of mob movement, of people rubbing shoulders and saying, "We are in this boat together."

One of the things which would have made the fruition of the plan extremely difficult is the fact that a paper lives or dies by personality. When forty or fifty are banded together they must select a single one to be the leader and articulate representative. Still, in any dream of a coöperative commonwealth I've always had the feeling that newspapers most of all were fit subject for some sort of socialization. I've never known even the most obscure reporter who didn't think he knew more about running a paper than the man who owned it. I've always felt that way myself. And once I was right.

The curious thing concerning the death of *The World* was the manner in which it became animate just before the final rattle within its throat. Within the last two or three years there must have been times in which the morale of the staff was low. Last night I went late to see the men I knew and had worked with long ago—that is, two years, or maybe three years, which is a long span in the life of any roving and rebellious columnist. I never found the paper pounding and pulsing quite so much as it did now—when it was dead.

We sat together in a very vigorous sort of democracy. At first I felt I might be out of place as one who was an ex-*World* man. But by 4 in the morning we were all "ex." We had ex-managing editor, ex-city editor and dozens of ex-reporters. For the first time within many months it was possible for somebody who covered a district to point the finger of scorn or accusation at somebody who had been his boss and spill his whole mind and emotion. You didn't have to "sir" anybody or say "very good" or "yes" unless you wanted to. Out of a situation which was certainly tragic to many there was at least a glimpse of that heaven in which we may all walk and between harp tunes look up and say with impunity to any passing angel or archangel, "Oh, is that so!"

Naturally, I have both hope and confidence in the new paper. Like John Brown's body, *The World* goes marching on. To heights, I hope. But something is gone. They aren't all marching. Men have dropped out. For them there will be nothing more on any newspaper, and I think of these casualties. I think of a profession which grows efficient and overcrowded. And to those who can no longer make the grade and who stand under the indictment of being not good enough I bow low, I swing my hat, as if it bore a plume, and say:

"Good, bad or indifferent, you have been in it. You belong. Some part of stuff set down on paper was you, and ever will be."

MORE OR LESS

James Joseph Walker spoke to a group of social workers at the City Hall on Wednesday, and he said: "I will confess I have been more or less shocked by the reports of the framing of innocent women."

But in this duel between "less" and "more" the former has won the day, for the city's chief executive is about to take a vacation of three or four weeks at Palm Springs, Cal., since of late he has been more or less under the weather.

I have no doubt that James Joseph Walker is ailing. In fact, I am surprised that he feels as well as he does. Much has happened of late which is naturally disturbing to any sensitive city official.

We all hope he has a helpful vacation. We would like to watch him return refreshed and swinging his right. He will see bright skies, snow mountains and a blazing sun in the lovely land to which he goes. Even the name Palm Springs is glamorous. It suggests an oasis set within an arid country. And there, I trust, the palms will be straighter and itch less than those of Tammany. And if mere scenery and sloth and sleep begin to pall the delights of the race track and the casino at Agua Caliente are within easy motoring distance.

But, though I grant that James Joseph Walker is sick, it seems to me unlikely that his health can be as precarious as that of the City of New York at the present moment. It is a pity that the mayor cannot take the metropolis with him on the trip. New York stands in need of scathing sunlight, fresh air and a fine rousing wind to cleanse its lungs and vitals. It is feverish and haggard from the invasion of infectious disease. Oh, yes, I think New York is by much the sicker of the two.

Apparently Mayor Walker differs with this diagnosis. To the social workers at City Hall he suggested the possibility that "it is only another case of shell shock, and I guess the city will get over it."

Any man, including a mayor, is entitled to his guess. But shell shock itself is a serious ailment. Quite often it results in a complete paralysis. And yet I think it is not the shell but the very substance of corruption which has shocked the city into a feeling of helplessness. We have every right to be shocked and "more," not "less," when several judges are proved to be crooked and certain police professional perjurers.

"Some of these reports have been exaggerated," says the mayor. Suppose only one woman had been framed. And even suppose that lone case had concerned a notorious harlot. Even then I think we should expect from the mayor something much stronger than "more" or "less."

More or less! The dead at least are definitely dead. There can be no more or lessing them back to life.

But Palm Springs is a pleasant place in which to sit and

dream and let the world go by. And possibly James Joseph Walker in his waking hours may find time to express the pious wish and the friendly prognostication that "the city will get over it." The hours will drift pleasantly while he is counting sheep and forgetting goats.

It is quite likely that the mayor stands in need of a tonic. Not, I think, a nerve tonic. But there is such a thing as sickness of the will. And the cure for that lies in getting down to cases, in putting a shoulder to the wheel, in being a real mayor and not just "more or less" Jimmy.

I seem to see a willingness upon Mayor Walker's part to shift responsibility. In the same pleasant speech to the social workers he expressed a grave concern over the failure of civic organizations and great newspapers. He said:

"While the reports are revolting, I am at a loss to understand why organizations like yours, why our great newspapers with reporters in every court, did not discover the situation until it broke out in headlines."

In other words, the press has held out on James Joseph Walker. Apparently no reporter took the trouble to tell the mayor the facts of life in a great city. Somebody should blurt out to him the news that there is no Santa Claus within the ranks of Tammany. At least, only for a very restricted set of good little boys and girls. And somebody should tell him of the birds and flowers and of the edge which the crane retains over his phonetic cousin in the district attorney's office.

The crane is mightier than the Crain and much more stalwart. The crane stands on at least one leg.

It may be that James Joseph Walker will sleep more abundantly and restfully under the palms, but if a parable could conceivably dissuade him from the trip I'd like to remind him of an ancient jest used by Charlie Case—a popular monologist dead and gone these many years.

This story had to do with a railroad journey which he took in the company of his brother Hank. "Somehow," Case used to say, "there happened to be forty or fifty sheep in the same car with us. And when the train stopped the brakeman pulled us out, and he began to beat my brother Hank. Now, Hank was always my favorite brother. I didn't want to stand there and see him abused. And so I crawled under the car to the other side of the track."

I don't think the mayor will really profit by his trip to Palm Springs. I don't believe James Joseph Walker can crawl under to the other side, though he go to the ends of the earth. No matter where he goes or what he says, he will still see. And he will hear.

DOWN AMONG THE ANTS

"That," said a man, indicating a needle point several hundred feet below, "is the Chrysler Building."

We were standing just below the mooring mast of the Empire State, on the 102nd floor. Everybody with a desire to grow philosophical should stand half an hour each week on this high platform.

It was the afternoon of May Day. In Madison Square the Communists were holding a mass meeting. Two inches further down the Veterans of Foreign Wars were to gather and after them the Socialists. On each rostrum there stood a man waving his arms and insisting that with him lay salvation, and behind the sweep of his fist nothing but disaster and rank heresy. And from 1,200 feet up each orator was no more than a tiny bug, and the crowd about him a passing swarm of ants. At that distance policies either political or economic blended into the extraordinary sameness of humankind when reduced to small dimension.

And so I would not recommend a philosopher's seat just below the mooring mast to anybody as a regular point of vantage. It might induce in him the greatest of all defeatist heresies: that nothing matters very much. Instead of eating at an apple, one may ascend a quarter of a mile if he would lose the sense of distinction between good and evil.

And this is not in any sense a sound point of view because most of us do and must live our lives upon the surface of the earth. Where practices and beliefs are to us a vital and even an essential thing, one yields even to slight blasphemy in regard to Providence if he gets too far aloft. It is, like this, from distances that captains of celestial industry regard our little planet.

It may be that certain grave injustices of pestilence and whirlwind pass as nothing since they are directed by beings who watch the world too microscopically. However, there is one way in which those ardent for betterment in life may find a stimulus in looking at the city whole and spread out utterly to the gaze. Even from 1,200 feet sparse bits of green stand out in the drab pattern of the brick and stone. This little smudge is a park. And even smaller is the tiny display of some isolated tree in a backyard. One gets a sense of the prison contours which we have raised against ourselves.

Here is Manhattan Island, which must have been a glorious garden spot before man came to civilize it. In the days of the Dutch it knew rivers, lakes and even a spread of jungle foliage. And now, looking down upon it, this land of natural luxury has become a record of squat squalor with a few exciting towers.

If we are to plan another sort of city with due regard for earth and trees and space to turn around, we must lift from their foundations whole blocks of stodgy dwellings. We have become too close and one shoulder rubs against another. It is an anthill in which we have left a little scope for elbow movement, but nothing for the soul of man.

Possibly we can still swing a cat in some of the confined cloisters in which we manage to live and breathe and—after a fashion—have our being. But looking at the set-up from an Empire State grandstand, it is easy to understand that few of us have a reasonable allotment in which to swing an emotion. And that, after all, is more important than throwing the 16-pound cat.

Again, one gets some notion of the prodigal wastage of our rivers. We sit, or might, upon an island blessed by rushing waters. When the Indians went away they left behind them groves and beaches coming down to the water's rim. All that is changed. For now a stream's edge means no more than a good factory site. And all along our borders stand the tall, black, grimy towers of the industries which prison us.

If this were indeed, as Jimmy Walker says, the Imperial City of New York, then some emperor ought to sit upon this pinnacle, and looking down upon gray spaces and those of brown, say, "With my thumb I will put in here a smudge of green and over at that corner a little yellow, indicating the rush of sun."

We must break down our walls and leave a smaller area lying within the shadows. From the mast it is all too evident that we have reared canyons against ourselves. That almost we dig ourselves down into the earth like miners seeking coal.

It is an exciting thing to see some building spurt up to the sky. The closer you get the better it looks. And yet you cannot escape the feeling, "Look at the millions who have been left behind within their sharp and deep-cut ruts."

THE AGITATOR

In recent years the word "agitator" is almost always used as a term of reproach. In fact, the imagination supplies the prefix "red."

And yet the most casual survey must show that all causes —conservative or otherwise—have been furthered by agitation. The chief complaint leveled against the agitator is that he takes people who are content with their lot and makes them dissatisfied. This is the charge hurled against labor leaders who organize strikes in districts where unionization was not heard of before. And the manufacturers like to say, as in the case of Gastonia, that everybody was peaceful and happy before the agitators came.

It may be true that even in certain industries where pay is low and living conditions severe a bovinity can exist until some outsider calls attention to the rigors and injustices of the situation. But this process of rousing men and women to a thought of something better, or at least different, is most certainly not confined to radicals.

Many wholly conservative people subscribe large sums of money for foreign missions.

Now, obviously, the missionary is always an agitator. He may go to a South Sea island where trousers are quite unknown and stir the savages into putting on garments by making them ashamed of their previous lack of attire. You may say that this is a harmful and busybody sort of proceeding. In the case of the South Sea missionary I agree, but my point is that the theory of "let well enough alone" has been constantly violated by many who hold the admiration of the conservative community.

Take the case of Woodrow Wilson. When he returned from Paris and began to preach his theory that salvation from international disturbance lay in the League of Nations he qualified as an agitator. I happened to be in favor of the agitation which he conducted. Nevertheless, it would be foolish to deny that he went into communities and endeavored to place in the hearts of men a dissatisfied feeling about foreign relations which had not been there before. These communities were content with the old order of national rivalries, or, rather, they gave small heed to them.

And so I deny that it is an intrusion to tell a socially maimed or wounded person that he labors under a disability. A striking case was much reported in the instance of a young man who had been blind from birth. The anti-agitation school, in all logic, should have been against the operation which gave him sight. Never having seen the passing show he could not have worried about it a great deal. And yet it was within his due that a window into the world should be opened up for him.

The Agitator

In somewhat similar fashion it seems to me an excellent thing that men should take occasion to tell workers in backward communities that $15 a week is a pitiful wage, even if it is the rate to which they have become accustomed.

And going back into historical precedent, it can easily be maintained that Jefferson, Washington, Franklin, Patrick Henry and the rest were agitators. It was not in the mind of every colonist to rebel under the slogan "No taxation without representation." In all truth, many of the inhabitants of the original thirteen States suffered no palpable burdens under British rule. They had to be aroused to their disabilities.

And it was entirely in accord with much of our modern editorial comment for the Tories to maintain that the revolutionists were spreading ill will in places where content had grown.

And no one would deny the reasonableness of fastening the title of agitator to William Lloyd Garrison. In fact, in his case, the epithet was constantly employed by the slaveholders of the South. It was their argument that Negroes who had never even known a dream of freedom were merely rendered restless by the strong words of the man in Boston. And restless they did become as the tingle of the abolition movement began to prick against dead nerve centers.

Few would insist now that the fruition of a dream should have been denied forever to these men, even if the vision was carried to them by an outsider.

The agitator in all fields of human endeavor is the person who insists, sometimes with violence, that the world as it stands is not good enough. This insistence partakes of a very necessary quality of life. Contented organisms have already felt the touch of degeneration.

In man or beast or microbe life consists of the desire to push out wider borders, to grow and move and explore domains which have been barricaded. Posterity has picked practically all its heroes from the agitators. They are the saints and the holy men of our religions.

And since this process of honoring the despised and the criticized has become so universal, we might sharpen our wits enough to refrain from hasty condemnation of all who would shake us out of lethargy. They may be disturbing. They may be a nuisance. But they are the corpuscles of the corporate being through which the waste and the stagnation of the status quo is turned into living tissue.

TWO-GUN CROWLEY

One hundred and fifty heavily armed policemen fought for two hours with gas and revolvers and ax and captured Two-Gun Crowley. With him they took his girl and his confederate.

It was good police work, sharp pursuit by the detectives and a difficult task carried out efficiently. In spite of the number of attackers the work was dangerous, for desperate armed men in hiding can easily pick off many who seek to dislodge them.

And credit should go to Commissioner Mulrooney. They say that he prides himself on being a good cop. That compliment he deserves, although some may withhold complete approval of his abilities as an executive.

But if the police came out of the Crowley man hunt with credit you and I did not. It is wasteful and an unimaginative way of life to spend so much effort and risk of life upon the capture of a criminal when such indifference and carelessness have been shown in the matter of his genesis. We should catch our gunmen younger and long before they have taken their posts behind a barricade prepared to shoot it out.

The existence of a Two-Gun Crowley is not accidental. In all probability he will be executed and the community will sit back with the feeling that the case is ended and a problem has been solved. Then we will wait until some other gangster very like him provides a similar city melodrama and a first page story.

Even more important than catching a Crowley, convicting and punishing him is the task of finding out what he is all about. You must dig for the whys. This is more vital than even the finest detective work in tracking down the outlaws. We need another sort of detective. It is up to us to create a class of men capable of solving the intricate and subtle trail which comes before the crime.

Here he is: Francis Crowley, 20 years old, 5 feet 3 inches tall, a little more than 100 pounds in weight. He was born in a New York slum. Before he was a year old his mother turned him over to a woman who ran a baby farm. His first job was with a gang of laborers, and he quit this after a little while to steal parcels off the rear ends of trucks. And a little later he became an automobile thief.

By now we have our subject well on the way to the final crimes for which he was arrested. And the law will concern itself with those episodes and leave the earlier trail alone.

It has been charged that many of the more modern students of crime tend to sentimentalize the criminal. It seems to me that the approach which they suggest is far more realistic than the notion that an electric chair can be a complete solvent for a social problem.

Take the background of Crowley: Slum-bred, undernourished, undereducated, underpaid. Not every man who goes through this mill becomes a vicious criminal. But I rather feel that may be the way to bet. At any rate, no one will pretend this furnishes a reasonable school for citizenship.

It would take money to tear down all the hovels in which the Crowleys are born. But it also takes a lot of money to catch the adult Crowleys. We might very likely need something as radical as free medicine and milk to raise up the slum children physically stunted by lack of nourishment and sun.

There is, I believe, a very possible connection between the meagerness of this man and his passion to play the desperado. He couldn't have been much good at heavy labor —this skinny 5-foot waif. To him a gun provided ego satisfaction.

I am not consumed with pity for Crowley the individual. But it would be dull not to realize that he, like his sort, is governed by precise rules of cause and effect. And that is where the guilt of you and me creeps in. We can get excited about a killer. Ten thousand stand to cheer the police in their dangerous work of digging him out of a top floor apartment. Very probably many of the citizens gathered around would have been glad to volunteer their assistance in the man hunt. The police cut holes through the roof to get at the desperadoes.

All right! But how about more radical digging and deeper cutting? Can't somebody lift for us the roof of the house in which Crowley was born? Let us have slits through the tenement walls of the place in which he lived. If he went to a city school we might inquire and try to ascertain in just what respects the system failed him.

It is true that as things stand he is an enemy of society. But inevitably there is some point along the journey where we failed him. I am not pretending that the task is easy or that psychiatry, to mention one phase of the study, has advanced to the point of ultimate wisdom. But we should try.

If the city had never produced more than a single Crowley it would be enough to track him down, try him and convict him. But we know of gangsters who have been and of those who will come after.

And so I suggest that there ought to be some court intent upon facts far more fundamental. The detectives of the force did skillful work in solving the problem, "Where is Crowley?" It still remains for us to meet that even more important query, "Why is Crowley?"

WALKING AROUND A GRAVE

President Hoover and Ex-President Calvin Coolidge did a soldierly job at the Marion shrine. It was soldierly in the sense that both Republican leaders paid a tactful tribute to a dead member of the party and left unsaid all those things which must have been in their hearts.

Mr. Coolidge, indeed, made no concession to the fact that the Harding administration constituted one of the gravest tragedies in American history. He went ahead and spoke very much as if the succession from Lincoln to Harding had gone on without a single spiritual break.

President Hoover added a few words of apology. But these were weasels—every one of them. He said:

"We came to know that here was a man whose soul was being seared by a great disillusionment. We saw him gradually weaken, not only from physical exhaustion but from mental anxiety. Warren Harding had a dim realization that he had been betrayed by a few of the men whom he had trusted, by men whom he had believed were his devoted friends.

"It was later proved in the courts of the land that these men had betrayed not alone the friendship and trust of their stanch and loyal friend, but they had betrayed their country. That was the tragedy of the life of Warren Gamaliel Harding."

But there is no adequate support for the theory that Warren Gamaliel Harding was an idealist sinned against by friends who betrayed him. Mr. Harding was, among other things, an effective and an experienced politician. He was under no illusion at all as to the forces and the methods which brought about his nomination. He had played the game with the Ohio gang long before he became the Chief Executive of the United States. He knew Harry Daugherty.

It is probably true that Warren Harding himself was not touched by the actual financial scandals which mired many of his friends and close associates. Yet this doesn't lift him clear of guilt. He knew these men. And when he put them into positions of power there was no reason why he should expect them to turn lily white between midnight and morning. He had every reason to believe that they would go on as they had gone on.

If President Hoover and Calvin Coolidge choose to spread a cloak of respectability, indirection and downright perversion of fact over the grave of Warren Harding it does not matter much in one sense. Although I do not possess the gift of prophecy, I am willing to assert that President Hoover's Marion speech will never stand in the school books alongside the Gettysburg address. The speech itself and that made by Mr. Coolidge will soon be forgotten. These addresses will be dismissed as mere set pieces of Republican partisanship.

But the effect will not pass away so lightly. A precedent has been set. Another lie will be added to the many half truths which are crammed down the throats of school children. No impartial surveyor of the facts has ever been able to find an adequate cause for our war with Spain.

Research has brought to light the information that all our demands could have been won without conflict. The episode ought to stand in even the most elementary textbooks as an example of what mass hysteria can do to a nation.

And, going further back, it was not an idealistic impulse which led us to fight Mexico and take for ourselves a huge slice of territory. I am not among those who maintain that America is always wrong. This criticism has frequently been leveled at any who dare to disagree with a single item of national policy.

Like other countries, we have behaved superbly in certain situations and ill in others. History ought to be a sort of bird's-eye view of the proposition from beginning to end.

From a height it is possible to see all things in their due proportion.

It does not bother me so much that myths have come to cloud the actual nature of Washington and of Lincoln. It would be better if the young student knew these men entire and had some comprehension of the complex mixture of strength and weakness which goes into every man. And yet if these two great figures have become to some extent plaster saints, in spite of the best efforts of the modern historians, the general conclusion is not so far away from the fact.

Both Lincoln and Washington add up as persons of supperb totals. It is against the great that the present crime is being committed. The Harding myth distorts an actuality.

Here was a weak and insufficient person who became President through the faults of a political machine. Very likely he meant well; I mean he was a kindly man on the whole. But he was no idealist. It is not enough to say that, since his administration was a ghastly mistake and a tragedy, it should be forgotten. The faults of American government should be studied just as closely as the virtues.

We ought to know and keep in mind the life and death of President Harding, so that a new generation can grow up firm in the resolve:

"Such things should never be again!"

And that both President Hoover and Calvin Coolidge omitted from their speeches.

ACTS OF GOD

The American Red Cross refused to aid the starving children of striking Pennsylvania coal miners. The reason given by Chairman John Barton Payne is that his organization is confined, by its charter, to the relief only of emergency disasters due to "acts of God."

On the other hand, the organization was conspicuous in its efforts to minister to the maimed and dying during the Great War. Is war an act of God? I doubt it. I don't think any intelligent human being can conscientiously worship a deity who advocated the slaughter of millions of innocents. On the contrary, it seems to me that the urge to fight for a cause, for better living conditions, for the right to rear and educate their children decently, as these Pennsylvania coal miners are doing, would find favor in the eyes of God.

If the American Red Cross is so finicky about living up to the letter of its charter it should have refused to render any aid to the American or allied armies. The excuse—"War is un-Godlike and uncivilized"—would have been sufficient to vindicate its officers. And—who can tell?—such a stand by a powerful organization might have made us pause and think and decide against entering the conflict.

And, again, if we are going to be technical, isn't everything we do an act of God? "God created man in his image" refers not to the physical aspect of man, but rather to his mental make-up. Man's desire to rise from his humble beginning and find a place in the sun would seem to emanate from his God-given ego. If the Maker had intended that

146

we should be satisfied with our lot he would not have given us eyes and ears and desires.

"The meek shall inherit the earth" has been misinterpreted. It does not mean to suggest surrender. There is such a thing as "the terrible meek." The plutocrats of that earlier era appreciated as much as do our contemporaries the effectiveness of slogans. And they worked them to death.

But getting back to Pennsylvania:

"The coal strike," said Mr. Payne, "was the result of an economic situation prevalent in that industry for the last ten years and may continue indefinitely."

Does that mean that the children of the miners will have to starve indefinitely? Let us assume, for the sake of argument, that the strikers are in the wrong. Is that sufficient reason for allowing their children, the innocent victims of these prolonged bickerings, to go hungry? Do we still adhere to the theory that the child shall suffer for the sins of his father?

Russia is more intelligent in some respects in handling its affairs. There the child is all-important. It is the business of the State to nourish, clothe and educate its children. The Soviet régime is leaving no stone unturned to rear its future citizens in the way they should go. That way may not be ours. But they merit our attention, nevertheless, by reason of their foresight. The ideals instilled in childhood remain. And hunger is not uplifting.

A hungry man, no matter how high his moral standards, is apt to slip back and become one of society's outcasts. Certainly a hungry child cannot be expected to feel nothing but love and loyalty for the country that permits him to starve. He doesn't reason. He just feels. And hunger is among the strongest emotions. In prehistoric times men killed because of it. And we shall never be truly civilized until hunger, disease and war are banned as unlawful and inhuman.

If the Red Cross refuses to recognize and help these children it is up to the state to do something about them. And if the Red Cross continues in its attitude of silly discrimination it might be a good idea for the citizens of the United States to keep the incident fresh in their memories when the next annual drive is on for funds.

When we help the street corner panhandler we don't stop and ask, "Are you hungry as the result of an act of God?" Here is a hungry man. For the moment that is all that concerns us. As long as we foster an economic system that necessitates the existence of charitable organizations it is their job to take care of the needy. By discriminating they defeat their aim and purpose.

Isn't it just possible, though, that Mr. Payne was more concerned with the good will of the mine owners than that of God? It may be that by feeding these hungry children his organization would offend a heavy contributor. And, after all, there are salaries to be paid.

MURDER IN THE FIRST DEGREE

The jury came in with a verdict of murder in the first degree. It so happens that I am thinking of a particular case, but it will serve as a text chiefly because it was a trial not animated by any touch of the unusual. There was no news in the conviction or the inevitable sentence. This was simply a run-of-the-mill sort of murder. A man with a bad record stabbed an enemy. Nobody could question the guilt of the defendant or the justice of the penalty. That is, nobody who believes in capital punishment.

But I saw the man stand up as he looked upon the jury and jurors looked upon him. I sat far back and could not tell with what twitch of the features he received the verdict. He had his hands clasped behind him, and all he did was to lock his fingers a little tighter as they told him that he was guilty. That could hardly have been a surprise.

He knew it all along. Nevertheless, the fingernails bit into his flesh. And as the fingers tightened it was possible to notice the play of muscles across his back.

"What a magnificent body!" I thought to myself. And then I remembered that those same muscles would flex and tighten once more as the community carried out its intention to flick him away like a burned out stub. It seemed to me a pity. It still seems a pity.

A lot of energy and time and vegetative planning went into the creation of those shoulder blades and the delicate mechanism of nerve and tissue. I could not keep from thinking of this John Doe as some sort of flowering shrub, because his individuality and his personal quirks and whimsicalities were not discussed during the trial. He killed a man and therefore must die.

There is a nice shiny surface of logic in the rule which holds that repayment for an eye must be in kind. A life for a life. It sounds like an algebraic equation. There is a sense of perfect balance. But the fiber of the reasoning is marred by a flaw. It does not constitute a literal transcript of the circumstances.

"Why," people often ask, "is there always sympathy for the criminal and none for his victim?" The answer is easy. The dead lie beyond our pity. By quelling the heartbeat of the assassin we do not set up a rhythm in the breast of the one who was stabbed. And if we pluck out the eye of an offender there does not exist a socket into which it may fit with any utility.

And so what we are really saying is not "A life for a life," but "A death for a death." We deal in depreciated currency. Nobody profits either in a spiritual or a material sense by the transaction.

Sometimes the victim of the knife or the bullet leaves behind him sons and daughters destitute by reason of his death. The killer owes them something very specific. And it seems to me that no very material adjustment has been made when the community comes to the bereaved ones to say: "The man who killed your father has paid the price. He was electrocuted at 6 o'clock this morning."

In all reason just what has he paid which is in any way tangible? Far from paying, he has been allowed—even compelled—to welsh out of a settlement. His crime constitutes an offense against certain individuals and against the community, and by all means I would have him pay. But the payment will have to be by service. Instead of being made to die he should be compelled to sweat.

Some few exist whose potentialities for social conduct are dim, but this does not hold for the majority of criminals. There is stuff there, even in spite of flaws and marks which mar them. The human body itself is not so much kindling wood to be lightly tossed upon the slag pile. I can think of no one to whom I would deny the chance for regeneration.

Possibly I am a little romantic, but when the dramatic

moment came in Cuba for the decisive yellow fever tests I think it would have been eminently fitting to pass the call for volunteers along the corridor of some death house. In that event the code of "a life for a life" would have had some meaning. Only under such circumstances can we justly say, "This man who killed another now has his chance to pay the price."

You see, the fault lies so close to our own home. The failure of the criminal is always a joint stock enterprise. We mark him as unfit to live among civilized human beings, but it follows logically that we were inept in fitting this cog into the machine we built. Repair shops have been built for motors, but we scrap men.

If it were compulsory for every citizen of New York State to attend an execution once a year we would be done with capital punishment. We—and I mean all of us—are content to be hangmen because we walk softly and do not talk of rope at our parties. We neither see nor hear nor feel, damn our eyes! And damn our hearts and heads and the life force within us, too!

Out of the all but eternal ages comes a human being delicately knit. Even though moronic, there is the wisdom of the centuries in his spinal column. God has joined together cell and muscle, and this we tear asunder. And I have come to think that perhaps I have at last identified that mysterious crime which worried me when I was a child. This supreme impudence of conduct may well be the sin against the Holy Ghost.

WILLIAM NUCKLES DOAK

Senators and Representatives in Congress are forever rising to their hind legs and hollering about entangling alliances. While they are on the matter I wish some one of the people's servants would take up a problem which both perplexes and grieves me. I refer to the power and the perquisites extended to Benito Mussolini by American officialdom.

He has but to crook a finger or raise an eyebrow when anything within our borders happens to displease him, and straightway somebody is called upon the carpet or sent to prison.

You probably have heard of Orlando Spartaco, who received a sentence of two years for raising a commotion during a visit of Grandi to Philadelphia. And yet, I doubt if you are familiar with the precise facts, since it was generally and erroneously reported that the young anti-Fascist had leaped upon the running board of Grandi's car. I have before me a transcript of the case as it was conducted before a jury and Judge Harry S. McDevitt.

Officer Richard E. West, being duly sworn, testified as follows:

"I saw the car entering Sansom, from 24th, and I also saw a lot of excitement on the north side of Sansom, about twenty feet ahead of the car, and a man was hollering something in Italian, I didn't understand. Then the fists started to fly; so I rode the horse down, and this man here was hollering . . . So I got hold of this man here and drug him from the crowd."

"Mr. Levinson: 'I want to ask the officer one question. I understood you to say that the fists were flying; you mean they were flying against this man?'

"Officer West: 'Absolutely.'

"Mr. Levinson: 'And you went in to rescue him from the crowd?'

"Officer West: 'Absolutely.' "

That is the entire vital evidence on which a young man was sentenced in an American court to a term of two years in jail.

Contrast this procedure with what happened following another incident which also occurred in Philadelphia a few months before the visit of Grandi. This time the visitor was Herbert Clark Hoover, the President of the United States. He had come to witness a world series game between the Cardinals and the Athletics. As the President left Shibe Park, a number of people in the stands shouted "boo," and made other derogatory sounds. Nobody was arrested.

Now, I am not endeavoring to encourage the practice of booing the President. I yield to no one in my dislike for Mr. Hoover, but I much prefer to vote and work against him than to make vague vocal outcries. I am merely indicating that whether it is bad sportsmanship, poor taste or what not, the forces of law and order in Philadelphia were prepared to accept the right of the citizenry to indicate disapproval of our Chief Executive. Then why be so tender about the feeling of Grandi or Mussolini?

I have a special and personal feeling for Orlando Spartaco because I once figured in a somewhat similar incident and received nothing more than a black eye. Happening upon an anti-Free State meeting, I heard a speaker declare that Michael Collins sold out for British gold. Collins had been killed only the day before, and to me seemed a heroic figure in Irish history. Accordingly I hissed. That was, if you like, an incitement to riot, only I happened to be the riot. It was the biggest black eye I have ever received.

Personally I have no enthusiasm for organized jeering sections, but I hold that the spontaneous right of raspberry should be denied to no one in America. Far from being sentenced to jail for two years, Orlando Spartaco should have been protected in his privilege of shouting the equivalent for "To hell with Mussolini."

I think it is about time that somebody informed all those in authority that Benito Mussolini is not a dictator among us. If the snoot of King George can be punched in absentio in Chicago, there is no reason why Mussolini should not be razzed in Philadelphia.

And in particular I wish to have this fact called to the attention of Doak, the deporter. William Nuckles Doak he was inappropriately christened. N. D. Doak, or Nuckles Down Doak, would have been so much more fitting. He seems to be under the impression that dislike of Mussolini is a sort of sedition which makes a man liable to be sent back whence he came.

All I can say is get the transportation ready. I don't like Mussolini, even if that means that I must live in Brooklyn.

WE THE TINDER

"The Lord's going to set this world on fire—some of these days. You better git ready!"

The beat of the song has been with me for a week. It began in a room where people were dancing, but they danced to "Who Cares?" I can't remember the lyric, but it's something about "if banks fail in Yonkers" and "I love you."

"Who cares if the skies fall . . . tum, te, tum, te, tum." But the Lord is going to set this world on fire some of these days.

We are tinder for the coming of a great revival. We do care, even if we still seem sodden to every spark.

Of course we care, even though all the dervishes whirl to some variation of the theme. America first. No dole. Rugged individualism. We have followed the pipers down into the pit of the valley.

"The Lord's going to set this world on fire—some of these days."

My eye runs over a batch of morning papers, and I see: "Dies Game, Grins in Chair." "Manresa, Spain—A republic of Soviets is hereby declared. All acting against it will be shot immediately." "Woman of Seventy Holds Thirteen Spades." "Madrid, Spain—'I am going to give them back as good as they send!' declares Premier Azana." "Bombay Thousands Defy Police Staves." "Pittsburgh, Pa.—Unless immediate relief is provided 2,300 persons in nearby mining regions will starve." "Japanese Threaten Chinese in Shang-

155

hai." "Thugs Steal $349,000 Gems." "Thuringian Villages Menaced by Starvation." "Trade Barriers Grow." "Calls on America to Arm."

Some of these days.

And so I turned to the brief paragraphs of Will Rogers. He has made himself famous because he sublimates American common sense. Here is what he says: "All Europe is looking for us to do all the debt canceling so don't send delegates with hardened arteries, as usual, but get some with hardened hearts, for these people are even rehearsing their crying now."

Some of these days.

People in Germany starve, and in the streets of London huddle ragged men and women. It's all a device to bamboozle Hiram Johnson and Alfalfa Bill Murray. But it has served to give Will Rogers a quip. That ought to warn these scarecrows across the sea. There's nothing like a good joke.

Men with hardened hearts. Yes, that's the old formula. They have been the rulers of the world. Did Caesar scruple or Napoleon blanch at the sight of blood? The Old Guard dies but never surrenders. Don't fire till you see the whites of their eyes. We'll hang Jeff Davis to a sour apple tree. Remember the Maine, and make the world safe for democracy.

The Lord's going to set this world on fire—some of these days.

Some of these days there will sweep across the mountains and the plains a great wind which will stir the surface of the waters and the hearts of men. Even those with the hard hearts will feel the throb of the new day as if it were a pulse. Some of these days.

And I remember no thunder of the prophets, but by that curious twist of associated ideas a scene from an old melodrama by Augustus Thomas called "The Witching Hour."

"You can't shoot that gun. You can't even hold it."

I saw them do just this at a Lambs' Gambol a few weeks ago, and I remember the startled look on the face of the villain as the revolver clattered to the floor.

And the men with the hard hearts will find, to their surprise, that they cannot hold the guns against the multitudes of marching men who come on and on from every corner of the globe. They will be invincible, for they bring with them no guns but the glory of brotherhood.

Some of these days.

It is said that such talk is fantastic and hysterical. There is a disposition to point out the hatreds of the world. An eye for an eye, a death for a death. And the deep abiding fear. Johnny, get your gun.

And the men of the hard hearts maintain that hatreds and fears can be eliminated by adjusting gunsights and sharpening the bayonet's edge. They would say that. They always have.

But some of these days—

GOVERNOR ROLPH SPEAKING

"Mooney was justly convicted," said Governor James Rolph Jr., of California, in "a firm and measured voice."

But the voice was not firm enough or loud enough.

And what was the measure meted out to Mooney? It should have included a fair and honest answer to just one question. By every dictate of honor and justice Governor Rolph was under obligation to take to his heart this elementary problem—"Guilty or not guilty?"

It now turns out that this was the one phase of the case to which Governor Rolph paid no attention whatsoever. Almost five months have passed since the last formal application was made for a pardon. Governor Rolph would have the world believe that during all that interval he was "studying" the case, that he lay down with it at night and woke each morning to cogitate complexities.

This is sheer fiction. Much is made by Governor Rolph and his associates of the fact that no new testimony was introduced. That is correct. The last hearing was no more than the recital of an ancient wrong. A brave man, whether a rogue or an honest executive, could have given his decision in ten seconds. Governor James Rolph Jr., of California, is not a brave man.

Even before he announced his surrender to big business, little business and apathy he indicated a lack of decent regard for the issue. His notion that injustice is a thing to be ruled upon at one's leisure indicated a bluntness of ethical sensitivity. And what came out of the silences into which the Governor traveled with Judge Matt I. Sullivan, former justice of the State Supreme Court?

In so far as the newspaper extracts go the learned jurist devoted himself not to a judicial finding but to an arrogant apology for a dirty deed. This man who sat upon the bench has the impudence to present the public with a mass of comment wholly irrelevant. I quote from the learned gentleman's report:

"For instance, Professor Einstein, the famous scientist, has joined the army of those protesting against the further imprisonment of Mooney and Billings. Unfortunately, this good man and great scientist knows as much about Mooney and Billings and the case against each as they know about Einstein's inexplicable theory of relativity."

So what? Guilty or not guilty? How can it conceivably be any part of the Honorable Matt Sullivan's job to discuss Einstein's mathematics or motives?

And again from the honorable one:

"The I.W.W. in practically every locality throughout the United States contributed liberally to the defense fund. Reds and radicals of every shade made their contributions. Workers in Russia and the United States likewise contributed. Anarchists, socialists, communists and syndicalists were in the list of donors."

But guilty or not guilty? Since when did it become a crime subject to life imprisonment for a worker to win the support of his fellows in his fight against injustice?

And just one more segment from the report of Matt the mighty:

"Mooney pleaders must be ignorant of the past life of Mooney, his record as dynamiter, his public and private utterances in favor of anarchy and revolution, his publication of the *Revolt*, his connection with the Blast and Blasters."

But, Your Honor, Mooney was not tried for the expression of radical opinions. He was not ostensibly tried on the charge that he was a militant labor leader who believed in direct action. He was sent to jail on the charge that he bombed a parade in San Francisco on July 22, 1916.

How say you? Guilty or not guilty as charged? Are you judge or herring tosser?

Mooney pleaders are not ignorant of the fact that Mooney is a radical agitator. He has made no secret of it at any time before his trial or since. We who demand his freedom know that, just as well as we know that Governor Rolph is a peanut politician and the Honorable Matt I. Sullivan is a convenient counsel for that same governor. And in these facts we find no adequate answer to the cry, "Guilty or not guilty?"

"Three of my predecessors," said Governor Rolph in extenuation—Governor William D. Stephens, Governor Friend W. Richardson and Governor C. C. Young—"to each of whom an application was made by Thomas J. Mooney for a pardon, denied such application."

And accordingly we are asked to accept injustice because it has been compounded by four timorous men instead of one. "This should end the agitation for once and all," says the *New York Sun*. Quoth the craven, "Nevermore."

"In a firm and measured voice." The governor had nothing to talk down but the whisper of conscience and the still, small voice of truth. He was louder for the moment. A breeze stirred the leaves. It was nothing. But the wind rises. Pin your ear to the ground, Governor. Listen to the rumble. It is not settled. It is not done. Truth can be and truth will be a tempest. Four little governors and a former judge will not be enough to stand before it. A lie may live and even wriggle after it has been spiked, but not beyond the sundown.

HE HAD IT ONCE

The boys who write the book reviews are pretty harsh with Rudyard Kipling. In mentioning his new volume of a little verse and several stories called "Limits and Renewals" they agree in saying that it is not much good. And the boys are correct.

And yet it seems to me that they pounce upon him with too much eagerness and glee. He was a great man when he had it. Of all living authors his chance of survival is the best. That is, if he will please refrain from turning wine into water in these his barren years.

This last endeavor of the master makes curious reading. Some of the tales are bad beyond belief, but as far as I'm concerned they do not wrench the heart as much as the pretty good stories. It is agonizing to find Mr. Kipling doing an imitation of Rudyard Kipling and not quite getting away with it.

The book contains at least four good tries. You cannot read these narratives without feeling here was a man who once must have been mighty.

I have a notion that Kipling may serve the writers of the days to come in the same manner in which Mulvaney was useful to the young recruits. Mulvaney, if you remember, was both preceptor and horrible example. He taught by direct and ricochet fire. And so it is with Rudyard. His works constitute an object lesson, I believe, in the barrenness which must come at last into the words and sentences and plots of all who strive to mix narration with conscious propaganda.

Without any doubt at all Kipling is the greatest story teller of our time. But at an early age he was ruined by the dream of empire. He began to see the superman as a British brass hat. All the problems of this world and the next were to be solved by accepting the theory of the white man's burden. Particularly if the gentleman in question happened to be English. "Let St. George do it" was the motto which Rudyard Kipling celebrated.

He was at the beginning too good a fiction writer to make his British all out of the same heroic mold. Some were dumb, and some were smart, and a few were even rascals. But, good or bad, these were the salt of the earth by which the savor of the universe would be perpetuated.

Already I am beginning to tread the path of those who would ambush the great man and riddle him with putty-blowers. After all, this is the Rudyard Kipling who wrote "Kim" and "The Jungle Book" and told the tale of "The Man Who Would Be King."

Men of far greater intelligence have strung words together, but not one is now alive who has done such magical and stirring stuff. As things stand we have the business of writing all mixed up with a working knowledge of economics and politics and the philosophy of Marx.

Even in his best day Kipling was an insular and insulated snob incapable of seeing the world in any terms except as the domain and preserve of the Widow of Windsor. He has not the slightest comprehension of India's aspiration for freedom. He does not feel or even come within rifle range of the newer ferments which agitate the world.

Distinctly Kipling belongs among the casualties of the

great war. It was too big for the scope of his canvas. He had trained himself to write of the intimate wars which went on each year when spring released the tribesmen of the hills. Conflict was another form of fox hunting carried on by gallant lads from back home who wore red coats and went into battle behind "The Drums of the Fore and Aft."

Yes, he did write that and also "The Brushwood Boy," which remains, as far as I'm concerned, the finest fantasy of our times. I suppose the great puzzle is not why Kipling writes so barrenly now but what possessed him in the years of his brilliance. As an intellect he does not belong in the same room—no, not in the same block—with Shaw and Wells. And yet he has a brave chance to outlast them both.

The thing he tried to prove is already more remote than the snows of yesteryear. Not even the British themselves still hold with any stanchness to the faith that they are the anointed of the Lord brought upon earth to brighten the far corners of the universe. The captains and the kings depart, but Rudyard Kipling remains to pipe his lay. He has the honor of being not only the first but also the last minstrel of the empire.

How could this sullen, crotchety, war-struck, middle-class little man ever have reached the heights which he attained? I haven't the slightest idea. All I know is that he did it.

In direct discourse he never gave expression to an idea which pressed as much as half an inch beyond the close horizon of Tory thought. But he wrote "Without Benefit of Clergy" and "The Disturber of Traffic." He is the Fuzzy-Wuzzy of English literature. It doesn't matter how he did it. The fact remains—he broke the British square.

AL'S HOUR

CHICAGO, July 1.—I'd rather be right than Roosevelt. And if I just had to be a Democrat, why, then I'd be Al Smith.

If and when Al fails to get the nomination I know a young producer who would love to feature him in an intimate revue, for in spite of competition Alfred E. Smith has proved himself the greatest performer of all the troupe now playing in Chicago.

This might seem merely the reiteration of a well-known circumstance, but for the fact that there was doubt this time before Al came through. He didn't rehearse very well. The Huey Longs, Alfalfa Bills and other acts from the small time seemed to have caught the public eye before the big show went on.

Even some of Al's best friends went around before the first night shaking their heads and saying that the hop on the fast one wasn't there any more. He was a good fellow when he had it, was about the best that they could muster.

And then Senator Walsh said: "The chair recognizes the Hon. Alfred E. Smith, a delegate from the State of New York." And there was for a split second that curious humid hush which comes just before the wind sweeps over the valley and the lightning begins to shoot its fangs at chimneys and tall maples.

It was so in the Chicago Stadium, for the storm broke in the topmost gallery and swept down across the forest of delegates and up to the platform wall and over. Al stood there with the wind of popular acclaim beating around his head and shoulders. And he liked it.

I don't know how he felt about it, but any man would be a fool to swap those minutes for a term, for two terms, for an eternity in the White House. When did 20,000 people ever reach out in that way and pat a President between the shoulder blades and cry out to him, "Attaboy!"? No, we vote for Presidents; we pull the lever and put 'em away and forget about them.

The galleries cried "Al! Al!" as if their hearts would break. And the man from Fulton Market smiled for a while and then began to weep. Suddenly he broke through the din with that curious voice, half Caruso and half Tenth Avenue. When Al speaks the nose has it. It cuts like a sharp blade, a fish knife, through the uproar. Al carries his own gavel in his larynx.

He began to operate on Cordell Hull, who was already cut and bleeding. "The fact," rasped Smith, "that the senator only found out in the last three days that there is sentiment for repeal is just too bad." With a right and a left, a left and right, Smith tore into the arguments of the Tennessee dry and the crowd stood up as if this were truly a main bout for a title and not merely a political convention.

Cordell Hull had quoted from a statement of Al's made during the 1928 campaign which was obviously far less dripping in its temper than the majority prohibition plank for which Smith was now speaking.

"That was four years ago," said Smith savagely. "Did the senator agree with me then? He did not. And because I happened to be four years ahead of my time, look what happened to me."

I think it is true that Al does move, and I am for the men

who know the difference between last year's little old camel and a present porcupine. And even so, I believe that the most progressive and radical of us should still adhere to some fixed point and tie the craft of our hopes to some ancient pier upon occasion, so that those who have been far away upon returning will know where to find us.

Al referred to the Republican Convention and said: "I promised myself to listen to it on the raddio." And the walls came tumbling down.

I suppose that among the many reasons which induced millions to vote against Al Smith four years ago not an inconsiderable number of thousands were alienated by the fact that he chose to call the instrument which brings crooners to our homes "the raddio." I did not sit in upon party counsels, but it is inevitable that this fact was brought to his attention by friends and advisers. But Al is no man to swap a pronunciation while crossing a stream. He will change neither a "d" nor a devotion no matter how the vote may go. "Raddio" it was and "raddio" it shall remain though it splits the Solid South and tears untrammeled Democracy asunder.

Accordingly, when his name was placed in nomination I did a thing which is against the rules of the Convention Correspondents' Union and of other organizations to which I am committed. I joined the parade upon the floor and shouted: "Smith! Smith! Smith!"

My cold-blooded, or at least my fairly tepid, newspaper judgment assures me that he isn't going anywhere. And yet the 20,000 and one other never had a misgiving. We'd like to go along.

A PROFESSIONAL STAMPEDER

CHICAGO, July 2.—What day is this and where am I? Please pardon the confusion. Probably we should never have taken that last ballot. But I can explain everything. I was sitting up with a sick convention. Yesterday, I think it was, or maybe tomorrow morning. I wonder what they put in that last ballot.

And never before have I had greater need for a clear head. I want to tell you all how love came to me at the Democratic National Convention. We have taken a little cottage on the banks of the two-thirds rule, where every prospect pleases and only man is vile.

The "we" refers to me and Prudence Ginsburgh, the trombone player in the Oklahoma Lady Kilties Band. It might be just as well to begin at the beginning, although that takes us all the way back to the nominating speech for William H. Murray.

He had just been named and the demonstration in his favor was on. I wouldn't predict about one, but I'll bet you could have heard two pins drop. And then into the hall blared Prudence and the Oklahoma Lady Kilties Band.

At first it was the idlest of impulses. Just youth and 4 o'clock in the morning and a fellow who had gone through the experience of having three flasks shot from under him. In other words, I decided to join the William H. Murray parade and to enlist for the duration of the demonstration.

Fate and the deadlock willed it that I should be marching next to Prudence Ginsburgh. At first no words were spoken. I cannot even say that our hands met. After all she was playing "Give Me Something to Remember You By" on the trombone.

As I remember, we were passing Pennsylvania. Or maybe Pennsylvania was passing in order to poll the delegates. At any rate, we walked together all the way from the sun-kissed delegates of California to the rock-ribbed goats of Maine. That is why I call her Prue.

A political expert from Washington says that in Oklahoma once around the Convention Hall constitutes a common-law marriage. But political experts are invariably wrong. After all, I merely inquired if she would like to be bound by the unit rule.

At first the talk was casual and in snatches. It seemed best not to try and carry on a conversation while Prue was playing her trombone. We had to exchange our confidences during those intervals in the music where no passages have as yet been written for trombones.

Since we were both marching in an Alfalfa Bill demonstration it appeared to be only tactful to broach some of the economic issues in which the great governor is so vitally interested.

"What do you think of the relationship between the debts and reparations?" I asked politely.

"I don't think anybody's got a right to pry into their private life, even if he is a Congressman," replied Prudence. Possibly the cornet just back of her right ear confused her a little, and so I added: "How about bimetallism?"

Now when a man asks a fair question like that and the girl replies: "You're telling me, Big Boy," I think he has a right to assume that he will not get far with the young lady by discussing the financial structure.

We turned to things of smaller moment. But it developed that she thought Alfalfa Bill was something you got from the feed store at the beginning of every month.

"Don't you take any interest in this great demonstration in which you are participating?" I exclaimed in shocked surprise.

"None whatsoever," she answered, and for the first time all the flash of witty banter was gone out of her voice. She was crying. Between trombone solos she told me her sad story. It seems that Prudence Ginsburgh is a girl who gets no fun out of conventions, because she is a professional stampeder.

She lives with her married sister in Tulsa and at almost any hour of the day or night a man drives up with the other Lady Kilties in a big bus and says: "Come on, Prudence. We're going out to stampede a convention." In the beginning she used to ask where the convention was sitting and what it was all about. Indeed in her early days she wouldn't take a convention unless she liked it.

But now the life has got her. She asks no questions. Racked by sobs, Prue confessed to me that once she stampeded a convention of the Anti-Saloon League.

The harsh life has calloused her to such an extent that she can't tell the difference between the Elks and the Single Taxers. It is her contention that "when you've seen one wild demonstration you've seen 'em all."

"But isn't there any difference," I wanted to know, "between Republicans and Democrats?"

"Yes," she admitted, "if the fellers pinch you as you go by, then they're Democrats. But it did happen to me once with the Farmer-Labor party."

"You poor child," I cried as I threw both arms around her. "I will protect you. I'm a Socialist."

And now the Democrats have nominated their candidate for the Presidency. But Prue and I won't care, not even a Franklin Delano Roosevelt can spoil our happiness.

BOO!

Some hold that it is very rude and wrong for galleries to boo at a political convention. I don't think so. It is a fiction to pretend that the non-delegate spectators are guests privileged to be present only through the generous courtesy of the party's representatives. The function of these outsiders is spiritual as well as material. Not only do they help defray expenses by purchasing tickets but they are the backbone of every demonstration and the very core of those "enthusiastic outbursts" which go out over the air and serve to convince listening America that all is well with untrammeled democracy.

These unpaid servants of the party cause sit faithfully through long hours and duly applaud the name of Jefferson and Jackson. They clap hands when told that Joe Doakes or William Gish grew up in a log cabin in order to prepare himself for the long fight against the special interests.

No oratorical flourish is too feeble to excuse these representatives of the rank and file from their obligation of shaking the rafters with coöperative fervor.

And so I say that they have every right to boo upon occasion in order to preserve a balanced ration. The human spirit, like the human body, demands its proper allowance of citric acid. There is such a thing as mental beri-beri which is not to be avoided without some tot of lime or lemon.

If the galleries at the Chicago convention had failed to hiss William Gibbs McAdoo on the night of the great surrender there would have been in that fair city a dangerous epidemic of bile poisoning. And suppressed bile poisoning, at that, which is the worst kind. But for the highly effective performance of the paying guests I would have taken on the business of booing all by myself.

It has never been my privilege to watch a more noxious spectacle than Mr. McAdoo made of himself, nor a freer and fuller recognition of that fact. Governor Franklin D. Roosevelt may have many excellent qualities, but few voters are likely to love him for the friends he has made.

Even under the best of circumstances William Gibbs McAdoo suffers from smugness. He is too palpably and completely satisfied with himself at all times to please anybody but Mr. McAdoo. No other man in politics is quite so glib in devising righteous reasons for deplorable conduct.

There he stood before the twenty thousand wreathed in a smile as broad as the gates of hell. He seemed quite unaware of the fact that the canary feathers in his whiskers were all too evident. "What price McAdoo?" chanted the galleries as the gentleman talked of party harmony and the welfare of his beloved country.

To be sure, it can never be said against Mr. McAdoo that he is a lost leader who sold out for a ribbon to wear in his hair. The pockets of the man bulged with the pledges and promises of the opposition. Incidentally, he had made room for this argosy of personal advantages by very quickly tossing into the gutter his own pledges and his own promises.

Indeed, as the man turned from side to side to cast a broad and malicious beam you could hear the clank of newly minted political preferment in his pockets. Franklin D. Roosevelt will let him be Secretary of State if things turn out according to the schedule. Of course, Governor Roosevelt has been known to change his mind. But William Randolph Hearst has promised to have McAdoo out to dinner some night, and he can count on that.

If William Gibbs McAdoo had taken the platform to say, "I'm jumping on the bandwagon now because I think I have made a very good deal for myself," the galleries might have accepted his report in silence, though a sullen one. But it was asking too much to expect them to keep quiet in the face of flagrant and hypocritical effrontery. You can't have your self-respect and eat it, too. The next time William Gibbs McAdoo arises to tell a gathering about his manifold sacrifices for the public good I hope he will have the decency to wipe the cream off his chin.

But in regard to Mr. Fitts I had quite a different feeling. Mr. Fitts was booed almost as heartily as William McAdoo, and yet he lingers in my mind as one of the convention heroes. I'm sorry I don't know his full name. Nobody else did. He was just Mr. Fitts of Alabama.

It had been expected and announced that McAdoo would lead the fight against the dripping wet plank, but the gentleman from California is no Horatius, and when he saw that it would be tough to hold the bridge he retired quickly to previously prepared positions.

In fact, none of the notable prohibitionists in the party

cared to put up a fight when they saw that it would be a losing one. I am informed that Cordell Hull has been heard of in certain sections of Tennessee, but he is hardly what you would call a national figure.

Mr. Fitts, I imagine, just happened to be passing by, and so they drafted him. He took the rap without any hope of reward whatsoever.

Most of his speech was lost in the confusion. All I can remember is the recurrent phrase, "I could stand here for an hour." And I think he did.

He was ineffectual, he was wrong and muddle-headed, but he was no quitter. And so I commend to the Democratic party, both severally and collectively, the name of Mr. Fitts of Alabama.

FRAU ZETKIN

In the parliaments of the world there have been many moments of great intensity. The very fact that legislative bodies are made up of conflicting forces affords the material for that clash of will which is the essential element in drama. But of all the shows put on by men and women gathered for the making of laws none can have surpassed the present opening of the Reichstag.

"I was born July 5, 1857. Is there anyone here older?"

This was the opening challenge of Frau Clara Zetkin as she stood at the speaker's desk, supported by two younger comrades of her party. It is the German rule that the session shall be called to order by the senior member of the Reichstag.

And so it fell to the grandmother of the German revolution to have the first word in a house in which the Communists constitute a bitter and a desperate minority. Frau Zetkin has been ill, and her voice was criss-crossed with the ravages of time and rebellious controversy.

And yet she hardly needed the strong arms of her supporters as she flung out her challenge. For she looked to the Nazis—row upon row of them, clad each in uniform for the first time in any Reichstag. It was at these followers and disciples of the mailed fist that she hurled all the strength of her seniority. They sat silent, with arms folded, for her frailty was a power which left them helpless.

"Is there anyone here older?" said the tiny, bent figure, flaunting her years like a flag in the face of her foes. And, of course, there was none. In 1857 the twilight of the czars was not even a dream. Kings walked on earth which trembled, and slaves tilled American fields.

But she did not come to tell them about the back of the book or to call the roll of mighty dead men. She spoke of a new world and a promised land this side of Jordan. And there was in the small, strained voice the intensity and anxiety of one who cannot wait.

The tradition of the chamber was broken when Frau Zetkin utilized the formal occasion for a fiercely partisan attack upon Von Hindenburg and called for his impeachment. The general is more than 80. Perhaps this is not yet a young man's world.

It was too serious and stern for comedy, but surely there was irony in this duel—a fight about tomorrow between those already weary with the years and days. It was as if two spent hourglasses should lunge and lock in final combat.

And, though a gulf has always been spread between the military chief and the violent revolutionary, there was evident a forgotten and unacknowledged kinship. Hindenburg has many times called on his countrymen to give force to the uttermost and to fight and die for the Fatherland. And with a voice so feeble that it could not reach to more than a few rows of the silent house Frau Zetkin called upon her followers to take up arms and check the threat of war by shooting down all who believe in ruthlessness.

She lashed with her tongue as cowards all who would not seek peace by wading first in blood. Her hoarse voice broke, and she leaned back for a moment against the arms of the two women who stood beside her. Yet each time she straightened again and cried out for men to man the barricades and solve the economic crisis with proletarian bayonets. There was in her no more compromise than lies in a belt of machine gun bullets.

And yet it seems to me that there sounded above the head of Frau Zetkin a cry which dimmed her words. The thing she is became much louder than what she said. A little old woman told the members of the Reichstag that salvation lies only in the fierce thrust of steel to be taken up by oppressed and embattled workers.

And yet she herself was the living, flaming proof that force does not lie only in the gun racks. A puff of wind, a touch of the hand could have thrust her from her place upon the speaker's stand. But there was none dared raise that hand.

She was for her cause a regiment, a brigade, an army with banners. The Nazis in their uniforms seemed no more than sulky pupils kept in after school.

I wish Frau Zetkin could have sat a little apart from herself and listened to the speech she made. Then she might well have known the supreme truth which she created and spread out for the profit of mankind. There is no force which can stand against a fierce, a free and stalwart spirit. The voice of such a one is louder than the roll of guns. And though it sags down to a whisper, it will be heard around the world.

DEAR COMRADE

I was strangely moved to come suddenly, in a newspaper, upon the item that Nadejda Alliluieva died during the night in her residence in Moscow. Beside the story there was a picture of a woman of startling beauty walking through a snowy Russian street and above it the caption, "Wife of Stalin, Soviet Dictator."

They order such things better in Russia, I think, for the official announcement said, "The friend and devoted aide of Comrade Stalin." Perhaps even to the point of self-consciousness there was the attempt to say, "Before all else she was a human being," and to make her death belong to her.

The Russian press made no mention of the fact that she was the wife of Stalin. Instead the announcement went that "she served the party and remained both active and modest in her revolutionary duty. She has always tried to improve herself and has been among the most active comrades in industrial activity in recent years."

Russia is trying to break down a great many precedents and traditions within the span of a generation. And, though the chief complaint against the state has been the charge that it minimized the importance of the individual in the interest of the mass, in this respect at least it has tried to single out the woman who died as a person in her own right and not one to be remembered as the woman who married Stalin and bore him two children.

I find a somewhat surprising touch of sentiment from the official channels of that land which has tried to banish sentiment: "To the dear memory of our comrade and friend, Nadejda Sergeivna Alliluieva, our dear comrade and the finest person, passed away."

The translation is quite possibly a little awkward, but in any case this is a strange state paper. It is as if some official or other said: "No, I won't be blunt. I will break the Spartan code."

On the day before she died Joseph Stalin reviewed a victory march of fifty thousand in the great square of Moscow. He stood erect and made no sign or said a word of the dear comrade who lay dying in the Kremlin. The state is the state and a man's inner agony something else again.

Perhaps it is the better way. But it is difficult. It has been tried, and whether or not it has succeeded is a fit point for argument. I think that in discussing the Russian scheme so much emphasis has been put upon its vital economic factors that we are likely to forget that it is also an extraordinary spiritual adventure.

I suppose few partisans of the cause will admit as much, but here, once more, there walks upon the earth the soul of Cromwell and of Cotton Mather. I do not believe in the philosophy of Puritanism, but no sane man can deny the toughness of its fiber. Under one name or another it has always held some corner of the world. It is a span from Sparta to Plymouth Rock and back again to Moscow, but there is a continuing tradition.

It must be obvious by now that even when the theological aspects of Puritanism are swept away, it still persists. I have known atheists as grim and sedate as any parson. Cards and high jinks are just about as popular in Moscow today as they were in Marblehead two centuries ago. You may ask a man to make sacrifices for the sake of the life everlasting or for the five-year plan, and his approach and attitude toward existence will turn out pretty much the same.

If the Puritan principle ever conquered any community entire I rather imagine that there would never more be cakes and ale. It is a discipline which makes for high efficiency, and no troop of cavaliers ever stands much chance upon the field when engaged by embattled roundheads.

But there is no heart and soul which does not carry within its confines some counter revolutionary factors. Puritanism in all its many world manifestations has abated, dwindled and almost seemed to die not because of pressure from the outside but because the Puritan himself is such an inveterate rebel that he must at times rise up to smite his own philosophy.

Thus I find it recorded in the dispatches from Moscow that at the school where Nadejda Alliluieva went to learn the technique of making artificial silk, "her name was tacked up on a bulletin board, with fifty others, last spring as having cut her classes three days out of sixteen." And once she was cited for failure to return library books on time.

Probably the world will never hear much of the story of

this one who lived in the shadow of a great man and still had stamina enough to die under her own name. I have always been less interested in the pattern of people than in their variations and aberrations. I am curious to know what a dedicated revolutionist does when she cuts her classes.

It is a strange and probably magnificent adventure which the Russians are conducting, but it seems to me that in the face of death they act about the way we all do. I wonder if they really think that they have abolished God by teaching the children in school that the state is an old gentleman with a long white beard.

APES AND ELMS

New Haven should be gay and all agog after its striking football victory over Harvard. But Yale is gloomy, suspicious and furtive, and all because of a little rumor.

Several years ago a fund was left for the care and rearing of apes by the psychologists of Yale. At first there was a feeling that it might be necessary to lower the entrance requirements, but this scare soon blew over.

Every prospect was pleasing except the climate. The anthropoids could "Boola Boola" with the best of them, but they couldn't stand the chilling breezes from the Sound. Some three years ago the suggestion was made that the colony should be moved to Florida. In fact, an official announcement was made to this effect. There was some comment in the newspapers at the time, in which, as I remember, I joined, offering appropriate condolences to the football coaches.

According to the present rumor, the transfer never took place. The coaches and the psychologists sat down in secret conference, and one of the football men offered a way out of the difficulty. It was a practical suggestion, and the psychologists had never thought of it.

"Africa is a moist, warm country," began the coach.

"Yes," replied one of the professors testily, "and the American Great Lakes are the largest bodies of fresh water in the world. What about it?"

"Just this," said the coach; "when the wind blows free and cold what does a Yale man do?"

"He goes out for hockey," suggested an assistant professor, trying to get into the spirit of the proceedings.

"No, no," said the football mentor; "I mean what does he wear?"

Since the psychologists were all trained observers, it didn't take the head of the department long to answer, "A gray suit of clothes with a thin green stripe, a sweater with a large 'Y,' a purple necktie, pink and magenta woolen socks, occasionally underwear—except in Sheff, of course, and a raccoon coat."

"Now you've got it," said the coach.

"You mean that we should give 'Y's' to all the anthropoid apes in the Yale ape farm so that they can wear sweaters?" the assistant professor asked. He was a little duller than the rest, which was the reason why they made him an assistant professor.

"Not at all," exclaimed the athletic instructor; "that would cheapen the 'Y.' Let them earn it like everyone else. Under proper direction an undergraduate is just as good as the best anthropoid on the campus any day in the week. I mean give the apes raccoon coats and then who on earth will know the difference?"

"Done and done," cried the professors and clapped their hands in glee. They swore a mighty oath of secrecy, and the janitor of the building where they met was let in on the compact so that there should be no leak.

Yale athletic prowess boomed mightily, and it was not until last spring that any inkling of suspicion crept out. It was an unfortunate occurrence.

I am not referring to the slight unpleasantness which was created when it was discovered that a gorilla had been selected for Phi Beta Kappa. After all, that was known only to the few who watched the poor fellow cling to the chandelier and chatter when they approached him with a key. No, I mean the little scandal which marred the last tap day.

"Go to your room!" said a senior to a stalwart athlete, slapping him on the shoulder. He went, but to the horror of all beholders he reached it by swinging through the branches of an elm, and in transit he paused long enough to heave down a few coconuts.

The story never got out, and all the newspaper correspondents agreed to suppress it. But I think that sound journalism should not only permit but require some mention of the extraordinary episode which occurred in the Bowl immediately after the Harvard game. After all, some 50,000 people were present. And I for one will not keep silent.

As the final whistle blew, a substitute Yale tackle bounded from the bench and ran to the goal posts. Some thought that under the excitement of the victory he was intent on tearing down his own posts. But he did nothing of the sort. Leaping high in the air, he swung from the cross-beam.

Even that could have been pardoned as a bit of youthful exuberance but for one little fact. He swung by his tail.

And so today there are gloom, suspicion, and furtiveness down at Yale. Indeed, it has grown to such an extent that whenever one undergraduate makes an offensive remark to another—be it in classroom, study or parlor—it is customary to answer, "Take off that raccoon coat!"

"THE CHOPINZEE"

I knew de Pachmann, who died in Rome last week, and among the artists he was rare in that he lived up to the most fantastic and fictional concept of the great musician.

If a playwright undertook to set him down as a character in a comedy any audience would be dubious as to the authenticity of the figure. It would seem as if the dramatist strained too much after a bizarre effect.

And yet the eccentricities of the man were not affectations. I always felt that a sound philosophy underlay his curious concert manners. I note that Leopold Godowsky has referred to him as a "miniaturist." "His field," says the composer, "was limited, but within its narrow range he was supreme and inimitable."

Underneath Godowsky's compliment I seem to catch some hint of a point of view which has always appeared to me heretical. I refer to that state of mind which withholds something from the artist who does not choose to spread himself across vast surfaces.

And that is a notion which leads us to such palpable absurdities as figures carved upon the sides of mountains and "the largest mural paintings in the world." Not to mention that giant motion picture theater which was but lately the world's largest music hall.

De Pachmann may not have belonged among the great pianists, but he was supreme as an interpreter of Chopin. It was some English critic years ago who referred to him as the Chopinzee. And there was much in this pun to meet the eye, for de Pachmann was curiously squat in figure, with long arms and hands disproportionately large. When the mood was on him he seemed almost to swing back and forth upon a grand piano.

I heard him play several times in his apartment here and once in a Carnegie Hall concert which infuriated many of the better critics. He had become old and his eccentricities had grown upon him, but he remained, for all that, in a state of grace.

To him a piano was an intimate instrument, and as a "miniaturist" Carnegie Hall presented a canvas too large for his scope or interest. He liked to play where four or five were gathered together. "There are too many fools in any thousand," he once said.

For reasons obscure and erroneous de Pachmann drew the impression that I was a person of musical understanding. It is true that I loved to hear him and sat as rapt as any connoisseur while he played. But when he talked to me in technical terms I managed to conceal my ignorance by offering only assent and never any comment.

They kept most of the notices from the old man after his last Carnegie Hall appearance, but he hit upon one or two which were severe and said to three of us who were his friends, "You liked; that is enough."

He was happily insulated against criticism, for anybody who praised him became at once a great musician and the rest were either ignorant or malicious. I think the attitude has always been a useful one to creative artists.

As a pianist I felt that de Pachmann was always reaching out and trying to bring people in closer to himself and the keyboard upon which he perched. His style of concert was not unlike what the older vaudeville theaters call a piano-logue. There was always a running fire of comment from the performer himself. "Bravo, de Pachmann!" he would say to himself in a loud voice as he played a passage and found his interpretation excellent.

And he would throw in little bits of autobiography and reminiscence as he went along. It was in Carnegie Hall, as I remember, that he prefaced one piece by saying, "I once heard Mme. Schumann play this. Oh, my God!"

During a waltz the old gentleman would sometimes get up from the piano stool, cavort about for a step or so and then sit down again. And always there was a muttering and a chattering from him as he swung high in the treetops in-toxicated by the sounds which he brought forth from the big black box.

Temperament is an ungainly thing unless it is part of the organic structure of an individual. I do not like to see any artist slip into a mannerism as if it were a garment. But these moods of de Pachmann were in his marrow.

It seemed to me then and it seems to me now that the finest of all who deal with sound and shape and color must be those who look upon their own creation and cry out aloud, "Bravo!"

BRING ON THE ARTIST

New names seem effective in the promotion of new worlds.

Technocracy, for instance, is sweeping the country on account of a new label, in spite of the fact that most of the assertions which it makes are entirely familiar. And so I think I'll try to start a movement of my own. It will be called "artistocracy" and must inevitably be in violent conflict with the theories of Mr. Scott.

If I understand the new messiahs they believe that we can be saved only by handing over our lives and beings to the engineers. The Utopia which I have in mind would be not only willing but grateful in its reception of the statistics of the technocrats. But we would like a different sort of leadership.

We have had enough of engineers, great or otherwise. We want the world turned over to the artists as generalissimos. Nor is this still another subterfuge by which fascism may be introduced under some other name. The artist has never been a dictator, since he understands better than anybody else the variations in human personality.

But he has been kept on the sidelines far too long. In every age the artist has been the critic and the counselor of the prevailing social system. Yet always he has been called in after the event. His function has been to scourge the follies of his day as satirist or to bind up the wounds of a bleeding world in this rôle as a sort of sentimental Red Cross worker.

Even in the last ten minutes of play there has been no

disposition to let him go on the field and actually take part in the play. And he has been held back because of the conception that he was visionary and impractical. Now, of course, he should immediately accept the impeachment and after pleading guilty say, "So what?"

His best argument is that the world has been run by realists, and look what they have done to it. I'm not quite sure that I would argue that Edna St. Vincent Millay should upon the instant become the president of the Chase National Bank. It might not be a bad idea, at that, and surely it would be less preposterous than life under the decisions of the little group of hard-boiled men who met after the great war to found a peace.

There was in that number one who had some fragmentary inspiration of the visionary. Woodrow Wilson, curiously enough, broke more trench lines than any general in the American army. He swept back resistance and dislodged gunners from concrete pillboxes by introducing a formula, by flashing before the world the dream of a new world.

It is palpable that he failed, and generally it is held that his defeat at Versailles was brought about by the fact that he was not sufficiently practical. The reverse is the case. Woodrow Wilson could not forget that he came up from Princeton to the Presidency.

He fancied himself as one who could meet the political bosses of the world on their own ground and conquer them, even as he got the better of the Democratic machine in New Jersey. He traded bits of his bright dream here and there for things which seemed at the moment practical. And whenever he bargained off some section of the rainbow he was hornswoggled.

The children of darkness are shrewder in their own generation than the children of light. A dream is so much more valuable than anything else that all who engage in such barter are sure to go away from the market place poorer than when they entered.

Woodrow Wilson needed a more clear-cut devotion to his vision. He was ruined and vanquished when certain European slickers paid him the dubious compliment of calling him a practical man.

I have said that there is a certain shrewdness in the children of darkness, but I would keep a strong string on that admission. The advantages which they gain either for themselves or their nations are largely fallacious. The time has come to shelve these men who cannot see more than twenty-four hours or even less beyond the end of their long noses. The world is now in a state where it should call upon the impractical for advice and counsel.

Many a crumbling civilization has been given force and meaning only through the contribution of its writers and painters and sculptors. One remembers both Greece and Rome not through their legislators but only because of the men who piled word upon word or marshaled marble blocks.

And so let us agree even before downfall that these are the important men in any community. Instead of having them mold memorials to something which is gone we should intrust them with a vital part in the plan of birth and growth.

The captain and the kings have departed. Call in the artists to make the bright new world out of their most shining visions.

WHERE MINK MEETS MINK

I have always been curious as to why Rome fell, and I have my own theory.

Very probably one of the causes of the decline of the empire was the fact that the patricians began to arrive late at the circuses.

Some commoner who was intent on watching a lion just about to devour a Christian suddenly had his view cut off by a dinner party which barged in half an hour after the beginning of the show. The usher came down the aisle and said: "Let me see your stubs. Are you sure you have the right seats?" And the people in the belated detachment couldn't seem to make up their minds whether Mildred should sit next to Jack or whether Betty should go in first.

By the time they decided that problem and allowed the poor commoner to have an unobstructed line of vision to the arena the Christian was gone, and nothing remained but a rather smug and satisfied lion.

It spoiled the commoner's fun for the whole evening, and when he got home he said to his family that the show was a flop and would be in cut rates within the week. He even spoke ill of the whole imperial system and ventured the opinion that Rome wasn't what it used to be.

You see, the patrician party insisted on carrying on a loud conversation all through the gladitorial combats. The poor fellow was so distracted that he didn't have any clear conviction as to whether he should put his thumbs up or down. As a matter of fact, in his irritation he kept them down, which was a little unfair to the victim in the arena, because what the serious student of the sport really meant was that he wished the cackling crowd behind him were all Christians and suitable for casting in the next blue plate offering to the lions.

I have a strong feeling that something of the same sort is going on today. The most effective propagandists for the radical cause are the very rich. Of course, the cult of flagrant bad manners does not extend throughout the entire length of Park Avenue. Here and there any fair-minded revolutionist would mark a white cross. But he wouldn't need much chalk.

It seemed to me that the worst exhibition of boorishness I had ever seen in the theater occurred at the opening of "The Gay Divorce," but at that time I had not attended the first night of "Design for Living."

There can be reasonable excuses for arriving late, but that is only a small portion of the indictment. Those who showed up anywhere from fifteen minutes to half an hour late came whooping into the lobby and down the aisles. The later they arrived the more noise they made as they swished down the aisle. One theater party, which occupied an entire row, swept in a full fifty minutes after the curtain had risen. And they behaved as if they were changing the guard at Buckingham Palace.

It seems to me that the ermined and sabled are under some illusion that they should be preceded by footmen with silver trumpets wherever they go. Nor does any signal to cease firing occur when Park Avenue is finally in its place and ready to see what the mimes have to offer. I want some day to see a Broadway opening without benefit of footnotes. I'd rather not be told by the lady just ahead that a line is "delicious" or "so quaint." I'd rather be surprised.

Indeed, since the play is hardly the thing, I suggest strongly to the leaders of New York society that they hire some one of the abandoned playhouses of the town and hold nightly receptions in the orchestra and the lobby, leaving the stage quite untenanted. As things stand now the later diners are under a sad disadvantage. At times when Mildred greets Mary a full four rows ahead the cheerful salutation is almost drowned by the hum of the actors' speaking lines. Some of our players have begun to forget the dictates of the recent realistic school and are actually audacious enough to try to make themselves heard.

And I would cite also the matter of intermission manners. It is quite true that many of New York's theaters are architecturally at fault. It is difficult under the best of circumstances to reach the outer air or lounge, and exit is hardly expedited by the current practice of those who reach the end of the aisle or a narrow doorway and there take up their stand, as if they were Spartans defending the pass at Thermopylae.

I wish that in my school days I had been a superb plunging fullback instead of a mediocre guard. Even so, when next I attend the theater I plan to equip myself with leather headgear, and when I get home I hope to find it all splotched with mangled ermine.

THEY WILL COME BACK

"And we are not coming back!" shouted a spokesman of Japan.

He was announcing the decision of his nation to leave the League and retain Manchuria. There came from the galleries some applause at this gesture of defiance.

But in spirit at least there was present an old gentleman full of dignity and years. He carried an hourglass and a scythe.

"And we are not coming back!" shouted the orator, filled with the fervor of aggression and the nascence of nationalism.

"Is that so?" said the old man under his breath. For he had seen the elephants of Hannibal go up to the Alps and over. He had watched the legions of Caesar tramp through the Druid groves of ancient Britain. He heard the tears of Alexander and saw the bloodstains on the snow in the retreat from Moscow.

And while the elders at Geneva talked the soldiers of Japan stormed Kailu and Chaoyang. They drew the ring more closely around Jehol, the golden city and the pleasant place of Emperors. And it was said in Tokio: "This is our destiny. Let the old men talk. We will act. History is on our side."

Of all inconstant allies history is fickle beyond the rest. It follows the call of a silver trumpet which may sound suddenly at night, and on that instant the forces of destiny, the horsemen and the footmen, gray as cats and big beyond belief, change sides, with banners flying.

Above the heads of this shadowy army on the march there flies the bird of victory, circling about and seeking some new standard upon which to perch.

Destiny never moves in straight lines but twists and turns, and, though the arc be great, it will return to its own citadel, which bears the curious name of Beginning of the End.

And in the great hall one may see the tattered banners of proud brigades and some other dim mementoes of empires that once cluttered the earth with their majesty and might.

The light is thinly filtered in. The dust lies deep upon the floor, but all who pass by may read upon tablets of brass the names of the men and of the nations which once were things of sound and fury. And there is some strange enchantment in the place, for it is possible for no one to speak of these dead and forgotten expeditionary forces above a whisper. There is no echo.

"And we are not coming back."

Oh, yes, you will, Japan. There is a force, and the empire of which you dream will trickle down until it is one with the lost lands of Julius Caesar.

Not in Japan alone but in many other quarters it is held that the word of the wise men matters little and that destiny is on the side of the big guns and the tanks. "Read history!" cried Matsuoka to the League.

Look well, oh, men of Nippon. Read history. Read it and weep, for it tells in every chapter of the downfall of imperial adventure and the strong tides which set for human rights. A decent regard for the opinions of mankind is not a thing lightly to be thrown overboard.

It has been said of the League of Nations that it has

proved impotent in the present crisis, I disagree. It seems to me that the reading of the roll, in which every nation except Japan and Siam voted for censure, marked a new manifestation of world solidarity.

I will grant that it did not on the instant check the armies as they moved over the frozen terrain toward Jehol. But it has put Japan upon the defensive in an important way. Even within the borders of the island empire doubt has been sown.

I do not expect to see the outside powers thrust Japan back from selfish adventure. I believe with all my heart that the better way will come from within the Japanese people themselves. Public opinion may seem to be no more than a fingertip laid upon the wrist in the beginning. But its force grows. It tightens. It is a mightier ring than that of men and machine guns which encircles the golden city.

They will come back.

THE TALE OF AN ANCIENT WRONG

A sailing ship came down the tide and cast her anchor over. She rode the long swell and waited for boats from the blazing coast to bear her black slaves. When they were below deck she picked up her pin and headed for America.

That was more than two hundred years ago. Yesterday in Decatur, Ala., a jury of twelve white men brought in a verdict of death against Haywood Patterson. The attorney general of the great sovereign state referred to him as "that thing."

They say it was a quiet courtroom and a gentle day down in Morgan County when the jury filed in after twenty-four hours of deliberation. But could none of them hear the wind in the rigging of the slave ship, the creaking of her timbers and the cries of the cargo?

That ghostly ship has steered her course around our coasts and even up into the back waters times innumerable. She seeks in vain a final haven. We, the grandsons and the great-grandsons of the slaves of the slavers, are not appeased. We have not forgiven the Negro. It is less difficult to forgive your enemies, but the persecution of the Negro continues because we have wronged him so vastly and so vitally. We are bound to the wheel of our damnation and try to stave it off with silly postures and cruel antics. Fear grips us, and we sheer off even from an act of simple justice.

Attorney General Knight could not even bring himself to admit that he was in the presence of a man on trial for his life. He had to take refuge in such a phrase as "that thing." He was afraid of the facts. He had reason to fear.

There was much panicky talk in the speeches of the men who pressed the case. "Show them that Alabama justice cannot be bought and sold with Jew money from New York!" cried Solicitor Wright at one point in the trial. And the attorney general, after deploring the injection of prejudice by his associate in the summation, went on to say: "If you acquit this Negro put a garland of roses around his neck, give him a supper and send him to New York City. There let Dr. Harry Fosdick dress him up in a high hat and morning coat, gray striped trousers and spats."

And that was because Dr. Fosdick had told Ruby Bates to face the danger of return and go back to confess that she lied when first she accused the Negro boys. And that was because the attorney general was afraid.

If human life were not at stake this Scottsboro case might take rank with the most inspired of all extravaganzas, but the shadow of the chair falls across such ironic ribaldries as the conviction of a Negro field hand on the ground that Alabama does not like the modes and manners of New York City. Instead of a crown of thorns, Alabama rhetoric pressed down a high hat upon this poor laborer.

But the irony of the situation swings wide beyond the borders of the state where the trial was held. Does the learned counselor from the Southland actually believe that the song of the slave ship never floats above the roofs of Harlem? Instead of the fantastic festival outlined by the prosecutor, what would New York really have to offer any Haywood Patterson? Morning coats and garlands? Not exactly. The great and free city of New York would afford him an opportunity to share a three-room apartment with nine or ten of his fellows. And only with the best of luck would he be able to pay the rent.

The South imposes rather more lynchings, legal and otherwise; New York and Chicago take it out in tuberculosis.

We have no right to sit in the seats of the scornful. Nor is it the part of wisdom to think of the Scottsboro case as a local issue. We will get nowhere if comment merely takes the form of attacks upon the legal machinery of Alabama and charges that Decatur opinion is blinded by bigotry. That would merely be a matter of the mote calling the beam black.

As a matter of fact, some wise words were spoken during the trial. "The world at this time and in many lands is showing intolerance and showing hate. It seems sometimes that love has almost deserted the human bosom. It seems that hate has taken its place. . . . Wrong dies and truth forever lasts, and we should have faith in that."

That was said by the judge—James E. Horton. Well, Your Honor, when it comes time to pass sentence of death how are you going to plead? Remember that you and all the rest of us are on trial for our faith, our integrity and our lowest common decency. What say you? Guilty or not guilty?

Speak up, man! Let us all speak up and prove that we are not guilty of this monstrous thing. Let us scuttle the slave ship in forty fathoms and stop that whine of the wind in its rigging.

THE BURNING OF THE BOOKS

They burned the books, but there remains a red glow in the sky. The fuel of the foolish was curiously assorted. Upon the Nazi bonfire were piled the works of some who never glowed before. I had not thought to live into a day when sparks would fly from Morris Hillquit.

The names of the great, the near and never great came to the crucible along with the words of the lame, the halt and the blind. Side by side the magnificent and the feeble words of those who merely meant well ascended to heaven.

Unconsciously the Nazis paid a singular tribute of respect to certain authors of small fame and rather meager merit. What wouldn't I give to have some forgotten book of my own suddenly become fortuitously a part of a pillar of fire by night! I really must buckle down to work and write something which Hitler does not like in order to be in on the next illumination. Yes, and I will even consent to call it to his attention.

Remarque, Ludwig, Mann, Karl Marx, Jack London and Ben Lindsey! It sounds almost like what some of the book critics call "a balanced ration." But why Ben Lindsey? He seems to me one of God's noblemen and also among the most fearsomely bad writers who ever set an earnest pen to paper.

They burned the books of Dr. Sigmund Freud. One of the barkers at the bonfire explained that the little man from Vienna had put too much stress upon "the animal qualities of human nature."

I cannot understand at all the philosophy of these nascent Nazis. They seem to be engaged upon a rather pitiful attempt to combine the school of blood and iron with sweet violets. If I can make it out the accepted author must be a combination of Nietzsche and Harold Bell Wright. It's a swell trick if they can do it.

But most of all I was interested in the burning of Dr. Freud. Sigmund Freud, like Karl Marx, is a writer who has been vastly discussed by millions who never looked at a line he ever wrote. To paraphrase a familiar spiritual: "Everybody talking about Marx ain't gwine there. Revolution! Revolution! Gwine to walk all over Karl Marx's revolution!"

And in some respects Sigmund Freud is in an even better position than Karl Marx to get a pretty good chuckle for himself out of Nazi goings-on. The little man who led the first expedition into the darkest subconscious can afford to smile at the most amazing demonstration of national neuroticism the world has seen in our time.

An American correspondent who reported the address which Herr Gutjahr made as the books burned writes, "It was a boy's speech, and it was received with boyish enthusiasm."

I think Mr. Birchall might have gone a little further than that. It was, as a matter of sober fact, a child's set piece, and the whole enterprise represented a retreat from reality into infantilism. The I.Q. of the Hitler movement can hardly rate anything above 6 years of age. At that stage any one of us would like to dress up in a uniform and play with matches.

But somebody really ought to tell Adolf's adolescents that it isn't funny any more.

The first time I meet a Nazi fooling around writing things with chalk on nice, clean walls and sticking his penknife into the furniture I purpose to fetch him a cuff over the side of the head and exclaim in a firm voice, "Naughty! Naughty!"

A HOUSING PROBLEM

The Tenement House Department has just made a survey which shows that New York City has 1,401,078 apartments.

That is a great many apartments, and I suppose they range from twenty-four rooms, with balconies and roofs, down to alcove, bedroom and bath. It is not surprising to learn that there are more than enough to go 'round. According to the recent census, two hundred and one thousand, or a little more than 14 percent, are without present tenants.

With such a wealth of equipment it is curious that the great City of New York should be faced with a housing problem. But the plain fact of the matter is that, even though vast armies of halls and kitchenettes and living rooms yawn for even so much as the echo of a human footstep, each day the marshal's men make their rounds and carry through evictions.

And so a vast acreage of sheltered space is left to mice and moths and whatever stray ghosts there may be, while men and women trudge mean streets seeking some place into which they can go from under the stars.

It doesn't sound very sensible. And it isn't getting any more sensible, for with the diminution of relief funds Commissioner Taylor has announced that it will no longer be possible to supply even the neediest with funds for rent. With a due appreciation of that gentleman's difficulties, it does not seem to me that the policy of public welfare has always been dictated by inspired wisdom. I am told by Mary Fox:

"The procedure during the whole winter has been that when a family was actually on the point of eviction a check would be issued by the Home Relief station to enable the family to get another flat.

"I have known of families," she adds, "who have hunted a week before they would find a landlord who would take them in once he saw the Home Relief check. The landlord's position was: 'If I take you in I will have to keep you and your family for several months, at the end of which time it will be necessary for me to pay a city marshal from $4 to $6 to get you out. I'd rather have an empty flat than accept somebody as a tenant who offers one month's rent for three months' occupancy.' "

Under the circumstances we have the almost fantastic situation in which one arm of the city government carts furniture down to the sidewalk and expels a family, whereupon the dispossessed are expected to go to another department of that same city government, with the dim hope of being put back in again in some other place.

Moreover, the cat and mouse quality in the administration of relief has resulted in the filling up of the poorest types of tenement houses. The owner of the worst slum tenement is the only one willing to take the risk of taking in the dispossessed, because his property is in such a condition that even one month's rent is so much velvet.

In addition to the empty apartments of the city there are also the huge number of hotels, which have for the most part been very slightly annoyed by the presence of guests in recent months. If the federal government is going to hire marginal farm lands in order to raise the price of wheat and keep the farmer from losing his home I see no reason why it should not also take over marginal apartment houses and hotels and insure the industrial tenement house dweller of some place to lay his head.

Some may object that housing should be a matter for the municipality or the state. Others may urge that the whole thing ought to be left to private initiative. Private initiative being what it is, I see no great hope from that quarter, but, whatever method is used, it certainly is not beyond human ingenuity to house everybody in any community which has grown real estate poor through vacancies.

And tomorrow is Mother's Day. This is a festival devoted

to sending flowers or candy to the appropriate relative. Or maybe you just buy a flower for yourself and wear it in your buttonhole in honor of your mother. The precise details of the celebration escape me.

But in any case there are a great many mothers of the East Side and elsewhere who will find that their token of the day is an eviction notice. There are thousands of families which do not even answer a knock at the door for fear it may be a marshal.

And 201,406 apartments are vacant. Who says that man is a reasonable being?

"THE WORST IS OVER"

I saw a money-changer in the neighborhood of the temple late yesterday afternoon, and it did not seem to me that he was on his way to catch an outbound train. On the contrary, he was headed up the steps, cool as a cucumber. "I wonder if the old place has changed," he remarked as we passed.

In all probability he will not find much alteration inside. There is some scaffolding still up around the main entrance, but the sign "Business as usual" is prominently displayed.

Reform has slackened. Within a month there has been a perceptible slowing up. It may be that the new deal was no more than a round of roodles and that we are all going back to the old game.

"Stocks Soar to New Highs," "Market Boils in Record

Session," "Pivotal Issues Up Ten Points." Front page prosperity is with us once again. Mr. Morgan is going to pay an income tax almost any year now.

But the trouble lies in the fact that a rich man's boom will hardly suffice to relieve the victims of a poor man's panic. The rise of stocks and bonds has very little to do with any upward turn in the employment curve. Shareholders may do extremely well even in periods when millions are out of work. Congress is fond of denouncing Wall Street in speeches from the floor, and yet it takes far too much for granted on no other basis than the rise in quotations.

Already there is a disposition to agree that the worst is over. If any dove has come fluttering back with an olive leaf we have a right to whatever cheer this bit of greenery may bring us. But the great trouble is that the lessons of the flood are quite so quickly forgotten. Arthur Hopkins once produced a play called "The Deluge," in which an assorted group of individuals was trapped in a house by the rising waters of the Mississippi. With death staring them in the face each member of the community began to have a closer understanding of his associates and a deeper sympathy. But the waters receded, and so did the little group which had seen a vision of Utopia.

So it seems to be with the government of the United States and with its inhabitants. When the banks were on the verge of ruin almost any sort of radical legislation might have been obtained, but the very institutions which were picked up out of the gutter have turned high and mighty overnight and are now arching their eyebrows and talking about paternalism and government interference. After a short burst of candor the Morgan inquiry has gone back into the secret silences.

Three months ago Congress was sufficiently frightened to cut out the pension graft. Now that there is a glimmer upon the horizon Congress wants to put it back again. The most discouraging thing is the conduct of the Farmer-Laborites and other so-called radicals in the House and Senate. For the tenth or twentieth time in as many years it is shown again that the vision of these men does not extend beyond the price of wheat. At 70 cents a bushel every man jack of them has slowed down to a walk, and by the time wheat touches a dollar they have all become rotarian Republicans.

It is true that President Roosevelt supplied the original motive power for certain measures which actually had in them some element of fundamental change. In spite of the slackening of the program I still think that Franklin D. Roosevelt is the one best bet in the present administration.

But part of the attempt to return to normalcy is within his own responsibility. Mr. Roosevelt was elected by a party which is badly split. Moreover, his appeal carried into voting camps of widely divergent views. At the outset he may well have been troubled by the thought that his mandate, although hearty, was far from explicit. The platform on which he ran was franker than is usual, and, even so, it left many loopholes for interpretation and was shrewdly silent on various vital issues.

In effect, then, Franklin D. Roosevelt came into power as a sort of coalition government in his own person, and he surrounded himself with advisers of many hues. The best men among his counselors are some of the members of the "brain trust" which has aroused so much easy parody from the old-line politicians. Roughly, the Roosevelt council can be divided into men who believe that they are dealing with a temporary emergency and men who think that fundamental and permanent readjustments must be made in the economic setup of the United States.

It is altogether impossible to reconcile these two schools. President Roosevelt must make up his mind which is his crowd. And he must make up his mind now. If the lads who have come to the great conflagration with a fire extinguisher are to prevail there will be no great point in getting into a fury about Congressional obstruction of the program. That program will not matter.

AN UNDELIVERED ADDRESS

I have not been asked in this year, or any other, to talk at a college commencement, but if I ever had the opportunity I think I would like to make an address about as follows:

"Seniors of Ooffus University, you are about to be graduated into an extremely lukewarm world. The chances are that not one of you will get any decent sort of job for the next two or three years. Now, what are you going to do about it?

"Two tragic things can happen to a young college graduate. He may come to utter failure before he is able to endure it or by some miracle he may strike sudden and unexpected success.

"Possibly I will be regarded as a little whimsical if I maintain that the latter is perhaps the greater tragedy. In support of my position I will seek solace in Scripture, which has often been quoted at commencements. I think it is true that it does not avail a man very much to gain the whole world and lose his own soul. And, after all, when I spoke of unexpected success I did not quite intend to include all that territory.

"What I have in mind is that the bright youngster of twenty-one or -two who immediately makes his mark is almost certain to be dependent upon luck, influence or some showy talent. None of these factors is to be enduringly prized. Genius, or even good second rate ability, takes longer than that.

"The man who succeeds fortuitously is apt to become convinced that he lives in the best of all possible worlds, or something very close to it. He is likely to found generalizations upon happenings which are, after all, no more than a lucky turn of the dice.

"But perhaps it is not necessary to waste much time on these exceptions. The average college man will find himself on the wrong side of a wall of joblessness and indifference. Nobody, as far as I know, has any next Monday morning remedy to save him from discomfort and actual physical suffering. The best that any commencement orator can do is to urge him not to blame himself for conditions over which he has as yet no control.

"A few voluble people still go about the world saying that the unemployed are victims of their own folly and sloth and that they would easily find work if they only wanted to. This is an evil thing, but it is much more evil if any of the dispossessed can be induced to believe such nonsense even for a moment.

"I hope that college has taught you the undoubted truth

that practically nobody fails without active collaboration. I would warn every one of you against the practice of self-examination and the recital of your own mistakes and short-comings.

"Do not spend very much time in searching your own soul, but try instead to understand the psychology of the group or class in which you belong. By the help of this process you will probably find that the thing which you mistook for a personal weakness or ineptitude is character-istic of most of your fellows in like circumstances.

"College itself is a token of a new order of society. Though individual worth is recognized and encouraged, the rewards are not in terms of financial preferment. Every college or university is to a large extent a communal, enter-prise. In any educational institution worthy of its name and fame an effort is made to apply the rule of 'From each ac-cording to his ability; to each according to his needs.'

"It is right and very logical that the colleges of the world should be the places of inspiration for radicals and vision-aries. In a rough and inexact way the fellowship of colleges is a working experiment in the practical possibilities of brotherhood. There are few places where the student who flaunts wealth and special privileges is highly regarded.

"Even the overemphasis on sports has in it at least the saving grace that the individual does his best not for him-self but for the team. And so it would seem to me that we might be much better off if alumni remained collegiate and sophomoric and did not swallow whole the standards of a world which is based upon a conception of human nature far more artificial than that which prevails in college.

"I would not have you seniors of Ooffus go out to learn from the world. It would be much better to make the world learn from you. You are going into a community which is illiterate. Some of them can read and write, but the vast majority of your fellow countrymen are wholly illiterate economically and politically. Keep your heads up. Do not be patient in that state of society to which it has pleased the depression to call you. Be skeptical of the authority of the wise men. Your professors, perhaps, were not so smart. The same will go for your bosses. You can't make mutton broth of your sheepskin, but keep it handy, just the same. Don't take the world as it is. This is no impregnable line of giants. Call your signals and shoot a play off tackle."

BACK TO BELLAMY

America's most authentic prophet died more than three decades ago and is not vigorously remembered for the moment in the land in which he lived.

I think there should be a great revival of interest in the work of Edward Bellamy, for notions which he expressed before the beginning of the century are just now coming into articulation and a few, indeed, into action.

The reasons for his decline are obvious enough. Bellamy was a Utopian. Radical thought is growing in this country, but the radicals themselves are impatient with men who seem to them visionary. The reproach is leveled at these idealists that they talk only of "pie in the sky."

Yet I think that the realists have slipped a cog in taking this attitude. It is false to assume that a visionary is a man who thinks only in terms of events beyond the horizon. In the strict sense of the word, anything which lies one-eighth of an inch beyond the end of your nose is visionary. For instance, if I say that it will rain hard at 10 o'clock tomorrow morning I am a visionary. Yet if that rain comes I must be accepted as a lucky guesser or a blame good weather prophet.

Bellamy guessed right about such a variety of things that I think he must be accepted as a prophet. His major error lay in the time element. He foresaw a much faster movement toward coöperation than has occurred. He died in 1898, firm in the belief that the "new deal" was just around the corner and would begin early in the twentieth century.

The "new deal" of which he dreamed was, of course, a far more extensive economic upheaval than anything which has occurred during the Roosevelt administration, and yet there are observations set down in "Equality" in 1897 which have a striking pertinence to the present program. For instance, I opened the book at random yesterday afternoon in order to find some paragraph to prove the essential modernity of this last century Utopian. Naturally I thought I would have to browse around a little to hit on anything available, but under my thumb lay a section which sounds precisely as if it had come from somebody's speech about the National Recovery Act in tomorrow morning's paper. Indeed, I recommend it to Donald Richberg for his next address.

Is there anything out of date in this observation by Bellamy?: "I mean that under competition there was no free play whatever allowed for the capitalist's better feelings, even if he had any. He could not be better than the system. If he tried to be the system would crush him. He had to follow the pace set by his competitors or fail in business. Whatever rascality or cruelty his rivals might devise he must imitate or drop out of the struggle. The very wickedest, meanest and most rascally of the competitors—the one who ground his employees lowest, adulterated his goods most shamefully and lied about them most skillfully—set the pace for all the rest."

We are just beginning to accept this contention now, in 1933, and it has had its first expression in the set of codes which have been submitted or happen to be still in preparation.

But Bellamy would undoubtedly hold that, while all this marks a beginning, it doesn't commence to go far enough. Although a Utopian, Edward Bellamy was not an evolutionary socialist. Certainly not in the sense of either believing or desiring that the ideal state of which he dreamed might be built up slowly, one beam at a time. This frail son of a New England preacher was a revolutionist. Indeed, I think he was the first American revolutionist.

This claim would be disputed in various quarters. Some might hold that 1776 was actually a revolution. Obviously it vitally affected the political state of our nation, but it seems to me that it had almost no economic significance. And so Bellamy is still my candidate.

Even fiercer opposition might come from the sterner radicals. They would be inclined to dismiss Bellamy as a mere reformer because he believed in a "bloodless revolution." The phrase is an unfortunate one and also unfair. When a man says that he believes in a bloodless revolution he does not mean that nobody will get hurt in a vast upheaval. People who get in the way of any flood tide will be swept away. And when I say, "swept," of course I mean shot.

But a good Bellamyite insists that force and violent action are a very minute part of an upheaval. "A great revolution," he wrote, "which is to profoundly change a form of society must accumulate a tremendous moral force, an overwhelming weight of justification, before it can start." And he added, "Revolutions which start too soon stop too soon."

In other words, heads which have been counted exert far greater force than heads which have been broken. A revolution founded upon the resolute will of a determined majority will never have to sit up nights to worry about counterrevolution.

A UNION OF REPORTERS

"You may have heard," writes Reporter Unemployed, "that, although the newspapers are carrying the bulk of NRA publicity, a number of the publishers themselves are planning to cheat NRA reëmployment aims.

"The newspaper publishers are toying with the idea of classifying their editorial staffs as 'professional men.' Since NRA regulations do not cover professionals, newspapermen, therefore, would continue in many instances to work all hours of the day and any number of hours of the week.

"The average newspaperman probably works on an eight-hour-day and six-day-week basis. Obviously the publishers, by patting their fathead employees on the head and calling them 'professionals,' hope to maintain this working week scale. And they'll succeed, for the men who make up the editorial staffs of the country are peculiarly susceptible to such soothing classifications as 'professionals,' 'journalists,' 'members of the fourth estate,' 'gentlemen of the press' and other terms which have completely entranced them by falsely dignifying and glorifying them and their work.

"The men who make up the papers of this country would never look upon themselves as what they really are—hacks and white-collar slaves. Any attempt to unionize leg, rewrite, desk or make-up men would be laughed to death by these editorial hacks themselves. Union? Why, that's all right for dopes like printers, not for smart guys like newspapermen!

"Yes, and those 'dopes,' the printers, because of their union, are getting on an average some 30 percent better than the smart fourth estaters. And not only that, but the printers, because of their union and because they don't permit themselves to be called high-faluting names, will now benefit by the new NRA regulations and have a large number of their unemployed reëmployed, while the 'smart' editorial department boys will continue to work forty-eight hours a week because they love to hear themselves referred to as 'professionals' and because they consider unionization as lowering their dignity."

I think Mr. Unemployed's point is well taken. I am not familiar with just what code newspaper publishers have adopted or may be about to adopt. But it will certainly be extremely damaging to the whole NRA movement if the hoopla and the ballyhoo (both very necessary functions) are to be carried on by agencies which have not lived up to the fullest spirit of the Recovery Act. Any such condition would poison the movement at its very roots.

I am not saying this from the point of view of self-interest. No matter how short they make the working day, it will still be a good deal longer than the time required to complete this stint. And as far as the minimum wage goes, I have been assured by everybody I know that in their opinion all columnists are grossly overpaid. They have almost persuaded me.

After some four or five years of holding down the easiest job in the world I hate to see other newspapermen working too hard. It makes me feel self-conscious. It embarrasses me even more to think of newspapermen who are not working at all. Among this number are some of the best. I am not disposed to talk myself right out of a job, but if my boss does not know that he could get any one of forty or fifty men to pound out paragraphs at least as zippy and stimulating as these, then he is far less sagacious than I have occasionally assumed.

Fortunately columnists do not get fired very frequently. It has something to do with a certain inertia in most executives. They fall readily into the convenient conception that columnists are something like the weather. There they are, and nobody can do anything much about it. Of course, the editor keeps hoping that some day it will be fair and warmer, with brisk northerly gales. It never is, but the editor remains indulgent. And nothing happens to the columnist. At least, not up till now.

It is a little difficult for me, in spite of my radical leanings and training and yearnings, to accept wholeheartedly the conception of the boss and his wage slaves. All my very many bosses have been editors, and not a single Legree in the lot. Concerning every one of them it was possible to say, "Oh, well, after all, he used to be a newspaperman once himself."

But the fact that newspaper editors and owners are genial folk should hardly stand in the way of the organization of a newspaper writers' union. There should be one. Beginning at 9 o'clock on the morning of October 1 I am going to do the best I can to help in getting one up. I think I could die happy on the opening day of the general strike if I had the privilege of watching Walter Lippmann heave half a brick through a *Tribune* window at a non-union operative who had been called in to write the current "Today and To-morrow" column on the gold standard.

THE ARTS OF INACTIVITY

Some people say we are having a revolution, and others deny it with either bitterness or gratitude.

Of course, the difference of opinion lies largely in the definition of the word. To many it isn't a revolution unless a lot of people are being "liquidated" and ownership is passing from the top to the bottom.

In this sense we certainly have had no revolution. But changes of a somewhat startling nature are already with us and may crowd in even more closely. For one thing, we are definitely on our way to a fairly general acceptance of the five-day week. To a certain extent this may defeat the purposes of NRA. In certain industries it is likely that the discovery will be made that there was a great deal of waste motion in the old-fashioned week.

Penalties for tardiness are going to be more severe. The three-hour-for-lunch club has received its death blow. In many factories labor will be vastly speeded up.

But I am not referring to these conditions. I want to comment on the fact that for centuries the proud Nordic has been living in an ascetic's paradise. Possibly all Nordics do not fall under this criticism. The British have had for many years a leisure class even among certain persons engaged in gainful occupations. Perhaps it would be more accurate to confine ourselves to the New England tradition.

Surely it was so among these pioneers, their sons and their sons' sons that work was sacred in its own right. This attitude was confirmed by hundreds of saws and aphorisms. The devil found work for idle hands to do, and the sluggard was advised to go to the ant for advice and example. And now the ant must sit and learn from his former pupil.

When the Pilgrims landed on Plymouth Rock they began to wrestle with the wilderness, the Indians and some of the harshest farm land the world has ever known. Although I have never attempted it myself, I have watched with great interest many people trying to plow the soil of Connecticut. Generations have been working on those bowlders, but as yet they have only scratched the surface. A conscientious man can spend any number of hours per day and still quit with his task incomplete.

A forty-hour week would have reduced the early Puritans to starvation. So, after the manner of all men, they made a virtue of their stark necessity. Even after the economic urge had abated your true New Englander insisted upon imposing punishing hours upon himself and everybody under his control. There came into being the American business tradition. It went to ludicrous lengths. Even in the fairly frequent periods when there was no business the slave of the tradition insisted upon going to his office and sitting around. He had a feeling that any curtailment of hours was in a sense a surrender.

He demanded that nobody should watch the clock. I hold that something startling, even if it isn't revolutionary, has occurred when all of us are asked as a patriotic duty to keep close tally of time and report the names of miscreants who violate the code. The old morality has given way to the new or, at any rate, it is edging over in that direction. We no longer respect the man who forces himself or anybody else to toil through unholy hours. We see him now not as the useful and thrifty citizen but the greedy individual who is warring against planned production.

Not only is the industrial world in a state of flux but it seems likely that the manners and folkways of hundreds of millions of people are about to be changed by the new style week. I see by the papers that a committee has been appointed to advise toilers as to what they shall do with spare time to which they have not been accustomed.

To be sure, unemployment has given millions a certain training in the arts of inactivity. But that is hardly the same thing. These people have been under the necessity of working upon the problem of the next meal and chasing the will-o'-the-wisp of possible jobs. Leisure combined with some spending power and the dull blankness of joblessness are not the same thing at all.

Just what will happen nobody can predict. I doubt that many toilers will report to receive hints as to what to do with an extra day off. I think that the International Organization of Amateur Radish Growers is likely to treble its membership within the next few years. I hope and expect that the crop of Sunday painters will be vastly augmented. All existing standards of golf are certain to be lowered by the influx of new recruits. The artisan golfer who is well known in England will soon be making his appearance here and challenging the supremacy of the idle rich. Glee clubs and amateur theatricals will flourish. The professional stage will come back into its own.

And it may even be that every now and then somebody will buy a book. And from the point of view of the publishers that will be authentically a revolution.

"I WAS NEVER MORE SERIOUS IN MY LIFE"

There used to be a play—there will always be a play—in which the heroine says, "I was never more serious in my life."

And in that phrase, while thousands paid not the slightest attention, I could write my autobiography.

Only yesterday a young man said, "Now, honestly, Mr. Broun, these so-called radical columns of yours merely represent what seems to you shrewd journalism? Am I right?"

And he was not right. It is perhaps a little less than logical to demand that everybody who means what he says should put on a hair shirt and go into the desert to eat locusts and wild honey. But if there is no other way I will do that. My weakness and infirmity of purpose are such that I should prefer not to make my reservations for another two years. But I could be speeded up.

If you grin upon occasion, or take a drink, or stay up after 1 A.M. you become immediately a playboy who is fooling around with notions merely for the thrill which he gets in shocking people.

I do think it's fun to shock people. It seems to me a square deal all around. And yet I have not been conspicuously successful in achieving anything of the sort. And on the few occasions in which I have succeeded the result has come quite unwittingly. My great surprise lies in the fact that people are startled by postulates which appear to me self-evident.

We live in a cockeyed world and I am astonished at such times as fellow passengers fail to grasp that fact. Today I can pick up any paper and find that somebody honestly believes that there will be an end of crime if only justice is "fast" and includes the electric chair and the whipping post. How can they think anything so fantastic? Boiling oil, the rack and thumbscrews have never worked so well, and so I do not understand why anybody should believe that effeminate modifications of ancient tortures can prevail. And I'm not fooling.

I read of Hitler and his scheme to make over a down-trodden nation in its own image and I am not only puzzled but aghast that he should seriously believe that any such scheme can possibly work. The conquering countries imposed terms upon the German people which are preposterous. But is it reasonable, logical, or even sane to say, "Because we have been beaten with whips we will attack with scorpions a minority within our own community to prove that we are virile and unterrified?"

And when I read of those who are exiled, disfranchised, scorned, expelled, I observe that these are the very names upon which the glory and the fame of Germany repose. Just who is crazy and insincere if I venture the mild query as to how culture can be created by uprooting its most significant exponents?

And when I turn from foreign news I observe that there is a movement on foot to prove the superiority of the white race by the commission of things unspeakable and cruel and wholly insane. "I'll show you the proof of our high civilization by lynching you to a tree." Does that make sense? It does not.

And through the world and its byways today the great push seems to come from those who wish to save face by treading with hobnails upon the heads of others. I am a little sick and tired of being classed as soft, bourgeois and sentimental if I say that human brotherhood could solve over night the problems concerning which men shake their heads and say, "It is too bad but insurmountable."

Who says so? It is said by those who have never given even a passing trial to understanding. It is said by those who cannot grasp the notion of a world in which we work for glory and not for profit. It is said by the keepers and the purveyors of mean advantage and destructive selfishness.

And I was never more serious in my life.

NOT BLOWN IN THE BOTTLE

When I was in Boston at the baseball game going through the pretense of being a sports writer I was subjected to withering humiliation.

Although armed with proper credentials, I felt self-conscious as I moved slowly toward the gate marked "Press." The feeling was not wholly psychic. After all, I had to fight my way through some ten or fifteen thousand fans who could not get into the park.

I think that when you find it necessary to put your elbow into the back of an innocent bystander you owe him some explanation. Accordingly, as I knocked down women and children and small adult Boston males I kept shouting at the top of my voice, "Member of the working press!"

I thought that my goal and my salvation were in sight in the presence of a large policeman by the gate. He would, I felt, be sympathetic to my version of "The Charge of the Heavy Brigade." Indeed, at a distance I almost fancied that I caught a gleam of admiration in his eye as I swept a little old lady out of the path with my right hand and simultaneously slugged a chubby toddler with my left. This blow was so swift and neatly placed that it all but drove the little fellow's lollipop through his windpipe.

After each fresh triumph I uttered my jubilant war cry, "Member of the working press!" But as I reached the policeman and bawled my slogan in his ear he shoved me to one side and said, "Just a minute, young fellow; give the newspapermen a chance to get in."

Not Blown in the Bottle

Almost instinctively the cop seemed to know that I was not authentically a reporter but only one of those blame columnists. I didn't belong. And on several occasions since the fact has been borne in upon me that even in the craft itself the members of the "I" cult are regarded as curious amphibians. The columnist has not the legs of a district man, the sharp ears of the rewrite staff or the all-seeing and powerful eye of the trained observer.

Such progress as he seems to make from time to time is done in sudden froglike hops, and, worst of all, he is a frog living at the bottom of a well. He jumps ten feet the first day and falls back eighteen. How long will it take him to get out of the well? Anybody but the columnist himself could give you the answer. He isn't going to get out of the well.

And yet as I look about this cylindrical chamber to which I am consigned from this time forth I see many things I like. And I would like it even better if the landlord could be induced to redecorate.

I am not alone in the well. The place is filled with newspapermen. A few agile ones crawl out occasionally by fashioning a rope of short stories, or they may use a novel as a ladder, or tunnel underground and become "counsel of public relations."

But the great majority of us are permanent boarders. As such I think we ought to grow more companionable and learn one another's front names and favorite hobbies. As far as I can ascertain, America is the only land of journalistic lone wolves. In other countries there are guilds, institutes, associations and what-not. There is a sense of cohesion and pride in the craft.

It might be a good idea to change newspaper work into

a profession. Then, like lawyers and physicians, we could have academies and learned societies through which distinguished service might be rewarded with laurel sprigs. And we could also be pretty stuffy with recalcitrants who do those things which no newspaperman ever should do.

But even if we are not professionals, at least we might have as much pride of craft as plumbers and masons. I do think that in a hit-or-miss manner we (I must insist on being inclusive) have arrived at a surprisingly high standard of working conduct.

While I would hardly care to point with pride at any annual crop of my own columns, I don't do anything which actually seems to me shameful more than six or seven times a year. And that, I think, is not much worse than lawyer's par.

And yet it isn't good enough. Certainly the general public doesn't trust the newspaperman. Ask any householder whether the greatest affliction is to have a doctor, a lawyer, a plumber or a reporter in the house, and I am pretty sure the newspaperman would win the pest prize hands down. Of course, some of this feeling may be blamed on the plays, the motion pictures and the short stories which profess to deal with newspaper life. There are exceptions, but when a play includes "Jim Swift—Reporter of the *Times-Telegram*" you can be pretty sure that presently there will appear a character compounded out of Iago and the protagonist in "Ten Nights in a Barroom."

I remember that within a few seasons a dramatist was hailed as a great realist because the reporter in the play was shown with a copy of *The American Mercury* in one pocket and a quart of whisky in the other. Life might be simpler and sweeter if this were true. I have never met a reporter who had a quart of whisky with him. And I could count the half-pint flasks on the fingers of one hand.

We are, if the truth must be known, a pretty fine lot of fellows. It is too bad the general public doesn't know it. It might be an even better idea if we realized it ourselves.

"ANY ONE AT ALL"

At the moment this column is written the marines have not landed. The latest news is that everything in Cuba will be readjusted in a satisfactory manner without the necessity for intervention.

But if we smile in a bland way over this arrangement it will be a smug smile and a shabby one. It is flagrant nonsense to talk of allowing Cuba to settle its problems in its own way just so long as its harbors are crowded with our destroyers and battleships.

When you thrust a gun into the side of a nation or an individual it is not essential to add, "Stick 'em up!" The man or republic at the wrong end of the weapon can get the idea even if no word is spoken.

Or, to change the figure, Uncle Sam is playing the part of a prestidigitator who says to his victim: "Pick a card. Any one at all. I wouldn't fool you for the world." But the pack is held in such a way that the volunteer from the audience who is seduced into believing himself a free will agent can't very well select anything but the seven of hearts.

If the Cubans select anybody but De Cespedes they are likely to find that the choice just doesn't count.

There is an argument to be made in favor of our playing the rôle of roundsman in Central and South America and among the Caribbean Islands. It is not an argument which appeals to me. I think any such policy is wrong from both an ethical and a practical point of view. And yet I think it is preferable to be frankly imperialistic rather than to sneak up on the smaller nations.

I think that our high-handedness in conduct in regard to our Southern neighbors has created rather less antagonism than our hypocrisy. As far as our diplomacy goes I can find in it no hint of a new deal. And the various letter and editorial writers who have protested against my low opinion of Secretary Cordell Hull, of the State Department, are invited to contribute all over again and point out in just what way the old gentleman has departed from the standard practices of well-established American dollar diplomacy.

And if I am told that Mr. Hull has no voice in the matter and never knew what was going on I will be inclined to answer that this was precisely what I said in the first place.

Without pressure on our part there would quite likely have been a good deal of bloodshed in Cuba. It is also likely that the revolution would have taken on an even more decided left wing tendency. But the problems of the island and the matter of our relationship are not likely to be solved by any arrangement which brings about a mere palace insurrection. Bad as Machado was in his own personality, the issue never was wholly one of the character of the executive. The economic agony of Cuba is similar to that of many countries in the world but probably a little more intense. The island has lived by and for a sugar crop, and under the depression the destruction of all previous values for that commodity has sown poverty throughout the country.

We have been gravely telling one another in the United States for at least three years that it is nonsense for anybody to starve in the midst of plenty. It may even be that eventually we will do something about it.

But in Cuba the case for coöperative industrial and political life is even more plain. It is, of all the lands I've ever seen, the one which most closely approaches Eden. Ease and abundance ought to be simple in such a spot. Moreover, the people are in many respects far more highly civilized than the inhabitants of North America. Although many racial and national groups are represented, Cuba has never wasted its energies in fierce prejudice.

How things went on under the rulership of Spain I do not know. There seems to be little doubt that cruelties were practiced by the Spaniards in the years immediately preceding the war of 1898. But in the long run the guardianship of the United States has not been an unmixed blessing. We put in plumbing for the cities and we conquered yellow fever. But in return we introduced large-scale capitalism and absentee landlordism. If the homeless Cuban has no place to lay his head it is largely because some one of our great corporations has bought up all the land.

The present situation is important as a symbol and a test. On March 4 it was said that the money-changers were to be driven out of the temple. I wonder whether anybody has remembered to tell that to the marines.

TEX AND THE COOLIDGE GOLD RUSH

Texas Guinan died in Vancouver forty-eight hours before Litvinoff arrived in Washington.

I do not want to strain in reaching for symbols, but these chance happenings carry to me some suggestion of the passing of an era and the beginning of another. Surely Texas typified the boom times of the Coolidge gold rush.

In the days of her glory she made New York a sort of mining town. The little New Englander in Washington issued comforting statements that loans were not overextended, and Guinan cried from the top of her high stool to the arriving customer, "Hello, sucker!"

In slightly different form both were saying the same thing. This was the land of easy riches for the lucky. The vein was deep and wide and handsome. Whoopee would never end.

As in the case of the President, there was a touch of cynicism in Miss Guinan. I think that both had some inner inkling that the party would not last forever. But neither one wanted to be a killjoy and spoil a perfectly good jamboree. Both remained a little aloof from the high jinks in which they served as promoters. Even after the accession of Hoover, Mr. Coolidge played the stock market very mildly and Texas never took a drink in her life.

I knew Texas very well and liked her enormously, but I must confess that I cannot remember any comment which she ever made upon the existing social order. When I ran for Congress on the Socialist ticket Miss Guinan came out as one of my supporters and made a speech at one of the rallies. I doubt that it touched the fundamental issues.

My comrades were more than a little shocked at Guinan's name being coupled with the campaign. It seemed to me fitting then, and it still does. If ever there was an authority on the idle rich and the wasting of the wasters Texas Guinan was certainly that woman.

Her night clubs did an actual social service in reducing to an absurdity the theory that only the men of means are fit to manage the intricate industrial machinery of this country. I have seen captains of industry and kings of finance playing leapfrog across the dance floor of Guinan's club.

I do not wish to suggest that Miss Guinan was boring from within when she managed to illustrate so vividly the fundamental triviality of certain rugged individualists. It would be a great deal less than accurate to suggest that I sat at a ringside table concealing a Jeremiah-like fury under my fine raiment. I went to all of Miss Guinan's various establishments many times and remained late. I went because I had a good time.

Sometimes a little after dawn there would be a small poker game after the big spenders had gone home and the place was closed. In this way I managed to cut down the overhead a little. Contrary to popular superstition, Miss Guinan played poker very badly. Probably after saying, "Hello, sucker!" through a long evening she found it restful to draw to three flushes and inside straights.

I doubt very much that Texas died rich, because anybody engaged in a profitable racket seems bound and determined to find some other in which the money may be put back into circulation. Texas lost prodigious sums in the stock market, although for a short time she had a fortune.

She was an extremely honest and candid person. The prices for mineral water and ginger ale were fantastic and the kitchen was generally a gag, but she was always the first to admit as much. Texas never sneaked up on any of the spenders who came into her place.

I remember once, at the behest of a young lady who was with me, I somewhat reluctantly ordered a bottle of champagne. Texas came over to the table and said: "Don't be silly, Hayward. You know we're charging thirty dollars a quart for champagne and you know it isn't champagne. Tell your young lady to take gin and like it."

Although never very successful as a stage performer, Texas was an expert as a night club monologist. Naturally, she was not quite as skilled in impromptu as the casual visitor might assume. If somebody went to sleep and fell off his chair Texas was ready with a remark. But she did not have to make one up. The situation had occurred before.

Yet when pressed by anything brand new she was equal to the occasion. Texas has been called brazen, but it was more than that. She had superb courage. Once I saw her walk straight between two very dangerous guests who were just about to shoot it out.

Litvinoff is in Washington. The new world of equal opportunity and the redistribution of wealth draws closer. I am for it heart and soul. The jazz age was wicked and monstrous and silly. Unfortunately, I had a good time.

THE FUNERAL OF TEXAS GUINAN

I went yesterday to the funeral of Texas Guinan and came away thinking about survival after death. If there is no continuation of individuality the cosmic scheme of things is built upon a blunder and I shall oppose it and all its works.

Possibly it is a mistake to generalize upon a particular emotion, but unless the dead have the same senses as the quick a very large and ornate ceremony was held for no important purpose.

I heard two pallbearers in conversation as they waited while a lane could be cut in the crowd to make way for the coffin. One said, "I know now that I would like to be buried on some quiet Connecticut hillside and not be brought to Broadway to be a disturber of traffic."

"Yes," said the other, "but this was what Tex wanted. She would have loved it."

There came up then a member of the mob, and tears were streaming down his cheeks. He wanted consolation. "Don't you think," he asked, "that this is as big as Valentino's?"

The police cried out, "Get back there, you!" A photographer shouted, "Tell the pallbearer with the eye glasses to look over toward the camera!" The newsreel men cranked furiously, and not a wheel turned for five blocks up and down Broadway so great was the crush of people. Every window in the hotel across the street was occupied by those who wanted to be told that this one was Paul Whiteman, Mark Hellinger or Earl Carroll.

It was Mark who printed the story about the deathbed

conversation of Texas. The doctor said she had only a few hours to live, and so she called her manager and discussed in detail the plans for the funeral. "I want," she said, "to lie in state at Campbell's. I want for once to give the people a chance to see me without a cover charge."

All afternoon I had a strong feeling that this was not so much a funeral for Texas Guinan as a funeral by Texas Guinan. All her own qualities of showmanship were evident. In life she always selected a room which was a shade too small because she felt that it was good business to crowd them in or even turn a few customers away. It was her contention that anybody who is turned away always comes back. The funeral certainly packed them in, even though 2 o'clock of a Sunday afternoon is still a little early for that part of the Broadway crowd which waits for the sun to come up to signalize the end of Saturday night.

Texas was dead. That much was certain. We heard the words of a priest, a ritual was read and outside "Taps" was sounded by a naval bugler.

All of us were wary. No one gave a hand to the priest or to the chaplain. Texas was dead. And yet I swear I seemed to hear the sound of wooden hammers striking tables, laughter and the click of cleated shoes against a hardwood floor.

There was something grotesque about the funeral. It wasn't just the slightly florid character of the ceremony. It wasn't that any wandering eye met some eloquent mask which plainly said: "I wouldn't have done this for anybody but you, Tex. And what wouldn't I give for a drink!" In fact, it seemed just a little silly to talk about Texas being dead. She remained a far more vital living force than numerous ones among haggard hundreds in the chapel.

The Funeral of Texas Guinan

I didn't go to the cemetery. That seemed far less appropriate than anything else in the ceremony. They had to drive all the way to White Plains. I think it was Texas who said, "Once you leave New York any town you strike is Bridgeport."

I honestly believe that Texas saw the funeral and took a very great pride and joy in the performance. It was almost as big as Valentino's.

The universe is intricate, and very nice adjustments are necessary to keep the planets from running into one another. In would be a fearful error in taste if by any stipulation Texas were barred from the knowledge that the police had to fight back the thousands. "The columnists made me. I want them to follow me at the end," Texas said before she died. They were there. And certainly it would be a pity if Texas did not hear a prayer in which the hope was expressed that she should be "a companion of the holy angels."

Not everything is for the best in this universe, but at least it does make sense. Somebody like Spinoza, let's say, may not even have leaned down from the gold bar of heaven to watch the camera men and the radio announcers. But I'm sure Texas saw it all and gloried in it. And if my notions about the hereafter are wrong in this respect, all I can say is that there must be something mightily amiss with the management.

A ROOM WITH A VIEW

Good-by, Al; take care of yourself.

"I am too old now," writes Alfred Emanuel Smith, "to be regular just for the sake of regularity."

And to indicate the violence of his repugnance against things conventional, respectable and upholstered, Mr. Smith has written an open letter to the Chamber of Commerce of the State of New York denouncing experimentation.

Moreover, in order to pound home the full extent of his rebellious progressivism, Al Smith has come out lock and stock and barrel for Grover Cleveland.

I still want to feel that Al is more liberal than some of the other leaders and publicists. I try to console myself with the thought that, after all, Walter Lippmann has come out for both Hamilton and Jefferson, and that Carter Glass is probably grooming George Washington. Yet it isn't age but solitude which puts Al out of action. He has been living too long in that ivory tower. It's a long way from Oliver Street up to that mooring mast imbedded in the clouds.

From his office window Al can nod to any passing plane, but the noises of the street, the words of the people and even their cries come faintly to his casement.

For instance, we had but recently a city election of no little importance, and since Al Smith ventured no opinion I suppose it is charitable to assume that the matter was not called to his attention. If Mr. Smith had been informed that La Guardia, O'Brien and McKee were running, I haven't a doubt that he would have boldly declared himself for Peter Stuyvesant.

As one who no longer cares to be regular just for the sake of regularity, Alfred E. Smith would have delivered hammer blows to free the city from the grip of Tammany had he but known what was afoot.

In my heart there has been a deep devotion to Al Smith. The Happy Warrior was worthy of his title. I am not saying, even now, that he has let down people who believed in him. He has let down Alfred E. Smith. The governor used to say, "Look at the record." It was his battle cry in every argument. In those days Al could make a fact or a figure ring like a bugle note.

And there is no evidence whatsoever that Al looked at the record before he prepared his open letter to the Chamber of Commerce of the State of New York. He wrote that piece while he looked out his tower window and gazed at the setting sun.

"If I must choose between the leaders of the past," writes Al, "with all the errors they have made and all the selfishness they have been guilty of and the inexperienced young college professors who hold no responsible public office but are willing to turn 130,000,000 Americans into guinea pigs for experimentation, I am going to be for the people who made the country what it is."

Now, the first person to say "baloney" to that would have been ex-Governor Alfred E. Smith. It might be well to remind the ex-governor of an appointment which he made to the State Labor Board. When he appointed Frances Perkins people said exactly the same thing which Al is saying now about "inexperienced young college professors." She was "a woman," "a radical," "a wife who kept her own name," "a visionary" and "a theorist."

Al and Miss Perkins worked together on some very experimental labor legislation. Chambers of Commerce hollered their heads off. The legislation was passed. It worked. By now it is accepted.

In a famous verbal duel with Cordell Hull at the last Democratic convention, Mr. Hull reminded Mr. Smith that the prohibition plank presented by the dry wing of the party was almost the same plan which Mr. Smith had espoused in 1928.

"Sure," said Al as nearly as I can remember, "but it took Cordell Hull four years to catch up with me."

Is this the same Al Smith who now wants to go back to Grover Cleveland? Indeed, Al seems minded to go even further back. "What the people need today is what the Bible centuries ago described as 'the shadow of a great rock in a weary land.' "

This is, indeed, a weary land, but the men and women grow weary of living in that deep shadow which is cast by the existing order.

Al should have his desk moved to a window with an eastern exposure. He has looked too long at skies in which the flaming red dulled down to green and purple and to darkness. And as the light faded he has thought of famous fights in which he dared the spears of giants. And does he think that with him died the impulse to take a crack at the forces of greed and error which he now nominates as preferable to the experimenters?

Look to the East, Al, and remember that the sun also rises.

"A FINE LESSON FOR THE WHOLE NATION"

Comment on the San Jose lynching constitutes an obligatory column.

In the beginning it seemed to me as if this thing were so monstrously and obviously evil that it would be enough to say calmly and simply, "Here is one more sadistic orgy carried on by a psycopathic mob under the patronage of the moronic governor of a backward state."

To my amazement I found not only condonation but actual praise for the lynchers in no less than three New York newspapers. I read of "the vigilantes" and "the pioneer spirit" and so on.

Let us examine the evidence to see if there is any reason at all to ascribe the deed to the full-flowered resentment of an aroused public spirit.

Here is the story of the lynching as told by an 18-year-old ranch boy who asserted that he was leader of the movement:

"I was the first one of the gang to break into the jail. I came to town in the afternoon and saw the crowd around the jail. I decided to organize a 'necktie' party. Mostly I went to the speakeasies and rounded up the gang there. That is why so many of the mob were drunk. The word got spread around that it was going to be a Santa Clara University student lynching. But I'm not a Santa Clara student. I didn't go to college. I knew Brooke Hart by sight, but never had spoken to him. I thought that his terrible murder should be avenged. I found that several hundred others thought the same thing."

In other words, a farm boy who came into town for a spree managed to hit upon a drunken crowd which was willing to defend the American home and its institutions for the fun of it.

Governor Rolph has called it "a fine lesson to the whole nation." And a New York newspaper says in its leading editorial, "Nobody that we've heard of or talked to appears to disagree with the mob or disapprove of what Governor Rolph said."

All right; talk to me. Or better still read these selections from a United Press dispatch:

"Thurmond was unconscious, and probably dead, when the noose was placed around his neck. He had been beaten and kicked senseless. A boy, not more than 16, climbed to the top of a shed and shouted in a shrill voice, 'Come on, fellows!' He was the leader the mob had been waiting for. A new cry went up, 'Let's burn 'em!' Thurmond's body was cut down. It was drenched with gasoline. A match was touched to it, but only his torn clothing burned."

Governor James Rolph Jr. has been quoted as saying that he would like to turn over all jail inmates serving sentences for kidnaping into the custody of "those fine, patriotic San Jose citizens, who know how to handle such a situation."

"Thousands of men, women and children looking on in carnival spirit cheered with a lustiness which could be heard for blocks."

"Both were dragged across the park, their bruised and torn bodies leaving trails of blood."

And so the fine old pioneer spirit of California, under the leadership of that fine old nature lover, Jim Rolph, has ended kidnaping in the great commonwealth of California. And what has it left in its wake? It has left an obscene, depraved and vile memory in the minds of thousands who stood about and cheered lustily.

"Some of the children were babies in their mothers' arms."

If it were possible to carry on a case history of every person in the mob who beat and kicked and hanged and burned two human beings I will make the prophecy that out of this heritage will come crimes and cruelties which are unnumbered. The price is too high.

Every mother and father of a son wants to have him protected against the danger of kidnaping. But how would you like it if it were your 16-year-old boy who climbed to the top of a shed and shouted in a shrill voice, "Come on, fellows!"?

Governor James Rolph Jr. has said with audacious arrogance, "If anyone is arrested for the good job I'll pardon them all."

It does not lie within the power of the governor of California to pardon the men and boys and women and children who cried out, "Let's burn 'em!" For them there is no pardon this side of the Judgment Seat. To your knees, Governor, and pray that you and your commonwealth may be washed clean of this bath of bestiality into which a whole community has plunged.

You, James Rolph Jr., stand naked in the eyes of the world. "I'll pardon them all," you say. Is this to be the measure of justice in California? Men with blood and burnt flesh on their hands are to be set free. Mooney must remain in jail. Freedom for the guilty. Punishment for the innocent.

Governor, very frankly, I don't believe you can get away with it. There must be somewhere some power which just won't stand for it.

TEMPERATURE 110

"The day will come," writes Bruce Barton in his weekly inspirational editorial, "when, compared to the word 'professor,' the word 'banker' will be a term of endearment."

Mr. Barton is agitated because "a member of the Brain Trust," who is not identified in the inspirational editorial, recently made a speech in which he suggested that the profit motive need not be the backbone of a happy society. Bruce Barton is definitely shocked by the suggestion. And the speech reminded him of an experience of his own. He was coming in from the country on a chilly morning, with a cold in his head and a temperature of 101 degrees. In the morning paper he read that Secretary McAdoo had taken over the Western Union and Postal Telegraph companies. This didn't do Mr. Barton's temperature any good. He began to see spots dancing on the wall, and disturbing visions filled his head.

"The following thought popped into my mind: Suppose, instead of taking over the telegraph companies, the government had taken over the advertising business (in which I was employed), would I be coming into town this morning? Answer: I would not. I would send a note to the office that I was ill, and I would apply for a thirty-day furlough. . . ."

I challenge Mr. Barton's answer, and I challenge it on the basis of his own testimony. He seems to have a horror of any sort of system in which a sick man may be excused from toil, and the thought of a furlough for the ailing appears to him fantastic. In other words, Bruce Barton loves work for work's own sake. Carl Sandburg once wrote a poem about a man who was "terribly glad to be selling fish." I think Bruce Barton gets a lot of fun out of peddling advertising.

This is not cited as a complaint. I think that people who have the capacity to get all steamed up about a job are potentially of great usefulness. Some of this energy is wholly wasted at the present time because the job may be one which has little or no communal utility.

"I came into town that morning," writes Mr. Barton, "because I was engaged in starting a new business in a highly competitive field. I was too sick to work, but I worked, anyway. And by that kind of work we made our business a success. It's the kind of work men do gladly when they are on fire with a vision of happiness and security for their families. It is the kind of work men who are merely cogs in a bureaucratic machine do not and never will do."

A bureaucratic machine has been set up in Russia, and under its sway a good many things take place which are not to the liking of a few Russians and a very great number of Americans. But not even the most severe critic of the Soviets has ever successfully put over the charge that the Russians are loafing. They are probably working harder than any other people in the world today. Even the energetic Bruce Barton would probably be called "Old Lazybones" in Leningrad. You see, the Russians, like Bruce Barton, are animated by "a vision of happiness and security for their families." Only they don't happen to see it in terms of the profit motive.

But the truth is that, with a vision or without it, man is the doggonedest worker of all the animals. The beaver builds dams and houses, but then he quits and sleeps or plays contract. The beaver doesn't bother to paint the dam or cover it with ivy.

I was in a show once which closed at the end of a ten-day run, part of which was in Newark, N. J. On the last night the audience consisted of two men and a boy who had been passed in by the press agent. Along about the middle of the second act a dancer sprained her ankle severely. She had two more numbers to do, and she insisted on hopping on in great agony in order to finish her stint.

To the best of my knowledge this painful tribute to the cause of art didn't even have the inspiration of a vision of happiness for her loved ones.

I, who am well below par in energy, contracted a bad case of flu last winter because I insisted on going out into a raging blizzard to do a five-minute broadcast. My family had nothing to do with it. They screamed and yelled at me. I just didn't want to have to sit home and hear somebody else doing my stuff.

A revolution might very well snuff out both Bruce and me in the first week, which would be a grave error on the part of the revolutionists.

At least, I'm sure it would be a mistake to shoot Mr. Barton. Advertising would be quite different in this world without profit. Instead of taking over teas and tooth powders Mr. Barton might be appointed by the government to popularize collective farms or to make people machinery conscious. Mr. Barton would be in heaven if he suddenly found himself the boss advertising man in charge of all the Lords, Thompsons and Thomases. Why, in a world like that Bruce would be blithely skipping down to work with a temperature of 110.

PAPER WORK

William James said that mankind must find a moral equivalent for war. Blow, bugles, blow, and let us put a ribbon with palms upon the breast of Travis Harvard Whitney. No soldier could have been more gallant than the man who crumpled at his desk in the Civil Works Administration. Before he would submit to being taken to the hospital where he died Whitney insisted on giving directions to his assistants as to how the work should go on. He was torn with agony but it was his commitment to put two hundred thousand men and women back to work. This was just something which had to be done.

I saw him once, and in the light of his death I am not likely to forget. He called up to say that if the Newspaper Guild would furnish him a list of unemployed reporters he thought he could place some under the CWA.

"When do you want to see us?" I asked.

"Come down now," he answered.

We expected to find an office and an office boy and probably a couple of secretaries, but Whitney had a desk thrust right in the middle of a large and bustling room. He sat there and rode the tumult like a city editor. There were no preliminaries of any kind. The tall, gaunt man with deep-sunken eyes began by asking: "Now when do I get that list?"

I've heard so much about red tape and bureaucracy that I didn't suppose he meant immediately. "It will take a little time," I told him. "We haven't got a very big clerical force or much office space, and of course John Eddy will have to check up on the names for you. Let me see—this is Thursday—suppose we get you that list a week from Saturday and then on Monday we can really begin to get to work on it."

He indicated impatience. "That won't do at all," he said. "You don't understand. This is a rush job. Every day counts. Can't you let me have part of the list the day after tomorrow? This ought to be done right away. Can't you call me on the phone tonight?"

"Where can I get you after dinner?" I asked.

"Right here."

"How late?"

"I can't tell. I'll be here until I finish."

Travis Whitney made good that promise. He worked all day and he worked all night. He knew he was critically ill when he took the appointment. Doctors had told him of the necessity of rest and probably of an operation. "I think I can last," was his rejoinder.

And he set himself to win that race. Two hundred thousand jobs before the end came. I think it was Lord Nelson who had an ensign lash him to a mast at the battle of Trafalgar. Whitney's courage was better than that. He chained himself to his desk by a sheer act of will.

The people around could see him grow dead gray in the late hours. Almost you could hear the step of his adversary advancing. But all he said was, "We must hurry." He felt not only the pangs of his own physical torture but the bite of the wind upon the bodies of men who walked the streets without shelter.

I don't know what the economic philosophy of Travis Whitney may have been. He didn't have time to talk about it. "Some day" just couldn't fit into his scheme of things.

His thought was of two hundred thousand jobs which must be made and handed out without delay. He had the harassed look of a flapjack cook in a lumber camp. "Right away" rang in his ears like a trumpet call. Maybe somebody came and said to him, "But don't you realize that you're not solving anything? This is just a temporary expedient. When the revolution comes—"

And I imagine Travis Whitney turned a deaf ear and only said, "Two hundred thousand jobs and this has got to be now."

He couldn't make the life force last until he had surged across the line. They put him on his shield and carried him away, and I hope that on his tomb will be written "Killed in action."

Unquestionably this shambling, thin man peering a little dubiously through glasses had a concern. It was a passion. I suppose it is a little difficult to make paper work seem as exciting or romantic as cavalry charges. But you see he had found his moral equivalent for war. And I rather think that when next I hear the word "heroism" my immediate mental association will not be that of any brass hat on a hill but of Travis Whitney bent over his desk. And maybe I will see him as a man against the sky. And I will hear him as he says, "More gently, death, come slower. Don't touch me till my job is done."

THE TRIBUNE'S GOBLIN EDITOR

Mark Sullivan suffers from insomnia. And when he drops off into fitful slumber by counting administration measures jumping over the Constitution he is tormented by bad dreams. The very milk wagons on Pennsylvania Avenue become tumbrils calling at the homes of those who refuse to accept the New Deal.

In the old days things were very different. Mark slept, Mellon slept and the President slept very well indeed. In the morning everybody but Mr. Mellon met on the White House lawn for exercise and when Mr. Sullivan threw the medicine ball at the President he was not called upon to aim at a moving target.

Herbert Hoover, there he stood the same on Monday as on Wednesday. He was no football quarterback like Franklin D. Roosevelt. No indeed, he was one of the goal posts merely waiting stolidly for somebody to tear him down.

I gather from the jeremiads of Mark Sullivan that most of the dirty work is done at night. It is then that Guy Tugwell sneaks out armed with chalk and writes "Capitalism Must Be Destroyed" upon the sidewalks of the town. Mr. Sullivan is convinced that the revolution is not only here but almost consummated. And as I understand it he has two major complaints. He maintains that the upheaval is being carried on secretly and that it is practically painless. When he shakes his head at night and finds that it doesn't roll on the floor you can bet that he is pretty sore about it.

"Is it unreasonable to ask," inquires Mr. Sullivan, "that

we have an opportunity to debate the new system and that the outcome of this debate determine whether we adopt the new?"

And that reminds me that I should in all kindness suggest a remedy to Mark Sullivan for his insomnia. I think he ought to read himself to sleep. I fear that his wild words suggest an unfamiliarity with what is going on in the newspapers of America. No debate indeed! The careless Mr. Sullivan must have shaped endless columns of pros and cons within the last three or four months. It seems to me that every editorial page is filled with violent denunciation of Rexford Guy Tugwell signed "Intrepid Home Owner," "Original Settler" or "Indignant Member of the Sixth Grade."

To be specific, might I ask the Republican Revere whether or not he has familiarized himself with the writings of Mark Sullivan upon this very theme? I think that with a glass of warm milk and two Sullivan columns the sufferer will soon find his lids nodding as in the days when Pippa passed, and Hoover said, "I've got nothing either."

In all fairness to *The Herald Tribune's* goblin editor I must admit that he has freshened his narrative from time to time. Only this week he introduced a new villain into the plot. It now seems that Professor Tugwell is not playing a lone hand in his effort to Sovietize America while Sullivan sleeps. Some of the blame falls on the head of Felix Frankfurter, who has recommended several young men who have received appointments under the administration. "Nearly all of them are graduates of Harvard Law School," adds Mark Sullivan ominously. It must be, I gather, that Roosevelt is a Red since he has allied himself with so many wearers of the Crimson.

"The country, I am sure," adds Mr. Sullivan, "would be

instructed, and also, I suspect, amused by a joint debate staged with Professors Tugwell and Frankfurter on one side, and on the other, let me say, Senator Carter Glass, of Virginia, whose word for the New Deal is 'insanity,' and ex-Governor Alfred E. Smith, whose word for it is 'baloney.' "

Well, I won't promise to be amused unless they come a little funnier than that. I didn't even rock with merriment at Mark Sullivan's own contribution to the debate, which was to call Felix Frankfurter "the happy hot dog." The funeral baked meats of Herbert Hoover's administration did so coldly furnish forth the national weal that I'm afraid the gag may fall quite flat.

And yet I'm all for the debate. The American Newspaper Guild will be glad to arrange a proper scene for the discussion. Professor Frankfurter must be carrying on his machinations rather slyly, since he has been an exchange professor at Oxford for several months, but I don't see why Tugwell and Smith alone should not be sufficient to fill any hall. But before the New Deal is riddled as something lacking proper and sufficient clarity I would like to have some definition of "the familiar American philosophy" to which Mark Sullivan is so constantly referring. Who qualifies? Is it true that Mark Hanna and Theodore Roosevelt fit neatly into the same classification, or Woodrow Wilson and Harry Daugherty? And what are we going to do about classifying Andy Mellon, who has always seemed to me the worst Secretary of the Treasury since Alexander Hamilton?

EMMA'S HOMECOMING

Emma Goldman is coming home. The State Department has agreed to admit the old anarchist for a three-month visit on the condition that she "shall not engage in any political activity."

This provision seems a little unnecessary, for Emma is 64 and the cause which she espoused is at the moment dead beyond the hope of resurrection. Miss Goldman seems to me a very gallant figure but also a futile one. She was cursed by a temperament with a fatal defect. She just couldn't compromise.

Curiously enough, mankind is fond of using the adjective "uncompromising" as a word denoting great strength and vigor and carrying the connotation of assured success. It just doesn't work out in that way. Hell is paved with great granite blocks hewn from the hearts of those who said, "I can do no other."

Darwin was right. The life force itself will not permit such inflexibility. Growth comes through selection, adaption and the happy miracle of accident. Anarchists have gone the way of antediluvian mammals. They lacked mobility and have become extinct.

Of course, if I had anything to do with the running of the life force I'd change all that. In principle and emotion I'm all for Emma and against Charles Robert Darwin. The only trouble is that he happens to hold all four aces. No political and economic ideal has ever been as pure as that which Emma Goldman advocated. Every man in his inmost heart wants not liberty but license. We may respect laws, tradition or custom, but we do not love them. However lightly worn, any restraint constitutes a chain which may snap us up short at the moment we least desire or expect it.

The human animal, at any rate, is by his very nature anarchical. The life force gave us an instinct and then proceeded to hedge it around with the high containing wall of circumstance. Emma Goldman was always a plump hausfrau type of person, but she was for going up to every wall and over. But the best which could be written on her tombstone would be, "It was a good try." She got nowhere, nor did she advance the fortunes of mankind as far as I can see.

Although of foreign birth, Miss Goldman's happiest days were in capitalistic America. Here everything was wrong, and the light of battle shone in her eyes continuously. Great wealth and abject poverty presented a situation in which Miss Goldman could make many converts in her cry against the regimentation of the human spirit and the human body.

Then up rose Russia and destroyed private capitalism. Emma Goldman applauded this vast earthquake, but she made the mistake of visiting the land of the Soviets. She should have known better. Russian radical leaders did make rather considerable compromises here and there, but in the main they were faithful to their program. The only trouble was that their fundamental objectives were not those of Emma.

When Emma Goldman spoke of revolution she meant the changing of human organization utterly. She meant the complete swing around the circle. Of course, she found regimentation in Russia. She found a highly centralized government which exerted great pressure upon the individual.

His home, his job and even his life were at the disposal of the ruling class.

"But don't you see," I suppose they told her, "that this is a different class which is doing the regimenting and exerting the pressure? The workers are in command. This is the dictatorship of the proletariat. We are in a transitional stage. Before we can abate restrictions and be done with courts and jails and any sort of compulsion we must first root out the old order and the old psychology. Restriction can cease only when the whole world has become proletarian. Then these things to which you object will slough off."

But, as I have said, Emma was an anarchist, not an evolutionist. While there was a soul in jail she was not free. An army was an army, though it was now red instead of cossack gray. She was never one for sloughing. She wanted to go after the economic order of the world, much as Carrie Nation attacked a saloon. You took an ax and chopped the world into the proper shape. That was your revolution. You didn't wait for things to drop of their own weight. You knocked them down.

And so Emma Goldman and the Communists didn't hit it off. She is an old woman without a country, a party or a following. Capitalism is wrong, and so is communism. The same goes for the Roosevelt readjustment and for the fascism of Hitler or Mussolini. There is no régime to which Emma Goldman can give approval. But she has her dream and her integrity.

Radicalism in this country used to be far more violent than it is today. And, in addition to being far more fierce, I think it had, perhaps, a greater measure of dignity. If Emma Goldman happened to pick up *The Daily Worker* of yesterday and chanced to see a dandy little essay on the second page entitled "In Defense of Ping-Pong," it may have helped to console her a little for the fact that she didn't compromise.

NOT A SURE SHOT

My dictionary says: "in-ev-i-ta-bl(e)—adj.—That which cannot be shunned, avoided, or prevented; bound to happen or be met with in the very nature of things; unavoidable; as, the inevitable conflict."

I wish that some of my radical, my liberal and my conservative friends would familiarize themselves with this definition. Very often I am asked by one group or another to join in meetings which are called to protest against "the inevitable world war which is upon us."

If hostilities are unavoidable I'm not interested. I cannot become enthusiastic about prospectuses which are issued upon the notion that after one more round this tragic folly shall not occur again. It is my belief that after another general conflict the only convention to be called will include the vultures, the buzzards and the scarlet poppies. I cannot see eye to eye with those who feel that after another fling the world can be made over. There won't be enough left.

Although both sentimental and romantic, I am not sufficiently naïve to deny that another war is possible. I will go further. It seems to me that another war is distinctly probable. The whole lineup of the nations is propitious for conflict. The stage is set even more completely for hostilities than it was in 1914.

But this second world war is not inevitable. It is within the power of mankind to prevent it. Wars are made by man. They do not fall under the defeatist phrase which classifies other catastrophes as "acts of God."

I won't fight. Now if that is true of you and you and you, there will be no war. Of course, I have read that the attitude of non-resistant pacifism is old-fashioned. I have even heard it pointed out that it plays into the hands of the war makers.

Some very stalwart pacifists have abandoned their position within the last few years. Professor Einstein weakened a little while ago and confessed a willingness to arm against the Nazis. Here in America that old war horse Roger Baldwin did a complete right about face and announced that he would not refuse to wear the uniform in the event of another conflict. He admitted that he had been converted to the Communist position, which holds that a non-resistant is a little more harmful than a man with a bayonet in the first wave.

Although I have read much about the new-fangled notion, it may be that I misunderstood it because it seems to me so very silly. The people who call conscientious objectors romantic fools assert that those who are against war should sign up and then bore from within. If you go to Leavenworth or Atlanta you lose contact with the masses and become quite useless in the movement.

At least that is the way the argument runs. But I doubt whether any of the people who advance this suggestion are at all familiar with the psychology or the physical formation of an army. When war comes it is extremely difficult for any citizen behind the lines to express himself. The preachers and the publishers are under careful scrutiny. They must either wave the flag or stand stock-still. But where on earth did anybody get the idea that within the army ranks free forums and Sunday night debating societies have existed?

Even the agitator who speaks carefully behind the palm of his hand is likely to be detected. The most difficult way to make a protest against armed conflict lies with those who are already signed up with the organization.

And I think there is another valid objection. Very few of us are 100 percent proof against the sound of fife and drum. A heady drug seduces civilians in time of war and makes them shout "Hip, hip, hooray!" But the lure of the infantry and the cavalry and the engineers is still more potent. Burnt children of this world, I warn you, dread the fire. Don't think that you can put on khaki and still avoid its subtle seduction.

When, as a war correspondent, I was instructed to wear a Sam Browne belt I came closer to militarism than I have been since or ever expect to be again. Indeed, I knew a radical who in a trench picked up a rifle and fired at men who were not foe at all according to his philosophy.

I believe that those who hate war should keep away from the sound of the bugles. I believe that they should cease to go about saying: "It's too bad, but inevitable."

Who says that it is inevitable? You and your friend in the corner! All right, I'll get 302 to cry you down. Possible? Yes. Probable? I'm afraid so. But mention "inevitable" and the many millions of us will reply: "You can't make war without us and you can't make war with us. We've made up our minds—no more war."

"Inevitable!" Oh, yeah!

THE FIRST ROBIN

"York, Pa.—With the temperature at 10 degrees below zero the first robin of the year was seen in York today. It was found dead on Penn Common."

Call me an old sentimentalist if you will, but this seems to me the most tragic news note of the cold wave. I like people better than robins, and there has been widespread and agonizing suffering. But, you see, this was the first robin. He was by all odds the pioneer of his clan. He flew up from the South days, weeks and months before any reasonable robin weather was to be expected.

Without doubt the rest tried to discourage him. They spoke of the best recorded experience of bird kind. "Rome wasn't built in a day," some other robin told him. And no doubt he was advised that if he insisted on such precipitate action he would split the group and no good could come of it.

Somehow I seem to hear him saying: "If ten will follow me I'd call that an army. Are there two who'll join up? Or maybe one?"

But the robins all recoiled and clung to their little patches of sun under the Southern skies. "Later, maybe," they told him. "Not now. First there must be a campaign of education."

"Well," replied the robin who was all for going to York, Pa., without waiting for feathery reënforcements, "I know one who'll try it. I'm done with arguments, and here I go."

252

The First Robin

He was so full of high hopes and dedication that he rose almost with the roar of a partridge. For a few seconds he was a fast-moving speck up above the palm trees, and then you couldn't spot him even with field glasses. He was lost in the blue and flying for dear life.

"Impetuous, I call it," said one of the elder statesmen while someone took him a worm.

"He always did want to show off," announced another, and everybody agreed that no good would come of it.

As it turned out, maybe they were right. It's pretty hard to prove that anything has been gained when a robin freezes to death on Penn Common. However, I imagine that he died with a certain sense of elation. None of the rest thought he could get there. And he did. The break in weather turned out to be against him. He just guessed wrong in that one respect, and so I wouldn't think of calling him a complete failure.

When the news gets back home to the robins who didn't go I rather expect that they'll make him a hero. The elder statesmen will figure that since he is dead his ideas can't longer be dangerous, and they cannot deny the lift and the swing of his venture.

After all, he was the first robin. He looked for the Spring, and it failed him. Now he belongs to that noble army of first robins.

Many great names are included. The honors of office and public acclaim, of ribbons and medals, the keys of the city —these are seldom the perquisite of men or birds in the first flight. These go to fifth, sixth and even twentieth robins.

It is almost a rule that the first robin must die alone on some bleak common before mankind will agree that he was a hero. And sometimes it takes fifty years and often a hundred.

John Brown, Galileo and those who sought goals before the world was quite ready are all in good standing.

The man who says, "That would be swell, but, of course, you can't do it," is generally as right as rain; but who wants to get up and cheer for frustration? In the long haul the first robin is more right than any. It was his idea. He softened the way for the others. And with him even failure is its own kind of triumph.

He is not the victim of dry rot or caution or doomed eyestrain from too close an attention to ledgers.

"Here I go!" he cries, and I wouldn't be surprised to be told that the first minute of flight is reward enough, no matter what follows.

And so in a metaphorical way of speaking I bare my head and bow low in the general direction of the ice-covered plain which is known as Penn Common. And I think that the brief address should carry the statement: "You were the first, and after you will come others. They will inherit the grubs and the nests and the comfort. But yours is the glory. You are the first robin."

CARTER'S CRACKS UP

Miami, March 10.—They all said: "You can't start back for New York tonight. You haven't seen Carter's." I replied wearily that I had seen enough gilded hells and watched sufficient roulette to last me for a couple of years. "Ah, but Carter's is different," was the answer. "It's like this," explained a baseball reporter. "Mancuso may not seem like a great catcher to the fans, but he's a ball player's ball player. And there was Leonard Merrick. You may remember that at one time he had no following to speak of, but every fellow novelist in England was crazy about his work."

"Yes, I know," I broke in. "Johnny Boyle is the tap dancers' dancer, and Matisse is the painters' painter. But let's just stick at Carter's. Why should I stay over?" The baseball writer drew a long breath and said rhapsodically: "They have sawdust on the floor. At the house table you may see a man faded for a thousand dollars, for ten thousand, for twenty thousand. And a few feet away an old lady will be playing roulette with ten-cent chips. The bar is made of unfinished pine. It is the old frontier. This is the sort of place which was known in the mining camps when our ancestors were winning the West from the buffalo and the Indians and carving out a new nation."

I replied that I didn't really feel up to winning the West and that I would compromise on Michigan Blvd., Chicago, but that under no circumstances would I consent to be paid off in buffalo robes.

But the look of the dreamer and the poet was in the eyes of the young sports writer. "Carter's begins where the ball for Cinderella left off. Under no circumstances go there before midnight, and later will be much better. Along about 3 or 4 you will see a curious sight—the ultimate in the busman's holiday. At that time the men who have been spinning the wheels and dealing the cards and swinging the birdcage in the swankier places will begin to gather at Carter's to play a little roulette or faro on their own from the wrong side of the table. To see Carter's is to understand the gold rush and the administration of President Polk."

I have always been interested in American history, and so I went to Carter's at 1:30 in the morning. The young man had spoken truly. Here was "The Girl of the Golden West" brought to life in a way which neither Belasco nor the Metropolitan Opera House ever achieved. George Bellows should have painted it. I can see the picture called "Old Croupier at Carter's." Here was a gambling hell without the gilt.

To be sure, some of the men behind the wheels wore the dinner coat which is the uniform of the craft, but others were in sweaters and shirt-sleeves. The older men stuck to tradition. Here is an old gentleman who may have worked in Canfield's. Or played there perhaps.

An artist could not fail to catch the semi-detached, slightly devitalized look in the face of any veteran croupier. It is a little like that of a receiving teller at a savings bank. I suppose all men who get very little money and handle a great deal must be introduced in that same manner. There is a look of benevolence, but you feel that this may be a mask.

The croupier or the teller has an appealing expression in his eyes. He seems to say as he takes your $20, "Now, I do hope you are going to leave this here with us and not be so foolish as to draw it right out again."

But while the teller is an extinct volcano, the croupier suggests that he might some time, under great provocation, leap across the table and say: "I want to be a sucker, too. I can no longer bear the burden of this percentage in favor of the wheel. I want to gamble. Here are my life savings. Let 'em ride on No. 17."

To be accurate, nobody did precisely that while I was at Carter's. But there was a Sicilian gambler who had just dropped $20,000 in the crap game. I saw the brother of Al Capone, and the old lady was quarreling about the $3.50 she won when her number came up.

Carter's was a museum piece throughout, for when I ordered a gin rickey at the bar I smacked my lips in delight. Before repeal went through Carter managed to lay in a few cases of the old bad gin. I could feel the shellac trickling down my throat like velvet.

Moving from table to table, picking up $10 here, $20 at another spot and occasionally making a killing, I was drawn again and again to the bar not only because of the fresh gin but on account of the interesting people one met.

"We were taking Carnera on a tour through Europe for publicity," said Charlie Friedman. "Leon See and I decided that it would be a good idea to show him off in the Casino at Monte Carlo. We were building him up as a big shot. Of course, we couldn't let Primo gamble himself. The risk was too great. He might win. Leon See said he would gamble for the troupe. You know, he's a Frenchman.

"Our little party attracted a great deal of attention as we moved toward a table. Leon is shoving dowagers and dukes out of the way. But on the first spin he bets nothing. He just makes a note in a little book. Twice more he does this, and I'm wondering. On the fourth turn he bets eight francs on the black, and it loses. He notes that down and stays out the next six spins. Then he puts eight francs on the black again and wins.

"That goes in the notebook, and he starts to sit it out again. By now hundreds of people are watching the big shot Carnera and his manager. 'What on earth are you doing, Leon?' I cried. 'It's a system,' he explained. 'If properly played you win $7 every hour.' Recklessly I pulled a ten-thousand-france note from my pocket and put it on the red. Thank heaven, we lost. Honor was satisfied."

I started back for another whirl and to my astonishment found that they were covering the tables. I protested. "Why, it's almost 5 o'clock, Mr. B.," said the manager. "The boys have got to get some sleep." So Carter's isn't really the old frontier, after all. I suppose the croupiers have to go to some other place to play a little hearts. I'm going back to New York, where men are men.

THE LINDBERGH EPIC

The life of Charles A. Lindbergh ought to remain an American epic. He belongs truly among our pioneers. At the moment his fame is somewhat dimmed, but I feel certain that his countrymen will rediscover him. Under the heat of passion he was bitterly assailed by practically all the newspapers of the land, and even some of his friends and neighbors turned against him.

Even at the height of his success Lindbergh was never a national idol, for there was nothing romantic about the man. His associates were the farmers of his own community. Wall Street hated him, for he waged constant warfare against those big interests which tried to challenge the authority of the government. He was largely influential in forcing the appearance of Morgan before a congressional committee. In his book Charles A. Lindbergh wrote:

"Politics and business, we were told, should be kept separate. The wealth grabbers told us that. . . . But the wealth grabbers did not keep their business out of politics. We were the only ones that tried to keep business and politics separate, and the effect was that we kept out of politics altogether, except merely to vote to give politicians power. When we get down to 'brass tacks,' however, we will discover that business and politics should go hand in hand and should not be separated . . ."

And Lindbergh was very definite in making a specific application of that principle in a memorandum which he wrote for the Presidents of the United States. He said:

"1. The federal government must establish a financial system that is independent of private monopoly control.

"2. The federal government must own and operate the main lines in the telegraph and telephone systems.

"3. The federal government must own and operate all the transportation systems."

And Lindbergh amplified this third point in his brief platform by explaining: "Mr. Presidents, no agency is more important than transportation, though it has not the controlling influence on commerce that finances have as finance is now regulated. The free interchange of commodities between the people is of the utmost importance, and travel as well. Therefore all transportation should be as near to actual cost as it is possible to have it. That being the case the government alone could handle it, and should do so."

"The postal system, to be sure," he added, "is successful when compared with privately owned business of any kind, but it would be preëminently more successful if the other services we designate were also operated by the government. It requires them all to make the success of any such as it should be."

A flier who testified in Washington on the question of government operation of the air mail said, "It is as contrary to American liberty as anything I have ever seen."

I doubt that Charles A. Lindbergh would have said that. It is true, of course, that he was not native-born, but he came from Sweden when only a year old and grew up and lived with American problems. Lindbergh was not a technical expert in aviation, but he made one memorable flight. He was piloted by his son, who later became the well-known flier.

Walter E. Quigley describes the incident in an introduction which he has written to a reissue of Lindbergh's book, which is called "Your Country at War." The first edition was suppressed by federal agents in 1918. In 1923 Lindbergh decided to run for United States Senator from Minnesota. Knute Nelson had died suddenly, and a special election was necessary.

"Lindbergh telegraphed his son who was flying an Army Jenny plane in the South, to come to Minnesota and drive him in the plane so he could cover more territory and attract larger crowds. Finally one balmy May afternoon when we were conducting a meeting at the fair grounds in Marshall, we heard the drone of a motor in the sky and a few minutes later the future Colonel Lindbergh landed in a nearby field.

"I rode in the plane to Redwood Falls, our scheduled evening meeting, and distributed literature from the plane. Next day father and son flew to Glencoe—their first airplane ride together. That afternoon when the Colonel was going to take off he hit a concealed ditch on the Miley farm and cracked up, so the airplane method of campaigning came to an abrupt end."

I wish Mr. Quigley had described the incident in rather more detail. It would have been interesting to know what Charles A. Lindbergh Jr. thought then of his father's fervid speeches in favor of government ownership. Possibly the young man was familiar with his passion for human rights. He may have heard him speaking when his father was in the House.

But this was the last campaign and Charles A. Lindbergh's last flight. He died the next Spring. And that was the end of his message. There was no one to take his place.

PASSION IN THE ANDES

CARACAS, Venezuela, March 28.—Don't pay any particular attention to this date line because I am really back in New York, but a few days ago I happened to be in South America and called at the capital of Gomez. The night before we slid onto the shallow port a man in the smoking room drew me aside and whispered. He was the passenger who knew everything.

"Word has just come by wireless," he said, "that the dictator is dying. They've sent an airplane for a foreign surgeon, and when Gomez pops off the lid will bust. There'll be hell to pay in Caracas in the morning. Nobody knows whether the revolution will be right or left or simply in the palace."

And so I went to bed feeling like another Richard Harding Davis. I would stride into the square at noon to the sound of musketry and machine-gun fire. And with three bullet holes through my hat I would hold the cable by sending the first chapter of Genesis as I wrote the thrilling tale of blood among the oil wells.

I decided not to go on the tour arranged by the steamer. I wanted to be mobile. "There will be a two hours' drive into the interior which will enable the passengers to see the curious huts of the natives." Of that I had seen enough, and, by the way, the natives are beginning to realize that their huts are curious and they are not any too well pleased about it. But that's the story of the Red Mayor in Trinidad and ought to make another column some time.

Always the shrewd arranger, I managed to hit upon a driver who spoke not one single word of English with the exception of the phrase "O.K." Caracas is 3,000 feet straight up a mountain. I was willing to face death in the afternoon but not in the morning. "American newspaper man in nasty accident when car falls 2,000 feet," is not much of a story. "Don't drive so damn fast," I said to the Venezuelan Barney Oldfield.

"O.K.," he answered and did the next curve on one wheel. I tried the pantomime they use in radio studios to indicate, "Stretch it out. Go slower." Barney said something in his South American Spanish and I couldn't be sure, but I think it was "No, I don't swim." At any rate it had no effect on his driving.

I tried sarcasm. "Let's fix it like this," I suggested, "on the straightaway you go very slow, but make it fast around the curves." This he seemed to understand, for he took the instructions literally.

And so I will never know very much about the road to Caracas. I remember mountains above me and hills leaping like waterfalls to meet the sea. Sky and sea and chasm pin-wheeled across my vision. Suddenly we leaped over a ridge and there before me lay a suburb done in pink stucco, looking precisely like a Flatbush builder's dream of Seville. I wonder what the Spanish is for, "A thousand dollars down and the rest on easy payments."

Yet here was flat land again and rest for the eye of the considerably shaken traveler who had just spiraled up around an elevator shaft. But as we progressed to the center of Caracas the color grew more brilliant. Every child was clad in purple and the little boys had ropes about their waists as if in monkish garb. Under the brilliant sun it seemed to the eye of the uninitiated traveler as if Caracas were in fête. The driver slackened speed for the first time as we approached the cathedral. And for the first time he understood when I indicated that I wanted to go in.

Out of bright sunlight I came into cool darkness merely flecked and not broken by the light of many hundred candles. And all about the walls and statues and across the shoulders of the worshipers I saw the badge of purple. And now I knew that this was the color of grief and mourning. And, of course, it was for the dying dictator that these people prostrated themselves upon the stone floors.

Holy Week had come to the foothills of the Andes.

I have seen church services in far and near places and many were impressive, but here for the first time I saw a people who seemed to feel that the passion of the Lord was actually occurring once again. Pilate was not a famous dead neutral who washed his hands in an ancient city long ago. At that very moment the Son of God was on trial before the Roman. An Indian woman older than any living being I had ever seen lifted her head from the floor to mutter her prayers toward the altar. Children in their purple smocks looked at the dancing lights and wondered. Once again Judas walked the earth and Christ was betrayed in a pleasant garden.

Many stood outside upon the steps under the sun and peered through the doors and down the dark aisles. It was as if they waited for some word to come to them from the mourners. Almost they seemed to say: "What news?"

And though the faith of the faithful burns high along that mountain shelf it imposes upon the worshipers a very special sort of agony. They wait in racked anxiety to learn whether the stone has been rolled away on Easter morning. To them the miracle is beyond question because they have lived through its occurrence.

Only one sleepy soldier stood outside the door of the palace of Gomez. In a café a waiter shrugged his shoulders when I asked him about the revolution. "In Venezuela," he said, "one finds it good not to talk politics."

But then he added: "Gomez is very old, and he must die some time. But he is a strong man and he has willed this thing. Like you and me and the beggar at the door, he will breathe until he has seen another Easter morning."

THE GRAND OLD GAL OF THE NORTH ATLANTIC

SOMEWHERE OFF CAPE HATTERAS, April 1.—When Eugene O'Neill wrote a play about a young man who went goofy over a dynamo I thought it very odd. Nor have I quite understood, save in some remote Freudian sense, the passion of many famous writers for some certain ship or skiff or coal barge. But now in late life I find myself in love with a liner.

To be sure, the lady is somewhat on the seamy side herself. She will be 28 on her next birthday. This affair between me and the grand old gal of the North Atlantic was no matter of love at first sight. Before we shipped together I had heard discouraging reports. "The greatest pitcher since Cy Young," said one transatlantic veteran. "And she can roll with Ol' Man River," chimed in another of the seafaring folk.

Even her agents sought in a measure to deter me. "Only one cabin is left," said the candid young man at the Cunard office, "and, frankly, we would rather not sell it."

"Oh, I don't believe in ghosts or haunted staterooms or anything like that," I told him.

"That's not it, sir. Nobody has died there yet. But this is an inside cabin, next the smokestack, and when you get to Trinidad it will be hot—devilishly hot. I don't like to see a man of your build going into it."

Somewhat stiffly I replied that my arteries were my own affair and that of my own free will I'd take the chance.

After all, when they lifted the lid from the Black Hole of Calcutta several were still alive.

At the last minute some less stalwart passengers canceled, and I was moved to a higher deck. It wasn't right up with "the white folks," but it had a porthole. That night, along about dawn, I awakened suddenly when a considerable consignment of Cape Hatteras water landed upon my chest and head.

"Cut that out, Junior!" I cried angrily. "Daddy detests practical jokes."

But then another wave came through. They were right when they told me that the *Mauretania* could roll. We managed to get the porthole closed and fastened, and even so I didn't like it. First I would see the scud of dank clouds, and then the room grew dark, and the only outlook was green water. Once I fancied I saw a fish peering through at me. I am no mariner or deep sea diver, and so I dressed and went upstairs.

A couple of chairs acting as running interference tried to put me out of the play, but I dodged and found a seat which was nailed to the floor in the deserted smoke room. Presently a steward appeared, and I began to draw him out about tempests and the luck of the *Mauretania*. Had he been with her long? I wanted to know, and he answered, "Ever since she was launched, barring a couple of years against the Turks at Gallipoli."

"And weren't there times, maybe, when you thought perhaps she might not make it?"

He thought for a moment and said: "Just one. Of course, we've had plenty of waves break over the bridge when she pitched. There was one that took off all the lifeboats on the port side. But you got to expect things like that. But once there was a following storm, and a wave broke over her stern, and for a little while there was about two or three feet of water right here in this smoke room."

"What did you do?"

"I looked down, and I said to myself, 'This is peculiar.'"

"Of course," he added loyally, "we don't get as many storms as other liners."

"Why not?"

"Well, you see, sir, the *Mauretania*—she more or less makes her own weather."

The old gal made good that proud boast. When they auctioned off the run I bought a low number, remembering the roll and pitch and the feel of the gale in my face as I stood ·on the deck. High field won. In a rough sea she knocked off almost seven hundred miles without half trying. And probably there wasn't any gale. When a ship slices along around thirty land miles an hour it's naturally going to seem breezy. And "slice" is the word. I've seen ships which pushed and wrestled themselves along, but the old gal is an inspired bread knife. She grinds as fine as the mills of the gods and a great deal faster.

In tropic moonlit seas I used to stand by the rail and watch the water rush by. It always seemed as if the waves were in full retreat, as if the sea said, "Here comes the grand old gal of the North Atlantic; make way for somebody that can run."

There is a certain startling quality in the amazing speed of the old gal. You feel a little bit as if Queen Victoria had suddenly pulled up her skirts and cried to Lord Tennyson, "I'll race you to the nearest pub and lay you four shillings against a mug of bitter."

Modern art has not touched the public rooms. It's all dark wood and tapestry and practically nothing changed from the beginning.

"That tapestry on the sofa you're sitting on," said the steward, "—we had that the first voyage. We just can't seem to wear it out."

He gave it a sort of grandpop-ought-to-get-well-or-something look.

"Well, how about the old gal herself? Will she go on forever?"

"I can't say, sir, but I can tell you what's kept us going. We haven't any of that newfangled stabilizing stuff. You shouldn't do that to a wave. You've got to meet the sea halfway and humor it."

"Like Dempsey rolling with Firpo's punches at the end of the first round," I suggested rather aptly. At least, the steward said it was neat. And so we talked of the famous men who had sailed and the poker games they used to play and of the great and gone. And ghosts did come into the room and rattle the glasses and order drinks for themselves.

I hear that when the time approaches to put the old gal away in lavender they'll tune her up and take one more crack at a new Atlantic record.

And when they saddle old lack of paint for that last roundup I want to go along. I put in my reservation now for that cabin abaft the smokestack.

CHUMMY CHARLIE

Charles M. Schwab came back from Europe and expressed regret when he heard that the squatter colony of veterans along the Hudson opposite his Riverside Drive home had been ordered to move along. He said that they had been good neighbors.

"We visited back and forth," he explained. "They had been up to my house and very kindly assisted us around the grounds in getting rid of the heavy snows last winter. Mrs. Schwab frequently drove down to visit them in their homes. And I also called on them many times. When we had a surplus of produce from our farm at Loretto, Pa., we were happy to share it with them. They had looked forward to staying there, I know, until business improved. We shall miss them. They were not bad neighbors at all."

This I have no doubt was the sincere expression of a kindly old gentleman who worked himself up from the bottom to the top of the steel industry. He had a neighborly feeling for men living in plain sight of his turrets who just didn't have the good luck to get the breaks. The assistance which he rendered was quite in the American tradition that the more fortunately situated should help the stragglers in a casual and friendly fashion without any outside compulsion. After all, what are a couple of heads of lettuce and a bushel of potatoes between friends?

But in the long history of Bethlehem Steel I assume that it is entirely possible that there have been other shacks where Charles M. Schwab never got around to pay a visit.

Chummy Charlie

During the desperate days of the depression I venture to assert that thousands of jobless employees never saw so much as a leaf of the Loretto lettuce.

Does this mean that Mr. Schwab in his own person is some sort of exceptionally tight-fisted villain? In my opinion it means nothing of the sort. He is from all the accounts I ever heard kindly, genial and reasonable. The hitch is systemic and not individual. The American tradition that we can muddle through hard times by dint of private charity, individual benevolence and voluntary giving has broken down completely. And of course it deserved to break down.

When a man asks for bread and receives a stone he has a right to be indignant, but I hold that he should not be satisfied when he asks for bread and gets bread. It is quite true that in the life we know there do arise situations so desperate that private charity must be called upon in lieu of better devices and more rapid ones. But in the long run charity does desperate things to the donors. It makes smug prigs who go about saying that they would like to give but that they are afraid of pauperizing people.

I used to know, for my sins, a lady who went around on Easter, Christmas and Thanksgiving leaving baskets. Each basket contained one raw turkey, two cans baked beans, one jar cranberry jelly, two loaves whole wheat bread, one pound butter, one stick peppermint candy for the kiddies.

I suppose this generous woman was one of the most objectionable persons I have ever met. She would come back from her rounds on one of the three feast days all puffed up with righteousness.

"I know it is only a little," she used to say, "but one does the best they can." Her grammar was even worse than her personality.

One day a man at her house took her up on her favorite remark and answered, "You're damn tooting it is only a little. Did you ever stop to figure what any of those people lived on between turkeys? And did you ever stop to ask by what right you go around and get yourself into a glow of self-satisfaction by distributing a little occasional delicatessen?"

The young man was set down as a rude person and never was asked to lunch any more, but I think he was right. I have known people to stop and buy an apple on the corner and then walk away as if they had solved the whole unemployment problem. I think that people should make charitable gifts but only on their knees and with the deepest apologies. The fact that such things are in any way necessary constitutes an indictment of every one of us.

We have so snarled up the world with our rugged individualism and our insistence upon the preservation of initiative and our bleating that we won't stand for regimentation and compulsion that the whole blame planet is likely to fall right on our heads.

I can't understand how people can go on parroting stuff about taking care of the needy in our own good American way. The device of private charity is not working now, and it never has worked. The only dignified and decent way to attend to such matters until the doctor comes is to have the government say, "So much is needed, and this is your share."

Any reasonable system of taxation should be based on the theory of "Soak the rich." The rich aren't going to like it, but they should, because in the long run it is the only system which will preserve their souls from the decadence of donations.

AROUND THE WORLD IN
FIFTY MINUTES

CHICAGO, June 5.—"You have been unjust to A Century of Progress," said Ernie, and I was puzzled by the indictment. "Oh, well, if you like, I think that you haven't been fair to the fair," he explained.

"Why not?"

"I think it was too big for you. It's like going to Moscow for a week-end and then doing a book about Russia. You were over there a couple of hours, and then you come back and write a piece saying it's no good. I'll bet you didn't even see the Hall of Science." I hung my head in shame.

"Just as I thought," continued Ernie. "You went to the wrong places with the wrong people. How did you get around?" I told him that I'd walked. "That was wrong, too. This is an educational exhibition, and you have to sit down and take it. Come along with me and see the fair properly."

Ernie told the taxi driver he wanted the gate nearest to the Hall of Science, so when we got out we had to cross only two bridges, walk half a mile and turn to the left. At that point we could see our objective in the distance. So we took rickshaws.

I picked a big, husky college boy, who told me he had been a tackle at Purdue, but at the end of two blocks I couldn't stand it any longer. Passersby would say: "Look at that little fellow dragging that great big fat man along. I suppose he thinks he's in China and that we're all a bunch of coolies."

I told Ernie it was too painful. "He can give you another cushion," he suggested. "It's my pride that's hurt," I answered.

"Well," said Ernie, "here's the best idea yet. I told you it was to be educational. This is the Avenue of the Flags and Exhibits of all Nations. Most of them have restaurants attached, and we'll creep up on that old Hall of Science, sampling the native drinks as we go along. Here's the Czechoslovakian place right here. Wonderful people the Slovaks, but they've only got a service bar. We'll have to sit down at a table." A blond girl in a brilliant red-and-black peasant costume came over to the table with the menu containing a list of strange stews and fricassees quite unknown to me.

"Bring us," said my mentor, "a couple of Martini cocktails."

The Italian exhibit just across the way was decorated gayly in red and green. Chianti bottles lined the walls, and a tenor sang Rudolpho's "Narrative." "Garçon," said Ernie, "two Martini cocktails in a hurry."

"Here in this one narrow street," he ruminated, "the cultures of the world are met. There is no East or West, but only Chicago. I want you to see the Chinese village. It's a bit of the Orient set down here in the new hemisphere. When Chicago was only a rutted wagon trail these people already had developed a civilization which still endures. They have erected in miniature the Golden Temple of Jehol. I think the name is Jehol, but at any rate, it was the playground of great monarchs who drank the wines of antiquity."

We crossed the street. Ernie pointed to the temple gates.

"Keep going," he advised. "That's the temple, but we want a restaurant. It's next door."

Twice he clapped his hands and a young Chinese came running with a scroll in his hands. "You fetchee two Martini chop chop. Can do?" asked Ernie. The Celestial assented.

"I think maybe that we might have a bite to eat before we tackle the Hall of Science. After that we can try the native beverages at the Belgian village, and I understand that the Swiss have one of the nicest layouts around here. The Swiss are a free and independent people who run hotels, but they tell me that the Hawaiians next door have the best food on the grounds, and they also put on a show about a native princess who sacrifices herself in a volcano. I understand she has to take off practically all her clothes to do it. Before the coming of the white man they were a primitive people."

The Hawaiian concession was the largest on the block, and at one end of the dining room stood a lumpy mountain made of cardboard. Occasionally steam came from its summit.

"Kelner, we want two Martinis and a menu."

A man with a deep baritone voice began telling the unfortunate history of the Princess Moana Luana. It seems there was trouble in the tribe and she decided to give herself to the gods of the mountain in order to appease them. The young lady who played the rôle seemed to me a shade on the hefty side, and I sympathized with her as she ascended the trail. At each curve of the road she discarded something. "Going to die for her people," murmured Ernie with emotion, and this time I paid for a round of Martinis. "She stands at the crater's edge," said the announcer. "She prays. She hesitates. She casts herself into the flames of the volcano."

And the princess suited her every action to his words. She disappeared from view behind a canvas parapet, and great clouds of steam arose and filled the room with smoke.

"What will you have, gentlemen?" asked the Hawaiian waiter attired in costume of his people.

"One pig's knuckle," said Ernie, "and a couple of Martinis."

Next time I get to Chicago I mean to see that Hall of Science. I understand that it is highly educational.

THE STRIKE-BREAKER

To me it has always seemed not only illogical but improper that police or national guardsmen should be employed to protect the functioning of strike-breakers in any industry. In theory, at least, the police and the guard are supposed to be the servants of the majority of the citizens. Governors and mayors are elected by the masses. Why, then, should public forces be turned over to private individuals for their personal advantage, particularly when that advantage happens to be disadvantageous to the common weal?

Palpably the strike-breaker is an anti-social member of the community. As a rule he has no political or economic philosophy whatsoever, but in any case in which he became articulate he would be forced by the logic of the circumstances to assert that his temporary gain should be protected even at the expense of calamity among the many. Certainly whenever a strike is broken the city or town, as a whole, is worse off than it was before. Men and women are added to the list of unemployed and there will be an inevitable tendency to worse wages and working conditions all along the line.

In Toledo the head of a mercantile house told me that the strike in the Auto-Lite plant was costing his store a loss of 20 percent of average business every week. I said to him: "That doesn't surprise me, but the thing which I can't understand is why the business men in this town or any other should take an attitude of opposition to the unions and get together at meetings to denounce 'outside agitators.' If I owned a business here I would be down on the picket line with a placard urging the employers to comply with the demands of the workers. The success of your store depends upon the purchasing power of the people of the city. Just out of self-interest you can't afford to have the men lose."

I think the same theory holds good in San Francisco. The guardsmen and the police are supported by the taxpayers, who will be assessed in order to win a victory for the owners of steamship lines and thereby lower the general standard of living and the general prosperity of all concerned with the exception of a few owners engaged in the industry now under fire.

I even doubt whether the immediate employers gain much from success in breaking a strike. Any such result must be among the most pyrrhic of victories. Strike-breakers are expensive, inefficient and unreliable. In the long run I'll wager that many a cost sheet will show that it would have been far more profitable for the stockholders to have granted the union demands at the beginning.

I have heard a few ill-informed and sentimental folk picture the strike-breaker as a rugged American who was fighting for the cause of individual liberty and the freedom of every man to work at whatever craft he may choose for his own. The strike-breaker is not like that. He sells his birthright for a few meager and immediate pieces of silver and heightens his own chances to be back on some bread-line a few weeks or months after the event.

It seems to me that the average American is not very quick to realize the enormous benefits which even non-union workers have gained through the force of organization. The very people who will readily admit that prosperity can come only through the heightening and stabilization of purchasing power are the very ones who complain of the "tyranny of the unions." One of the familiar arguments is the citation of certain open shop employers who pay wages equal to the scale or even better. But people who mention Ford and other manufacturers as friends of labor lose sight of the fact that many a boss keeps wages up in a desperate fight to keep his employees from unionizing.

If there were no possible threat of organization all wages would drop to the intolerable levels established by the law of supply and demand. One does not need to be a complete technocrat to realize that with our present surplus of unemployed, wages would be next to nothing save in the case of a very small number of highly skilled individuals. And even they would suffer, since there are many jobs in which ten indifferent performers can approximate the efforts of one highly competent performer.

Much has been said about the American standard of living and the necessity of its preservation. That standard has been rather rudely battered about in the last few years, but where it still exists the credit must go to the unions, which have kept wages up and hours down. The non-union man is a person who reaps where he has not sown. He comes at the eleventh hour and receives his penny. He is willing to profit by the aggressive efforts of others to whom he has given no support. Worse than that, he stands ready to stab in the back the very people who have made it possible for him to command a competence.

And so I say that he is an anti-social force who decidedly does not deserve protection at public expense. I would not have him torn limb from limb by angry mobs. I think both the police and the guard have a proper function in strikes. I feel that they should in emergencies be called out by mayors or governors under the order, "It is your job to see that not a single strike-breaker enters this plant or so much as one wheel turns until the employers have made a fair settlement with their men."

MR. HEARST AND MR. LIPPMANN

It takes two sides to make a general strike. I cannot go along with the trend of editorial comment which fastens the blame for a difficult and dangerous situation upon the union members. For instance, Walter Lippmann notes in passing the assertion that the action was thrust upon the workers by the refusal of the ship owners to concede two reasonable demands. Apparently Mr. Lippmann is disposed to disregard this charge as a matter of no importance.

"But what," he writes, "is the state of affairs that has actually been brought about by the decision of organized labor to fight the ship owners with a general strike? A conflict between one group of employees and one group of employers has been transformed into a conflict between organized labor on the one hand and, on the other, the general public, the city, the state, and perhaps ultimately the federal government."

It seems to me that Mr. Lippmann grossly underrates the intelligence of the general public. And I think he is unfair in charging an entire community with moral cowardice. "I do not know," said Edmund Burke, "the method of drawing up an indictment against a whole people." Even when the problem has been scaled down to a single city I doubt if Walter Lippmann is competent to draw up such a scathing indictment of San Francisco. As I understand his contention it preaches the belief that every citizen under the stress of acute discomfort will be willing to lose sight of principle and knuckle down to an acceptance of the will of private capitalists.

In the present situation Mr. Lippmann enunciates a radical doctrine to which I cannot subscribe. He seems to argue that the whim of a small group of ship owners ought to be dignified under such terms as "the city, the state, and perhaps ultimately the federal government."

Mr. Lippmann, I think, is far too cynical. America is not yet ready to let a small and pernickety group of employers identify themselves as embodying the state, the city and the federal government. The public has rights, and one of them is to go back constantly to the original problem involved.

Any member of the public has a right to say: "Why should I have to take all this grief and turmoil simply because a small group of willful men insist that in their hiring halls they will not permit a reasonable apportionment of the jobs?"

William Randolph Hearst joins Mr. Lippmann in a bland denial of democratic principles. "Every service essential to the life of the community," writes the elder advocate of safety first, "must be taken in hand by a special corps of citizens representing the best intelligence and directing power within the city. Private pursuits must be laid aside and the most experienced and efficient men in the community must dedicate their abilities to its service and to its rescue from this all-embracing threat."

Quite obviously Mr. Hearst goes a bit beyond the position which Walter Lippmann was prepared to take just around the time of the last deadline. Mr. Lippmann has said no more than to express the attitude of certain confused people in a particular community. Mr. Hearst, or his agent, seems to suggest that now is the time for America to try the experiment of out-and-out fascism.

I am aware that this word has been employed a little carelessly. Only the other day a rooter at the Yankee Stadium was incensed because the umpire called "Strike!" when a ball passed a little below the knees of Babe Ruth. Rising to full height, the embattled fan shook his fist at the official and shouted out: "You Fascist!"

But when anybody begins to talk about a little selected group taking charge of affairs and wiping out the threat of the masses I think that we are being urged to take the road down which Hitler swaggered.

I will agree with all the editorial writers who view the

San Francisco situation with alarm. But I think they are looking in the wrong direction. A few have even seen the San Francisco strike as the beginning of the proletarian revolution. To me it seems another march on Rome. Look at the facts—a small group of employers brought about a strike through refusing to make certain minor though vital concessions. It is now suggested that an alliance of "efficient men in the community" should take over the task of administering civic affairs.

Ironically enough, this little knot of faithful thinkers might quite possibly be made up of the same small number of employers who fomented the general strike. Their action may not have been as stupid as it seems. Possibly the business men of the coast decided that this was the proper time to take things over.

Fortunately the 40,000 men who are out constitute an army which is fighting for our rights. The police and the national guard ought to stand with them shoulder to shoulder because the union members constitute the only barrier which lies between San Francisco and a brown shirt front.

The workers are fighting for the union—and I refer both to their own and that one in which we all live and have our being. You cannot indict an entire nation. No more can a free people fighting against tyranny be terrorized by cannon, tanks and the various gases which make those near at hand a little sick. Sometimes you can even get the effect here in New York.

And so I still think that the lawless employers should be restrained, and if they don't like it here I see no possible objection to sending them back where they came from.

281

HORSES WITH THEIR HAIR DOWN

SARATOGA, Aug. 6.—I think it was Sherwood Anderson, in his story "I Want to Know Why," who first aroused my interest in what goes on at a race track in the early morning. Anderson has a feeling for color and for form which is far beyond me, and I can't possibly make you see the horses galloping along the rim of the sun before the mist has lifted. The best I can do is to advise you to get some trainer to ask you down. I doubt if there is any more lovely sight in the world.

A race with your own horse on top, or thereabouts, provides a stirring picture, but, as in the theater, I like the rehearsal better than the performance. In the dawn the horses let their hair down. They are more natural and twice as articulate in the morning. Seemingly they do not feel that it is necessary to put on airs for the trainers, stable boys and clockers. They snort at each other as they pass by, and I presume it is a language.

For years I have been under the impression that race horses were beautiful but dumb. When I mentioned this opinion to Max Hirsch he was shocked and quickly put me in my place. But he was kind enough to ask me to come around to his barn and look for myself.

But I am not the type ever to get very chummy with a horse. The smallest wager which I put on the back of any of the noble animals is treated as if it were a load of lead. Even the finest of the topnotchers stops to a walk when he feels the pressure of my $2 upon his neck. Even the simple matter of handing out sugar to the colts and fillies is marred by me. I almost lost two fingers from my better hand in passing around the sweets in Saratoga. Horses realize instinctively that I have only the slightest knowledge of what it is all about, and they treat me contemptuously.

But Maxie Hirsch knows the language. You could have knocked me over with a selling-plater as I watched him discuss a weighty problem with one of his two-year-olds this morning. He was schooling some of his young horses in the use of the starting gate. One of them insisted upon kicking at the padded sides of the stall and rearing up on his hind legs. Hirsch walked quickly to the horse's head, but he never touched the bridle. With complete unconsciousness and great earnestness he said: "What's the matter with you? You're three years old; haven't you got any sense at all?"

It would probably be an exaggeration to say that the horse hung his head in shame. But he did pay attention and he stopped his prancing on the instant. Maxie walked some ten or twelve feet away from the gate and said: "Come on out, slowly." The horse walked to him with all the alacrity and precision of a well-trained dog.

"Now go back," said Hirsch; "back into the stall," and the horse did exactly that. I had an uneasy feeling that I was watching black magic and that if Hirsch had said: "Go over to my cottage and chew Walter Lippmann's column out of the paper," the horse would have done it.

To be sure, I'll admit that Hirsch would have to tell the horse what Lippmann was talking about. But what would be fairer than that? Mr. Lippmann is a sort of mild medical missionary to the men of Wall Street. They worship together at the shrine of the unknown God. Or, possibly, it would be a nicer use of English to say "the unidentified God."

But my point is that after several years of preaching to bankers and brokers, Mr. Lippmann has begun to look like a banker and broker. And certainly in the early morning Maxie Hirsch distinctly suggests a horse.

Naturally I mean this in the best sense of the word. During the training period Mr. Hirsch seems to be constantly motivated by the feeling, "Now what would I do if I were that horse?"

It seems to me that in following this formula Maxie Hirsch is by at least a couple of lengths more severe than Walter Lippmann. The mere fact that you understand the psychology of a banker or a race horse should not inevitably commit you to approval.

Maxie Hirsch remains a sentimentalist. Even when confronted by sheer fractiousness he cannot quite forget that he knew the culprit's sire and once won a bet on his dam.

Horsemen, as a rule, are too much overawed by a sense of greatness and prestige. The get of Galahad or Man O' War tend to be placed upon a pedestal before they actually have won the right. All the trainers I know ignore the behaviorism of John Watson and string along with Charles Darwin. And they make mistakes. As a husband and father the great Man O' War has been no more than a moderate success. I believe with Jefferson that all horses are created free and equal.

But, good or bad or non-winners, any one of them looks of stake quality all over when he starts to run through the mist and up to the morning sun. These are steeds worthy of the young Greek lad Apollo.

Others may have rain on the roof, the noise of distant surf

or a cricket on the hearth, but give me the drumming beat of hoofs against the dirt in the early workout.

Never again will I complain of bets which go astray. Even the poorer horse merits more than I can ever afford to lay upon him. I do not like to hear racing referred to as the sport of kings. It's much too good for them. On the contrary, from horse to visiting columnist we are all equal upon the turf or under it.

I INTERVIEW A COLUMNIST

Early this morning I ran into a newspaper columnist who is a close friend of mine, and we were both complaining that neither of us had an idea for the next column. "Would you submit to an interview?" I asked. "What do you mean 'submit'?" he replied. "When did I ever run away from a chance to get into print?" But after a few seconds' consideration he added, "I think you had better not use my name or identify me in any way, because I have a vague feeling that I am walking along a road on which banana peels are being spread in my honor."

"Are you a labor agitator?" I asked.

"I hope so," he answered. "At any rate, I mean to be."

"How can you square that with the fact that you are reputed to have received a high salary for a number of years?"

"I have $125.70 in the bank right now," answered my fat friend gloomily.

"Please do not evade the issue," I insisted. "You could have saved your money. You've probably wasted it in gambling and riotous living." "Sure," he said, "I could have saved it up to buy Peruvian bonds. Or maybe I could have saved up enough to be in just the right state of mind to do columns about the cussedness of workers who demand their rights and forget to be polite to the boss."

"But you're still quibbling," I persisted. "Rumor has it, again, that you've signed a contract for a number of years, so that, no matter what happens, you at least have security."

The young man answered obscenely, and for at least a minute it seemed quite useless to take notes. After a final splutter he continued: "Once upon a time I worked in a large metropolis on a morning paper. It was a liberal paper. Up in Massachusetts two innocent men were being railroaded to the chair. As I remember, one was a shoemaker and the other a peddler. I got mad, I got so mad that the editor told me not to write on that subject any more. I got madder and went on a one-man strike for six or seven months. Then, like a fool, I went back, and in another couple of months I got fired. And during all that time I had a contract and what you call security."

The man annoyed me, and I broke in sharply. "Don't try any of those martyr airs on me," I told him. "You never went cold, and Heaven knows it's palpable you never went hungry a day in your life."

This time he grinned at me with that charm for which he is noted. "But I will, Heywood; I will," he answered. "In fact, I'm beginning to feel that I must. But mostly those are not decisions that you make arbitrarily. They are forced on you. If you are willing to wait until next pay before the money is put up I'll lay you $100 to $10 that I will die in abject poverty and spend my declining years in want."

"You needn't hold the pose on my account," I assured him. "I've read the same amount of Freud as you have. I think we both recognize the Messiah complex which crops out in columnists at bars along about 4 in the morning. Quit weeping into your gin rickey."

I thought for a minute he was going to punch me, and, as we are both of a size, it might have been a good bout, though a short one.

"Look here, Broun," he said, growing more formal, "there's a point where all kidding ceases. You and I have known newspaper men better than either of us who were tossed on the scrap heap with charm for a coat and a 'so sorry, old fellow,' in lieu of an old-age pension."

I tried to mollify him. "Yes, I'd heard that you were one of a crowd that was working to try to improve conditions for editorial workers." But then I couldn't resist my traditional skepticism and suspicion of sham. "Still, they tell me," I added, "that in your case it's just a lark and that you go around making speeches and attending meetings just to show off."

Instead of getting angry he answered quite mildly, "Anybody who says that is a liar." And he quickly added: "That isn't fair. I ought to say he's mistaken. I had the same suspicion myself, because I am an old showoff. But I put myself on probation. A year has gone by, and so I know it isn't a lark. It's a job and the most thrilling enterprise to which a man can commit himself. In the labor movement I know which side I'm on. I'm for the workers. I hope you'll believe me."

And, as a matter of fact, I did.

A MAN I LIKED

A man I liked was Raymond Hood and, though he has left many monuments, he will be missed by the magical city. Mr. Hood was almost the only person with whom I dared to discuss architecture. Although I am brazen and bumptious, I would hardly have rushed into his field like a nudist running to a fire if he himself had not opened the way. He did not seek security, as so many technicians do, by giving you a bland smile and murmuring, "You wouldn't understand."

Now, of course, I haven't the slightest comprehension of costs or any other elements of stress and strain which enter into the job of an architect. Mr. Hood took a larger view. He was willing to listen with interest and complete disagreement to any layman who said, "I don't like the cut of your American Radiator Building."

I wouldn't have said that. On the contrary, I think that this gilded structure is a happy combination of the art of the architect with that of the pastry cook. This is not a sneer. Whenever I look up at that strange collaboration of gold and sable I start to hum unconsciously, "Happy birthday to you." It is the sort of skyscraper which should be crowned with tallow candles.

Even if you look down the list through the ages Raymond Hood will stand out among the architects of all time as one who had the fortune and the genius to conduct radical experimentation with mass and color. Many have had this privilege on canvas or with clay, but it is rare for a man to be allowed to play around with steel and glass and stone in this fashion. I got the impression that Raymond Hood rather resented the fact that there remained a necessity of having any truck with stone or brick. Toward the end, at any rate, he thought of his buildings almost solely in terms of steel and glass. Indeed, the McGraw-Hill Building is practically nothing but eyes and bones.

If Hood had lived a little longer I think that Manhattan might be even more magical than it is today. Under his guiding hand other towers would have floated to the sky, trailing behind them lines marked by lights within the building. Raymond Hood is the architect who glorified the greenhouse. And in his use of brittle and tough substances he did get away from the obese quality which mars much of city architecture. His buildings did not cumber the earth. Take, for instance, the *Daily News* Building here and the *Tribune* Tower in Chicago. In both instances the passerby gets the effect that the structure is poised upon one toe and eager to float or fly. Yet there is the sense of strength. Hood could do you a skyscraper which was ready for a fight or frolic.

I have no idea which was his favorite. I imagine it was the building he had just completed or, better yet, the one he was about to do. I am not prepared to say whether the *Tribune* was regarded by him as a Cinderella among his structures, but on at least two occasions he explained, "Well, he wanted Gothic."

Possibly I should not have suggested that Raymond Hood was quite the wholly emancipated architect who could go out and do precisely what he wanted without regard to the whims of his client. He worked for at least two of the most temperamental gentlemen in America. Once he felt that he had reached paradise. This particular newspaper proprietor said no more than, "Do me an eight-million-dollar building." It seemed the ideal commission, but naturally there was a catch to it. After the plans were all completed the client looked over the blueprints and said: "I want a handball court here on the roof. I can play against this wall here."

"But that won't work out well," Hood explained. "That's the wall of the directors' room. If you play handball against that it will make a great deal of racket. It will annoy the life out of them."

"That's precisely why I want it," explained the client.

As I have said, Hood would listen and argue about architecture far into the night even with adversaries who never built anything more than a sand fort. "If I say I don't like your column," he told me once, "I can't see any reason why you shouldn't take a crack at my turrets."

He felt that an architect had no right to deny the right of public criticism. "It may be my building," he explained, "but it's their skyline."

I see no reason why he should not be one of the happiest inhabitants of heaven. There's so much work to be done. He will look at the streets of gold and the many mansions of jade and jasper, and then if he carries with him something of his mortality he'll say, "Not that; let's have steel and glass." And if he is still the man he was, which I most fervently believe, already the riveting machines have begun their fanfare within the pearly gates.

ALL IN A SPIRIT OF FUN

BUFFALO, Aug. 31.—As the taxi came around the first corner after leaving the station something went "Bang!" a few yards to the right. "Trouble at the plant?" I asked the driver. "No," he answered. "The state convention of the American Legion." I was a little flabbergasted, and my surprise grew during the day.

The state convention for which I was headed was that of the A. F. of L. I found the gentlemen sometimes referred to as "labor agitators" sedate, business-like and wholly concerned with the job in hand. It was the Legion, which annually passes resolutions about "the red menace" and the sanctity of private property, which was tearing Buffalo loose from its moorings.

I am told that the Hotel Statler put most of its furniture in a safe place the day it agreed to be the official headquarters of the legionnaires. Indeed, so little respect did the veterans show for capitalistic thrift that I will be returning to New York bareheaded. A battle-scarred hero from Lockport thought it would be a good joke to cram an ice cream cone down on top of my old straw hat. Judging from the laughter of all beholders, it was a good joke.

Mind you, I am not sore. I had used that hat for two summers. It was impossible for me to wear it any more and still remain class conscious. And speaking of class consciousness, I realize for the first time that on many occasions I have done great injustice to the American Legion.

In my column I have assailed this or that Legion gathering as potential fascist fuel, because I read in the newspapers some flag-waving oration by an official or some stuffy resolution condemning recognition of Russia.

These pieces were set down in ignorance. When dispatches said that thirty thousand or forty thousand veterans gathered in this city or that roundly denounced some pacifistic person I took the news at its face value. That is always a bad way to take news. An afternoon in Buffalo has taught me that a Legion convention, in so far as the formal proceedings go, is just a gag. They say that thirty-five thousand veterans are here for the session which is current.

Judging from the clamor in the lobby, the sound of explosions in the street outside and the volume of "Sweet Adeline" from just across the court, the newspapers have gravely minimized the numbers. Look into any nook and cranny of Buffalo and you will find that the name is Legion. If there are any less than a million of the merrymakers I am a sucker at sound ranging.

And yet scarcely more than a thousand persons have listened to any of the speeches or formal resolutions which went on in the great hall where the solemn deliberations take place. The average veteran does not go to a convention to throttle the red menace but solely for the purpose of getting rid of personal inhibitions. In this effort he is singularly successful. I haven't seen so much as the shadow of an inhibition within half a mile of this hotel.

When the legionnaire starts for home after a three- or four-day session his eyelids are naturally a little weary. He has, in most cases, a family to which he must report. That, after all, is why he went to the convention. On the way home he has to think up an answer to the query, "Well, what did you do at the convention, Ed?"

Ed is no idiot. He isn't going to go home and say, "Well, most of the time I was in Room 323 drinking whisky sours and gin daisies with Ray and Bill and Mr. Murdoch—and, by the way, have you heard the story of Mae West and the left-handed paperhanger?"

If Ed made a report like that he would never attend another convention. He may have shed all his inhibitions in Buffalo, but by the time he gets to North Tonawanda he carefully replaces them. Ed has to have a story, so on the way home he buys a newspaper and finds out what happened on the floor of the convention.

His eyes may seem a little red, but his views are straight true blue. "Why, Martha," he explains, "on the first day we took up the problem of communism. The state commander made a brilliant address. He took us back to Washington and Jefferson and Franklin Pierce and asked us what any of these men would have done if alien agitators had suggested the overthrow of the American Constitution at the behest of Moscow.

"The next day was mostly committee meetings, and I had to stay up a little late. And on the final day we had a series of patriotic rallies. By a rising vote we adopted the following resolution in regard to patriotism in the American schools."

Ed then reads the resolution, and everything is jake, if he can raise the money, for him to go to the national convention at Miami in the fall.

I speak not from theory but knowledge. Early this afternoon I was invited into a Legion oasis, where there were beverages. I was faithful after my fashion. "I'd love a drink," I explained, "but I think you ought to know that I am a dangerous radical agitator. Or at least I hope to be."

"What do we care about your religion?" said the veteran nearest to the bottles. "Will you take soda or ginger ale with your rye?" I took soda.

STAYED ON TOO LONG

Once, when I was an actor, two fellow members of the cast were sitting in the dressing room discussing my frailties while I was out front doing a monologue. The more kindly of my critics said: "I don't quite agree with you. Heywood is improving—very slowly. But there's one thing he can't ever seem to learn, and that's how to get off the stage." I think that General Hugh S. Johnson's weakness was much like my own. In his passing from official life I must admit a liking for the man even though he seemed to me singularly unfit for the post he held. It was not always so. The general might have retired at the end of the first three or four months in a blaze of glory. He was and still is, I suppose, the best ballyhoo man Washington has ever seen. And I do not regard this as a small gift.

He started on his crusade with an evangelical fervor. He was one-half Billy Sunday and one-half the Captain Flagg of Laurence Stallings' "What Price Glory." Add to this a pinch of Cromwell. There might very well have been more Cromwell and less Sunday. There was no quiet along the Potomac in the early days when General Johnson clattered up and down the great open spaces of the Commerce Building. He was in himself a brigade of cavalry. In those days many of us believed that the artillery could not be far behind. The big guns would arrive in time. The ringing words of General Johnson would be made good by an actual display of force.

The reasons for his retirement are numerous. They have been piling up for months, but the immediate cause seems to be the violent protests against him by union labor, and these protests are well founded.

But let it be remembered that in the beginning General Hugh S. Johnson actually struck terror into the hearts and minds of those men who fall most readily under that easy label "vested interests." He was a Fuzzy-Wuzzy who broke the plutocratic square. Perhaps "broke" is too strong a word. He nicked it. The ranks re-formed, and the general never made a second successful charge.

I am one of those who believe that his intentions were at all times honorable. He failed partly out of ignorance, partly out of a fundamental weakness of character. It didn't take the tough boys very long to find out the general's violence of expression was what the Freudians call "defense mechanism."

He frightened them at first because the performance which he put on as the uncompromising dictator of industry seemed so plausible. Few men are as eloquent as General Johnson when the spirit moves him. He is the best phrase maker of a political generation. Although it was a husky baritone, he could make words sing, and the tune was one of fervor and determination.

I think the newspaper owners were the first to find him out. I believe the code which the publishers gained in Washington was the decisive defeat in the career of General Johnson. It was perhaps his most difficult problem. He had to deal with men who were the masters of public opinion. For just a little while he stood as one of the boldest men in America. For a week, maybe ten days, he took the attitude that he would and could tackle the united force of the American press. Then the newspaper owners began to crack down, and Johnson understood for the first time precisely what that phrase meant. Johnson gave in.

From that day on he was a licked man. There was an emptiness in even the bravest words he uttered.

Perhaps this theory which I advance is over-simplified. Hugh Johnson never understood the psychology or the philosophy of trades unionism. I don't think he was unfriendly, as many labor leaders contended. He was just dumb. He had too much to learn and unlearn.

It cannot be said even now that he is the darling of big business. He swatted his own class vigorously for a time. And though his crusade collapsed, something remained. When the history of this whole period is written I think General Johnson ought to receive credit as an early pioneer in the drive to wipe out that familiar smug slogan, "Nobody is going to tell me how to run my business."

And so over the political grave of Hugh S. Johnson I think somebody might drop a wreath. And also, of course, a dead cat.

NATURE THE COPYCAT

This is the best of all world series because it has set the seal of greatness and authenticity upon the name and fame of Ring Lardner. When the Tigers and the Cardinals met in the first game, or, to be more precise, "clashed in the initial encounter," I had a somewhat personal sorrow. "What a pity," I thought to myself, "that Ring is dead. Just think of the wonders he could work with Dizzy Dean and Daffy Dean and Schoolboy Rowe and Ducky Wucky Medwick."

And I expressed to Edward Angly my feeling that destiny had blundered badly in not arranging to have Ring in the press box as the Deans moved into the box score. "But don't you see," explained Angly, "that Lardner invented Dizzy Dean. Here is Elmer the Great come to life. Could any author ask for more?"

No author could ask for more. It is the supreme triumph to build out of your own head some clearly defined character and then to find the man not only walking the earth but bestriding the headlines. In college I was told that after Goethe wrote "The Sorrows of Werther" suicide became popular in Germany and young men milled about, killing themselves all over the place. Naturally, Goethe must have felt very much complimented. These young men had read his book and taken it to heart. But imitation is not the sincerest form of flattery. I am not thinking of a mere slavish copying of accepted models. After all, millions of girls in America once aped the curls of Mary Pickford, and Miss

Pickford, while a decidedly adequate actress, has never been quite a genius.

The tribute now being paid to Ring Lardner I would rate as greater than that accorded to either Mary or Johann Wolfgang Von Goethe. Lardner never saw Dizzy Dean, and the ace righthander of the Cardinals in all probability never read a line of the American author. Ring took a phrase here and there from ball players with whom he was associated, gave a little closer study to big Ed Walsh, the spitball king of the White Sox, and then mixed his notes with that prophetic thing called inspiration. And then he set upon the printed page a man called Elmer.

I have talked endlessly with baseball writers, who ought to know, about the works of Ring. Naturally, they were all admirers. But there were certain reservations. "It's swell stuff," was the general verdict, "but of course it's a little exaggerated. Modern baseball isn't like that. There couldn't actually be such a mug as Elmer."

These reports were accurate enough. When Lardner limned his famous character no such person existed. The dust was there, and the moisture for the making. But there was need for the breath of life. It has been given to man to make images in the same manner in which he himself was fashioned. Of course, this is not within the power of every man. The miracle is reserved only for the truly creative artist. And that is a phrase which ought to be used sparingly. It is a good trick when a writer can go out and set down with accuracy some living being whom he has observed with fidelity. He holds the mirror up to Nature.

But that is not the furthest reach of literature. There are a few who venture forth and say with divine arrogance: "I see it this way. Let Nature catch up with my conception."

And it is undeniable that life is a copycat and can be bullied into following the master artist who bids it come to heel.

Nor do I think that this extraordinary feat is wholly reserved for the writers of fiction. Pie in the sky may well become tomorrow's earthly manna. I think specifically of Edward Bellamy, long labeled in the American mind as a mere Utopian. And yet some part of his dream has been made good, and more will follow.

But I have no desire to get into the deeper waters. The scope of Lardner's work was probably too limited to make him a likely candidate for enduring fame. Still, posterity has cashed in on longer shots. However, for the moment I will confine myself to the fact that he has scored a startling triumph this side of the days which are without end.

Before there was a Dizzy Dean, Ring knew him from head to pitching cleat. And when the lank righthander pulls the string and lets a fast one go I seem to hear applause from high Olympus. And as the strikes chug by there is one who leans down from the golden bar of Heaven and exclaims, by every right in the universe, " 'Ata workin', Dizzy!"

THE FIRST TRAVELER OF THE LAND

CLEVELAND, Nov. 14.—The man at the Grand Central Terminal noted down the number of my car and berth and, looking over my shoulder, said, "Good evening, Mrs. Roosevelt."

The First Traveler of the Land

In her place in the line stood that inveterate traveler who is sometimes called "The First Lady of the Land." It seemed to me that she was going about her business with far less fuss and swank than anybody could possibly imagine.

One lone policeman stood at the gate, but there was no sign of attendant Secret Service men, and once through the gate Eleanor Roosevelt was on her own.

I was reminded of the fact that some feminine candidates in the last New York State election asserted that it was unfair for the President's wife to go on the stump for a friend, because her power and prestige might distort the issues and influence the minds of voters.

Yet at the beginning of this railroad journey I was struck by the fact that Mrs. Roosevelt neither asked nor received any special favors. And this was not only a compliment to her own unpretentiousness but also to the fundamental democratic feeling of America.

It is unwise, perhaps, to build up towering theories upon small incidents, but I am reënforced in the hope that, in spite of many ominous symptoms, America is not yet ready tinder for any fascist movement. Surely there is no other land in which the wife of the Chief Executive could travel with so little flutter and commotion.

I am not endeavoring to stress the fact that Mrs. Roosevelt is happily possessed of a high degree of ease and independence. This I believe to be the fact, but at the moment I am more concerned with crowd reaction. Any one of two dozen motion picture stars would have created far more stir in the station. In fact, even a minor Hollywood luminary would have been gravely disappointed if her leave-taking had attracted so little notice. And this calm acceptance of the fact that the wife of the President was taking a solitary trip on the 11:40 from New York to St. Louis had nothing to do with any lack of recognition. Even Mary Pickford in her long-curl days was no more easy to spot than Mrs. Roosevelt.

My original conception was heightened and confirmed by breakfast in the diner. The only hint of self-consciousness in the manner of Eleanor Roosevelt is the rapid way in which she strides through Pullmans, and this, I think, is less to be attributed to the fact that she is the wife of the President than to the circumstance that she is a shade aware of her tallness.

The table which she took was just ahead of mine. "Grape-fruit," I said. "Orange juice," was the order of Mrs. Roosevelt. With a certain bitterness I assumed that there would be little breakfast for commoners until she had been served. As a matter of fact, I beat her by thirty seconds on the fruit and by a full minute on the scrambled eggs. The steward sauntered over and said, "Sometimes I read your column with great interest."

I took this as a trade jest and answered, "You know who that woman is who is sitting at the next table?"

"Sure," he replied. "It's Mrs. Roosevelt. She's traveled with us lots of times."

And subsequently he did take occasion to wander over to her table to ask whether the coffee was all right and to remark that it was certainly a most unpleasant morning. But he asked me the same question and made the same observation. The waiter took everything in his stride, and nobody kowtowed or spread out the red carpets. Mrs. Roosevelt was just a fellow traveler.

A little later, in the lounge, the man to my right remarked, "That was Mrs. Roosevelt who just went through." He gave it out merely as a news report. And as another reporter I would like to add that I have not seen any person in the public eye go about her business with less swank and ostentation.

Quite possibly somebody will write in to inquire whether I believe that all the ills of the world will be promptly solved because the wife of the President is exceedingly well mannered. Let me reply now that I do not think so. Nor am I ready to assert that many dangerous trends are now afoot in spite of the fact that the President's wife is a person who manages to be democratic without effort or condescension. I merely say that to me it seems a small but useful indication of the national temper. And can't we let it go at that?

"THE WRECK OF THE *HESPERUS*"

I was a child prodigy myself. That is, at the age of 5 I always required 12-year-old pants. But the present flying squadron of precocious infants leaves me a little cold. In part this is due to ignorance. The inward significance of an I.Q. test is to me mysterious. For instance, one little lad who got by with *magna cum laude* was praised for the assertion that he hated arguments. Now, it does not seem to me that this is a state of mind conducive to future leadership.

As far as my own experience goes, the useful people of the world are not only ready to argue but eager and enthusiastic for the clash of minds. The world is run, and always will be, by those men and women who not only will argue at the drop of a hat but are also prepared to furnish the headgear and the primary propulsion.

If I were the father of a 5-year-old prodigy, which I am not, I would say to the little freak, "Come ahead and argue with me or I'll bat your ears off. Now, now, come on, don't sulk and be sullen. You have the right to set your needs and requirements on the record, and if you insist on keeping your mouth shut I'll lick the life out of you in order to prove to you that you ought to be a free and independent individual."

Of progeny I have but one, and barring the fact that he is a brilliant villain in school theatricals and a competent editorial writer I can see in him no manifestation of extreme precocity. Yet father and son are doing about as well as could be expected, because when I issue orders, ukases and ultimata he answers, "Why?" and is always ready to put up a battle for his privilege of doing whatever he pleases.

In the papers yesterday I find a still more alarming competitor for the title of All-America prodigy. This is a little girl called Theresa McGinty. There is nothing in the story to indicate any kinship to the gentleman who went to the bottom of the sea. Nevertheless, without wanting to seem unchivalrous, I would be inclined to put the little lady at the foot of the whole class of aggressive infants.

According to statistics produced by her proud parents, Miss McGinty could "recite seventy poems and sing nearly fifty popular songs when she was 2 years of age."

I think that word "nearly" is a dead give-away. Who wants to hear a song "nearly" sung or a poem approximated? Even if Miss McGinty could do "Trees" completely at this early age I doubt that I would be amused. There isn't much fun in listening to a child's assertion that Gunga Din is a better man. There isn't much fun any more in hearing anybody recite it. In fact, I would hardly pay 5 cents to be an auditor if Mr. Din himself could be raised from the grave in order to tell us all about his exploit.

If too much bitterness seems to creep into these remarks I must fall back upon the autobiographical assertion that I realize how much pain and anguish I afforded to all concerned in my own infancy. Each Christmas from the age of 1 year up I was trained to deliver, at the foot of the tree, a short poem in German. I didn't like it and, with a few election districts missing, neither did anybody else. But it was a rule and a tradition.

Of course, I always got stuck after the second line and had to be prompted, which didn't help the general hilarity very much. And to my dying day I will remember the peculiarly bleak Christmas festival at which Jack Kirk, a neighbor's boy, was stung by professional jealousy into attempting "The Wreck of the *Hesperus*" on his own account.

Nobody asked him and nobody could stop him. It was the impulse of the moment and he was less than completely prepared. Still he did get through several stanzas and then foundered on the phrase "A frozen corpse was he." He paused for thirty seconds and repeated, "A frozen corpse was he." Some kindly elder tried to get the party going again by applauding and shouting, "That was fine, Jack." But the determined little lad was not to be pushed into the past tense like that. He had started his poem and he was going to stick to it. For the third time he repeated, "A frozen corpse was he." It sort of put a damper on the whole proceedings.

I got a new sled, an orange and a stick of candy, and yet I went to bed that night without much of the usual elation connected with Christmas. The sound of the reindeer and the jolly laughter of the fake Santa Claus, who turned out to be Uncle Fritz, did not ring in my ears as I lay in my tiny crib (I required a 14-year-old size) and waited for the sandman.

He was tardy. He was kept away by another individual who seemed to be clanking up and down the corridors. "A frozen corpse was he."

HOME GIRL MAKES GOOD

Ring out, wild belles! Mrs. Harrison Williams has done it again. She succeeds herself as "the best-dressed woman in the world." Of course, her success is America's success, with possibly an assist being scored for the Paris dressmakers who voted the award. But whatever goes to France, the title remains in America.

I wonder how it feels to be the best-dressed woman in the world. That is one of those things I am never going to know. As far as I can guess, the feeling must be half exaltation and half a sense of responsibility. Personally, I would add to that a little nutmeg.

In the spring of 1906 I received two votes as the best-dressed senior in the graduating class of Horace Mann High School. Richard Weeks Jr. received ninety-eight and was duly elected. Even so, it was too close for comfort, and I have participated in no competition of the sort since.

Still I have some inkling of the strain under which Mrs. Harrison Williams must live. While I was running for Best-Dressed Senior in the graduating class of Horace Mann High School I often spent as much as three or four minutes in the morning deciding which pants I ought to wear. The gray or the blue? The blue or the gray? I generally decided to take the ones which possessed the closest approach to a crease.

Picking a necktie was the great ordeal. I had six, five of which were birthday presents. That took a bit of doing. Naturally I couldn't wear the orange one with the purple spots every day in the year, and yet in my eyes there really was no substitute.

But I mustn't try to push Mrs. Harrison Williams out of the picture. She, too, had problems which she was compelled to solve in order to win the title of "best-dressed woman in the world." Some folk who do not understand the psychology of dress will be cynical and say that the title goes to whichever little lady spends the most money at the best shops. I will admit that the odds would be at least four or five to one against anybody who tried to capture the championship by wearing little things she just ran up on the machine in her spare moments. But we cannot dismiss the factor of good taste. Next to good credit it is almost everything in the matter of being well turned out.

Ill-informed critics seem to think that it is merely a matter of so many frocks for evening wear. They overlook rough-age. The well-dressed woman will come out on the grouse moors on a braw day all bundled up in some sort of wind-breaker which a Dartmouth student would hesitate to wear to a freshman beer night. There's the art of the good dressmaker. He or she can make his or her client look chic for those occasions where there's some sense in being chic and hardboiled as all outdoors when that effect is called for.

For years I have been preaching that a dissonance in dress is not sloppiness but a new art form. Of course I am not the discoverer of this fact. Herrick mentioned the matter in a poem—"A slight disorder in the dress," &c., &c.—and there used to be a Bohemian poet in the village who hired a friend to wear his collars for the first six days. But if you want calculated carelessness today you must pay the price to those who know how to put creases in the wrong places.

No story of the rousing victory of Mrs. Harrison Williams would be complete without mention of the gallantry of the runner-up. Princess Sixte de Bourbon Parma lost by less than a length. Her handicap is discreetly mentioned in a United Press dispatch which says:

"The Princess Sixte, whose husband died recently, is still in mourning, but this spring will wear gray and black and white. Her mourning even now is of the smartest kind, and she is as distinguished in it as she was in her former gay attire."

You can understand her problem. Indeed, in fantasy I am sitting by the transom of the boudoir. Stella, the French maid, has just gone into the closet and come out with something done in black ostrich feathers, jet beads and a small pink bow on the right shoulder. Madame is furious. "Non, non, Stella," she says in perfect French, "I would be more triste."

"It looks pretty sad to me," says Stella in her blunt Gallic way.

"My heart is breaking," says the Princess Sixte with great dignity, "and already I am late for my fitting. Anything at all will do and particularly that little knickknack which came from the shop this morning." And with that she flounces out.

You've got to hand it to the Princess Sixte de Bourbon Parma. Under a strain like that I think she did magnificently to finish in the money.

THERE ISN'T ANY SANTA CLAUS

Almost any day now *The Sun* will reprint the letter from a little girl about Santa Claus and what the editor said in reply. I am sorry I can't remember the names. This annual tribute to Santa Claus has always left me cold, and I grow more chilly to the piece as the years roll on.

In the first place, the little girl showed a reasonable degree of skepticism. She was just about ready to throw off the shackles of an old myth.

The editor clamped them on again. He didn't tell her the truth. Possibly this bad precedent may account for many editorials on other subjects which have appeared from time to time in various papers.

I am all for legends and fairy stories and ancient customs. A folk story is generally true in spirit no matter how fantastic its details. It is a sort of parable built upon the accumulated wisdom of the ages.

But I have a grievance against the figure called Santa Claus. Unlike most myths, the tale of the old gentleman and his reindeer glorifies an untruth. It warps the minds of the very young with a most pernicious notion. To be sure, the average girl or boy finds out the fake about the age of 3 or 4. The child of 6 who still believes in Santa Claus I would set down as definitely backward.

But even after the literal belief is gone there lingers in the mind a yearning for some other sort of Santa Claus. Oppressed people of various kinds sometimes go from the cradle to the grave without registering any adequate protest against their lot. They are waiting for the sound of the sleigh bells. Santa Claus will come down the chimney and bestow those rights and necessities which they lack. He may be the inspired leader, or he is sent in the guise of some governmental agency or act of legislation.

Naturally, it would be folly to deny that leadership and legislation may nick deeply into many problems, and for my own part I do believe in a paternalistic government. Even so complete reliance should not be placed on any of these three factors or even on them all in combination. There isn't any Santa Claus. Groups of men and woman can obtain their hopes and desires only by massing together and going out to fight and agitate for their objectives. It is far more satisfactory to pick an orange directly from the tree than to find it in the toe of your stocking.

Harsh names are hurled at those who go out telling little children that Santa Claus is a fake. These disciples of the whole truth are called cynical and crabbed and spoilsports. But man must find out sooner or later that he stands on his own feet and this information might as well come early rather than late.

If anybody intrusted a baby to my tender care I would spring the truth about Santa Claus the instant the child could walk. I'd say, "And now, fine fellow, you have achieved the art of locomotion. You can go just as far and as fast as your feet will carry you. Forget about the reindeer. They make indifferent draft animals and singularly tough steak. Let me hear no nonsense out of you about Santa Claus. You and I are rational human beings up to the extent of our ability, I hope."

I even wonder whether children do get a great deal of fun out of the old gentleman in the sleigh. No very warm memories linger in my mind. He gave me a wakeful night once a year. Always I waited with rather more fear than anticipation for the sound of his fat belly scraping down the chimney. It gave me a sense of insecurity. If Santa Claus could sneak up on me in that way so might the bogey man, or any evil witch of whom I had read in the fairy books.

As a matter of fact, it was my annual inclination to sell Santa Claus short. My invariable bet was that his gifts would be disappointing. You see, I took the story very literally. It was said that Santa Claus would be lavish and generous with only those children who were very good and had a year's record of complete compliance to all the orders of their elders. No wonder I was bearish on the entire proposition!

In childhood, as in later life, everybody hopes for more than he is likely to get—particularly if the gifts are to be dropped in his lap. The Santa Claus myth has made for more disappointment than joy, if you look over the statistics very carefully. I know of many districts in the large and crowded cities where the old gentleman couldn't muster as much as a single vote. Of course, from my point of view, it would be better to hold the election the day after Christmas rather than the night before.

The question may be asked, "After we have shot Santa

Claus what can be put in his place?" I think we don't need a single figure. How about just centering the spirit of the day around the factor of universal fellowship? Not one Santa Claus but a hundred million!

ICE AND EAGLES

WASHINGTON, Jan. 29.—The pottage which they are serving hereabouts has fallen off in quality. The brand that is offered now goes under the curious label, "something just as good." Men in high position gaze in bewilderment at strangers who grow excited and say, "But don't you remember that the section said . . ." At this point all the keepers of the eagle blink wearily and answer, "We are busy men. Don't waste our time. Please be realistic."

The days of 1933 are done. That was the age of fire, but now the glaciers have come down along the banks of the Potomac. As an occasional visitor to the nation's capital I can remember as if it were yesterday the period when the world was being made over.

Men ran, not walked, along the interminable corridors of the Commerce Building, and each and every one had a look about him of dedication. God was in his heaven and "idealism" remained in the dictionary. There was even talk of cracking down great palisades in the economic structure of the United States.

And now in these same corridors and offices men say, "But let's be practical!" They do not raise their voices as they did once in speaking of plans and projects. In fact, above the conversation one can sometimes hear the clank of ghosts rattling their chains cheerlessly. And why not, for these are the rooms where many bright aspirations have died. And some, perhaps, were done to death.

Washington is now the city of a dream that was. Its motto has become, "We Do the Best We Can." And I think this is always a defeatist sort of talk, for it seems to me that those things which can be done are never carried out. It is the history of human beings that mankind never accomplishes anything but the impossible. The same civilization which has created machines capable of flying across the broad Atlantic has never produced anything competent to open the window in a Pullman.

Of all the various sects in the city only the tribe is faithful to its ancient ideals of 1933. Mark Sullivan and the members of his clan are still maintaining that the administration is racing Hades-bent for socialism. But Mr. Sullivan, I fear, is one who would impose traffic laws upon the turtles and ask the snail to moderate his reckless progress.

The plain truth of the matter is that the movement which was once known as the Roosevelt revolution turns out to be a carousel for kiddies. And in the big tent of NRA the patrons ride the horses and the zebras about the circuit. Some of the passengers play the game avidly because the signs all say that there is a brass ring which may be snatched by some fortunate one who will be handsomely rewarded.

And occasionally the trophy falls to one of the devoted dervishes, but when he comes up to the booth to claim his boon he is informed that as a reward for his industry he may go right back to the carousel again and be taken for another ride.

On the whole, defeats cause less woe than victories. This Washington of the glacial period becomes animated only when the news is bruited about that somebody has won something under NRA. When that happens the sirens sound and the police, the fire department, the cavalry and the tanks are sent to take it right away from him.

Nobody need worry any more that Washington is going left. Indeed, nobody need worry that the Washington of today is going anywhere.

THE MAN WHO CAME BACK

John Puckering, a market gardener of Arley, England, died the other day and came back to tell about it. On the whole he regretted his return. It seems to me fair to say that John Puckering was dead. He was pronounced dead by the doctors. He lay upon an operating table, and for 150 seconds there was not the slightest sign of a quiver in his heart. Dr. Mills massaged the heart, and after two minutes and a half it began to beat again. John Puckering is back among the quick and growing cabbages.

In all his fifty-eight years nobody paid very much attention to Mr. Puckering. "How are the carrots and the onions?" some customer may have inquired, but nobody was interested in his ideas about the empire and still less his conception of the cosmos. I fear a little that John Puckering may have returned to a somewhat impaired artistry. From now on one can hardly expect him to suffer agonies over the life and death of eggplant or young radishes.

Even when he meets the select few of the world who have flown the broad Atlantic the market gardener of Arley has a right to smile in a superior way, for he has crossed over the vast expanse of Jordan River. Columbus was a recluse and Marco Polo no more than a hitch-hiker compared to Puckering.

It is true that the report which he gives of the life beyond is a trifle vague and shadowy. "It was," he says, "as though I were looking into a great place, something like a hall, though I cannot recall having seen either ceiling or walls. There was a good light, and I saw crowds of people. So many were there they seemed like a multitude at a football match."

It may be that heavens of infinite variety are provided for all the elect. The paradise of Puckering does not precisely suit my fancy. When I go to my just reward I do not wish to be a part of any football crowd and hear the cherubim and seraphim continually cry out that they are going back to Nassau Hall.

It would hardly be heaven for a Harvard man to find himself bound through all eternity to the gloomy prospect of watching his team furnish mincemeat for the Tigers. Nor is it soul-satisfying to contemplate the everlasting snake dance of the Princeton lads down through the jasper streets and up to the golden bar of heaven. Who wants to be a Cambridge angel and under compulsion to tread featly among the half-pint flasks of the victors?

But the rest of the testimony of John Puckering, of Arley and the Hereafter, is much more comforting.

"The people stood in a circle," he says, "and I noticed

that there were no children among them. They looked natural, with healthy faces, and they appeared to be dressed as on earth."

All of that is swell by me. Existence would be more restful if I were not so constantly summoned from my work to the telephone to hear a piping and an eager voice say, "Papa, I want $2 straight on Boom's Pal in the seventh race at Hialeah. A dollar on Our Mae at New Orleans in the fourth. That's on the nose, too. And 50 cents on Sweet Chariot to show in the eighth at Santa Anita."

"Dressed as on earth" also has its attractions. The blue suit and the brown which I have now are adequate, and to me the thought of wings and a long white robe has always been alienating. I would prefer, again, to walk all over God's heaven in the black shoes I now possess. I've broken them in. It would be a nuisance to have to ask some other angel to wear my sandals for the first two weeks.

"I was deeply impressed with the happiness which shone in their faces and which was so intense that I felt as though I should not have minded joining them."

Spoken, John Puckering, like an old Puritan and a true one. The most that the sight of joy could raise in him was a sense of acquiescence. Possibly, for the first time in his life, he was moved to feel that one could be both happy and respectable.

Perhaps somebody may ask whether I believe that John Puckering, of Arley, went to heaven for 150 seconds. I hope so, but how can I tell? All I know is that he was dead. Where was he? There must be somewhere the land of happy faces. At least there ought to be!

A RIDE WITH ROOSEVELT

Washington is looking for a new slogan and thinks that maybe it has been discovered. Any administration which can get three or four months to the slogan is doing pretty well. The newest one will be built around the assertion which Mr. Moffett, of FHA, made to the President. He assured him that the depression was over, "but the country doesn't know it yet." I offer without charge, "Pinch yourself and see if you're prosperous."

But I don't want to stand behind any such advice. There are too many dressed in rags and other fabrics which would come apart under any pinching process. And there are too many millions who will still be unemployed no matter how hard they try to convince themselves that the whole thing is a nightmare.

Yet there are quarters where the pinching might be very effective in restoring a placid mind. Mark Sullivan, for instance, could easily assure himself that Roosevelt isn't turning Socialist after all. Ogden Mills, "Spirit of 1776" and "Disgruntled Patriot" need only start their circulation going in order to find out that none of the violently radical things which they feared the administration might do are in the picture any more. In fact, if I were an entrenched capitalist I'd leave a call for 8 in the morning on the theory that once again the call has come for Privilege to prance it as Queen of the May.

Money, I've been told, isn't everything, and there may be something in what they say. Certainly the very rich have slight capacity for contentment. They always ask for more. Even when their cup runneth over they continue to complain. And, seemingly, there is sincerity in their wailing and gnashing of teeth. It is still possible to find industrialists who honestly believe that President Roosevelt is going to slap them around in one way or another. Viewing with alarm gets to be a habit.

Big business is not content with the change in Presidential practices. It also requires that even those precepts which have been worn transparent should be abandoned. There must be a new slogan. And it will have to be something about recovery. "Readjustment" has been "withdrawn for revision," which is the polite way of saying that Cain's big white horses are stampeding at the stage door.

About the best which can be said is that it was quite a ride we had. The temperature was low and the snow upon the steppes hard-packed and white. Possibly that explains why some of the boys thought the New Deal sleigh was headed straight for Moscow. They forgot the wolves who always furnish way stations for the travelers.

Fast went the sleigh, but still the wolves surrounded it and yipped in unison about the Constitution and Thomas Jefferson. Presently the driver threw them a liberal. But he was caviar to the pack, and their howls redoubled. In the beginning the key men were tossed out one by one. It was hoped that General Johnson might be tough enough to stay the hungry animals for a little, but he proved no more than lunch spread for sandwiches.

On came the wolves, and on and on. They wanted red meat, their appetite being whetted. For a time the experiment was tried of tossing out not men but New Deal planks and labor boards and codes. Had these been hewn of oak or ebony they might have proved a problem for the lupine molars. Things being as they were the wolves soon shredded them into penny willow whistles.

Nobody ever thought of giving the wolves a smart cut with the whip, and still less of pumping lead into them. The beasts must be placated. This was to be a partnership. Indeed, on several occasions the sleigh came to a halt while the driver called out, "Any wolf who really wants to reform and will promise to be a good wolf and quit rapaciousness can come in the sleigh and ride with us." Quite a number accepted the invitation.

The driver seldom looked around and it may be that he is really puzzled about the disappearance of the buffalo robe. Even some of the shivering passengers profess to think he was deceived. But so were they. Maybe it was the fault of the horse. He ran like mad and made a perfect circle. The sleigh drew up before a well-remembered door.

"Why," said the driver, "we're back where we started. But just the same the ride was very bracing. We must try it again some day."

CHARLES EVANS HUGHES AS PORTIA

It is the unanimous decision of this column that Chief Justice Hughes has given the finest performance of Portia ever seen in this country. And, for that matter, Justice Mc-Reynolds was no slouch as Shylock.

As in the famous case in Venice, the issue hinged upon

a bond. The Venetian litigation took up a pound of flesh, while the Washington controversy was concerned with "25.8 grains of gold nine-tenths fine." But in each instance the issue was drawn as to the sanctity of the last drop of blood and the last ounce of gold.

The opinion read by James Clark McReynolds, of Tennessee, and that delivered by Mr. Shylock, Wrong-Side-of-the-Tracks, Venice, Italy, were strikingly similar. The Southerner and the Semite both contended that a contract was a contract no matter what damage and what suffering its execution might entail. The court, they contended, should limit itself to the simple question, "Is it in the bond?" "That's all," they said, "one needs to know."

From a strictly legalistic point of view, I think it must be admitted that McReynolds and Shylock were more logical than Portia and Hughes. The Chief Justice and the lady approached the problem in somewhat devious fashion. Neither one was quite bold enough to say that circumstances may alter contracts and that agreements must be bent and molded according to the public weal. In regard to the government's own obligations Chief Justice Hughes followed the reasoning of Portia very closely. Both said to the litigant in effect, "Of course, your bond is sacred and binding, but just try to collect it and see what that'll get you."

It would, perhaps, be a little less than accurate to say that Chief Justice Hughes spat upon McReynolds' gabardine. But, at any rate, he made him good and sore. Spectators in the court of last appeal heard for the first time a stump speech from the bench when the learned Justice from Tennessee departed from his script to declaim, "The Constitution as we have known it is gone."

It is rather lucky for Mr. Justice McReynolds that he made that crack before any of the pending sedition bills are passed. He might, under proposed legislation, be jugged as one attempting to cast doubt upon the wisdom and integrity of the highest tribunal in the land, which is the safeguard of our liberties. After all, Justice McReynolds got away more easily than precedent would sanction. Nobody took away his property and condemned him to be a Christian.

When I was in school the teacher said that while "The Merchant of Venice" was an interesting play, Shakespeare's interpretation of the law was flimsy and inaccurate. That may have been true then, for the Minnesota mortgage case and that litigation regarding the Georgia utilities company had not yet been considered by the nine old gentlemen in Washington. Shakespeare merely ruled somewhat ahead of his time. After a lapse of more than 300 years the Supreme Court is just beginning to catch up with him.

Portia and Chief Justice Hughes were both unconsciously motivated by their economic position. Shakespeare was shrewd enough to "class-angle" his heroine. She might quite probably have argued just the other way if the appellant had been anybody else than Shylock. She was dealing not with a proletarian issue but merely a nasty squabble between two profiteers.

Nor can it be said that the present five to four decision by the United States Supreme Court is a ringing declaration that from now on the Constitution shall cease to be a straitjacket but a more roomy garment, allowing full play to present and pressing human needs. And, even so, I find in this closely drawn verdict some crumbs of comfort for progressives. I seem to see a tiny fissure in that great Chinese wall called Property Rights which has been set up to keep us all away from human rights.

A bond is a bond. All right, so be it. But the time may come when it is something else. An intolerable human burden, for instance.

I am wondering, for instance, if Cordell Hull can continue to maintain with a straight face that the Soviet government had no right to outlaw those obligations incurred by Kerensky in his effort to stifle the Russian revolution.

THE DEATH OF A HAITIAN

"There seems," said Westbrook Pegler in a recent column, "to be a fundamental vulgarity about capital punishment which cannot be escaped no matter how esthetes may strive to render it attractive."

Peg was speaking of Hitler's hatchet men, and I think his observation is profoundly true. But I would like to note one exception. I am against all forms of capital punishment, but if I am ever on the spot where I must stand and can choose that form of execution which is least degrading I would select the firing squad.

A good many years ago I received an assignment to report a death house story in Sing Sing. I broke the code of my craft by asking to be excused, and Arthur Ruhl covered the electrocution. He was back in New York after a long stay in Mexico during troublous times. I saw him in the afternoon some hours after he had watched the victim die at dawn.

"I don't blame you now for dodging," he said. "It was pretty messy. I have seen a great many people killed, but this was much worse than I expected. It is cleaner in Mexico. You don't mind it so much when a man stands up in front of a wall under the morning sun and sky. It seems more honorable."

Although I do not speak from experience, I have collected from time to time secondhand testimony which convinces me that the firing squad remains the best method which humankind has hit upon for purposes of liquidation. In spite of my principles I once heard of an execution in which I would not have minded taking a part on either side. A gentleman in Haiti told me with some pride the manner in which his grandfather happened to get shot.

"My grandfather," he explained, "was a candidate for President. There were two others running for that office, and the battles back in the hills lasted for several months. By that time all sides had suffered numerous deaths and casualties, and a conference was arranged. By common agreement it was decided that my grandfather was entitled to the election. The war was over.

"The old gentleman was a fool or an idealist as you choose. He started from the hills to ride to Port au Prince to be inaugurated. But he neglected to bring his army. He traveled light, accompanied by a single mule and one aid, who was the prospective Secretary of War. In a lonely pass his former foes entrapped him. With proper politeness he was informed that the gentleman's agreement had been voided. He was not to be President of Haiti, after all. His rivals purposed to remove him from the race immediately.

The Death of a Haitian

"My grandfather took this decision with good grace. He readily admitted that he had been criminally careless in starting for the capital without his army. But he asked his adversaries to grant him one request. For a period, however brief, he had been the de facto President of the island. Haiti, as a land of fine tradition, could not afford to let an ex-executive be shot in muddy riding breeches and an old khaki shirt.

"The stay which he requested need not be one of long duration. Only a few miles back, another aid, the Secretary of the Navy, was proceeding with a mule and a leather trunk containing my grandfather's dress uniform. He asked the indulgence of being shot in garb which was fitting to his temporary estate.

"This seemed fair enough to the other presidential candidates, and they sat down at the edge of a grove to smoke and swap reminiscences of the late unpleasantness. The sun was not yet high, and the time passed almost like magic as each of the three generals admitted tactical errors in the conduct of the campaign.

"Presently the mule came 'round the bend, and my grandfather quickly changed into his dress uniform of gold and scarlet. Cigarets he had, but he lacked a match and borrowed one from his nearest rival. With steady hand he took a light, inhaled deeply twice and said, 'Gentlemen, I am ready.' There was a roll of musketry, and he fell at the foot of the tree of reminiscence. Honor was satisfied all around. There were no complaints. It was merely what you in America call a recount."

CHARLES A. BEARD

ATLANTIC CITY, N. J., Feb. 26.—I have seen nothing more dramatic than the substance and the manner of Charles A. Beard's attack upon William Randolph Hearst. Undoubtedly the effect was heightened by the fact that this was a teaching group meeting sedately on a Sunday afternoon abaft the Boardwalk in the Rose Room.

I am aware that Uncle Charlie, as he is known to educators, is the dean of American historians, but I gravely suspect that there is actor blood in his ancestral line. It was my assignment to play the stooge for Dr. Beard. This was not a plot. My only advance information was that the old gentleman would make a set address on educational problems and that toward the end he would say something "fairly direct" about Mr. Hearst.

Accordingly, I did a Maxie Rosenbloom, and although I pawed once or twice in the direction of San Simeon, I let nothing fly from the shoulder. In spite of the characteristic flaw that grave things were treated lightly, it was a pretty fair speech until Uncle Charlie got warmed up and made it seem as pale as the ghost of Hamlet's father.

For that matter, the professor himself began a little apologetically. He was an old man and not sufficiently nimble witted to speak extemporaneously after the manner of his brilliant friend the young newspaper columnist from New York. And after a little more mendacious matter of the same sort Uncle Charlie announced that he would be compelled to stick to the paper which he had written on the historical approach to education.

He rattled a sheaf of prepared pages ominously and proceeded mildly enough to outline the theory that teaching ought to be "a scholarly, balanced presentation of the facts."

But at this point the old historian, who once met General Grant and didn't like him, looked up from his manuscript. In addition to actor blood I think that maybe Uncle Charlie has in him a strain of American bald eagle. He gave the moment its slight dramatic pause as he seemed to be sighting some moving object on a mountain peak many miles away. And then he said slowly, "Some people, I am told, don't want this kind of teaching—among them William Randolph Hearst."

It reminded me of Madison Square Garden and the instant when a man from Maine mentioned the Ku Klux Klan by name for the first time in the Democratic convention. Other people had hinted and suggested, but Uncle Charlie said "William Randolph Hearst" right out, just like that. And he continued to point.

"An enemy of everything that is noblest and best in our American tradition." "No person with intellectual honesty or moral integrity will touch him with a ten-foot pole." "Only cowards can be intimidated by Hearst."

I began to wonder what my friend had meant when he said that the old gentleman would say something "fairly direct" about Mr. Hearst. But I didn't have much chance to wonder because I was up on my feet cheering with the rest.

Teachers and school superintendents and deans do not differ from other people under exciting stimuli. A professor of mathematics was standing on his chair whistling through two fingers. A chemistry teacher in the center aisle was leaping two feet off the ground every time Dr. Beard stuck the knife into the editor again. All but three people out of a possible 900 seemed intent upon hitting the sawdust trail.

And the dean of American historians had not once raised his voice. He dealt with William Randolph Hearst in as dispassionate and detached a manner as he might have used in discussing the failings of some Iroquois chief now dead and gone. And when he was done he said, "I have made copies of my remarks if the gentlemen of the press are interested, so that there need be no mistake about what I have said."

I must insist that under any definition of news which I have ever heard it is distinctly news when Uncle Charlie leaves his Connecticut farm to thrust a straight, a steady and an accusing finger in the face of William Randolph Hearst. But, with a few honorable exceptions, American newspapers either spiked the whole speech, as too hot to handle, or decided that Dr. Charles A. Beard, dean of American historians, was fit for their columns only after the most radical sort of censorship.

And this, too, I suppose, is a part of "The Freedom of the Press."

MR. JUSTICE HOLMES

Mr. Justice Holmes almost rounded out the century, and the circumstance of his great age was one of the factors which made him important to the modern world. He served as a constant reminder that most of the things called out-landish and new-fangled had been a part of human thought in the years which were gone before.

Decidedly it was a healthy thing to have on the Supreme bench a man who touched the tradition of Thoreau and Emerson, at first hand. He was not one to be moved into sudden panic by the prospect of change, because in ninety-three years he had seen so much of it.

Had Oliver Wendell Holmes served on until that noon when Justice McReynolds announced in trembling tones the destruction of the Constitution I rather think that Justice Holmes might have been a shade amused. He would have regarded the diatribe of the Tennesseean as one of those groundless panics which often seize upon the young.

There was something a little strange in having a man thrice wounded in the Civil War passing upon the problems of utility corporations which rendered services unknown during the youth of Mr. Justice Holmes. The economic setup in which Holmes was born had been all but swept away by the time he began to render his great decisions and his great dissents.

And yet in some respects the march of events indicated no forward progress whatsoever. Certain aspects of American life moved merely in circles. The soldier of Fredericksburg retired only a little while before the Scottsboro case was up before the court. Mr. Justice Holmes saw the rise and the fall of populism and progressivism. He rendered judgment in such litigation which was hailed by many as making a new nation or wrecking an old one. And when neither thing happened it may well be that Oliver Wendell Holmes buried himself a little deeper in the Latin poets and arrived at the notion that the United States Supreme Court was set on a plane somewhat lower than the throne of God.

I do not mean to say that he was not concerned with the dignity, the honor and the integrity of the body on which he served, but in very many of his decisions he steered clear of the conception that a final legislative veto has been intrusted into the hands of nine wise men. Certainly he did not favor any strait-jacket conception of the Constitution. He supported only those denials in which he felt that some specific prohibition of the act in question could be found. The silence of the Constitution always seemed to him to imply consent.

Much has been made of the dissenting opinions of Mr. Justice Holmes, and I venture to say that an examination of these opinions will find the court just about catching up with his point of view. But Oliver Wendell Holmes was by no means habitually a deviationist. His mind kept a little ahead of the trend of the times, but, like the rest of humankind, he was motivated and touched by his own social background and by the temper of the land in which he lived. I have always felt that during the great war he lost touch for a time with his own liberal philosophy. The bugles and the drums stirred in him old memories and opened ancient wounds.

But in his seventies and eighties there was more elasticity in Holmes than was resident in younger men. He had made a fast recovery from the bullets of the Civil War. Just so the shrapnel fragments of the later conflict did not permanently affect him.

It would be foolish to say that Oliver Wendell Holmes was a radical at any stage of his career, but he did fight for the free field of complete human expression. And, curiously enough, it was in his latest years that he seemed most receptive to those ideas which some call dangerous.

Certainly his cronies in the last decade were recruited from the ranks of men upon whom much of the force of the vigilante drive has fallen. I have particularly in mind the close association of Felix Frankfurter and the Justice. Men were welcome in the house of Holmes who never appear in Hearst editorial pages, save grotesquely pictured as wearing whiskers and bearing bombs. Perhaps the Justice remembered back to the day when Thoreau rebuked Emerson for staying out of jail.

"The riders in a race do not stop short when they reach the goal. There is a little finishing canter before coming to a standstill."

This was part of the last public utterance of Oliver Wendell Holmes before he took his gear and went before the judges to weigh in. And since the racing metaphor is his own, I think it is not inappropriate to say that on the chart against the name of Holmes should run the familiar caption, "Closed fast."

NEW LAMPS FOR OLD

Place a rat within a maze and he will not remain forever fuddled. After he has scampered down blind alleys several times and come against dead ends he will begin to learn the lesson of the labyrinth and come at last into the way of freedom.

Man does not show a similar aptitude. With brazen stupidity he insists upon a lacerating journey through the wire and into trenches where the grass has hardly yet had time to heal the scars of shellfire. And he orchestrates his folly with a roll of drums, the blare of bands and patriotic speeches.

Senators, great editors and holy men who speak through radio pounce eagerly upon all existing international machinery for peace and cry that it should be scrapped because of its antiquity and ineffectiveness. And yet these same men continually do cry for the modernization of every implement of war.

I would not hold in my heart such bitterness for those who killed the League and later stabbed the Court to death if any one of them had mentioned a single substitute for the devices which they so wantonly destroyed.

To be sure, they brayed of "isolation," but that's an alley choked already with the dead of young America. And "preparedness" was mentioned even in the very shadow of the white crosses which bear testimony that here is one more dead end in the experience of the nations.

When we scrap a battleship we lay two keels to take its place, but the demolition of any machinery set up for making international peace is accompanied with no new sowing. In those fair fields we scatter the ashes of lost ideals and sterilize the earth with such salt cynicism as "Let them stew in their own juice."

And already the bitter broth begins to bubble and fills the corridors of the world with its deadly fumes. Oh, yes, "let them stew in their own juice," but that juice is the lifeblood of all mankind, and it is thicker than the mountains and deeper than the seas which are supposed to assure us a private prosperity and a separate peace.

We are the chosen of the Lord, and in our self-anoint-ment we dream that by the simple device of never lifting a finger for fellowship we can remain secure upon our lofty plateau even though the watchfires dance upon the rim of our horizon. Moses smote the rock before the waters gushed forth, but we are to be safe and sanctified through inertia and the grumbling negation of a Cain rejecting the respon-sibility of brotherhood.

Look well, you Coughlins and you Hearsts, upon this world in which you ask us to disclaim all citizenship. Al-ready the tramping of the millions across the sea sets up a tremor in the wheat fields of Nebraska. And we are to save the world from the great delusion by keeping our pow-der dry and training our youth in the art of war!

I am told that in a prison a single inmate sometimes begins to pound a spoon against his metal dish and that presently the whole tier and then the furthermost corridors of the jail will be engulfed in the din as all within the walls are drawn into the mad rite, not even knowing why. There is just such horrid magic in the beating of a drum.

The League of Nations was a poor thing, and the World Court represented little more than a feeble groping for some new way among the nations. It was easy to point out the flaws and even the dangers in this machinery of peace. Will Rogers was very comical and Father Coughlin very pious. We rejected foreign entanglements and pinned our faith again in Bethlehem, Pa.

Down the blind alley of preparedness and self-sufficiency we scamper once again. The old roads have failed tragically, and, even so, we have not yet set foot upon any new path of freedom. "New gas, new guns, new airplanes"—this is the inspiration of the statesmen.

But let us cry "No!" If the old League was bad, all the more we must set about the building of a new one. If the Court could not function, then we must create one which can. In time of war we must prepare for peace.

There must be some way, and it is not the way of the gunmaker or the manufacturer of munitions. Now, this very instant, we must join all the peoples of the world in raising a cry to build not ships or shells, but some giant plow to furrow under the teeth of all the dragons.

HARVARD INDIFFERENCE

Harvard should take something for its sense of humor. Indeed, it would not be too drastic if some of the undergraduates were to lose their kiddie-kar privileges for at least a month. According to the news reports, the peace demonstration at Cambridge was pretty much broken up by more than 2,000 members of the Michael Mullins Chowder and Marching Club.

"The Mullins group," says the *Herald Tribune* story, "paraded the yard and the purlieus of Cambridge in true imperial German style—goose stepping, giving the straight-arm salute made popular by Adolf Hitler, and singing war songs. . . . All shouted 'Heil! Down with peace! We want cannon!' and other slogans until the university and Cambridge police put an end to the festivities.

"John Roosevelt, youngest son of the President, was among the supporters of the jokesters. He appeared amused at the vain efforts of the anti-war strikers to keep their meeting going in the face of such hilarious opposition."

I gather, therefore, that the object of the Mullins march was one of mockery, and that the cry of "Down with peace! We want cannon!" was intended to be awfully, awfully funny. But I would not call it hilarious. Rather, here was horror heaped on horror. It was as if the hangman's son were playing with a noose of thread. Not hilarity but hysteria was the note which was sounded by those voices. Two thousand strong they cried aloud: "It isn't true. It can't be so that anyone would mark and number our young bodies for the burning. That is the monstrous dream of an idiot and fair meat for a Hasty Pudding charade."

"Heil!" shouted the members of the Mullins Chowder and Marching Club, and there was, I suspect, almost a treble note of terror in the cry of "We want cannon!" They scoff at guns who never felt the earth tremble under the drum of a barrage.

"How heavy your guns are tonight, Mr. Mars. For what do you make preparation?"

"The better to bayonet you, my dears. You'll have to put your foot upon his chest before you draw that blade out right. That man behind you moans. He's still alive. Mop up, you fools, and leave not one behind you who, in his last agony, might toss a grenade."

Once I saw a soldier do a tap dance in front of his own wire until the machine gunners cut him down. He had mixed fear and brandy, and when he laughed it was not amusing.

There is, of course, the urge in all of us to delay the facing of reality. In our youth we cling to myths and legends in which the giants and the dragons of the world are pictured as pushovers for all little folk who live in the shadow of the beanstalk. And as we outgrow this fear we put on other armor of lighter metal and raise up to protect our hearts a certain shield called "the humorous approach." The device is a cap and bells set upon a field of motley. And you will find followers of this strange device even in the trenches of the front line. We who are about to die salute the zero hour with verse and chorus of "Hinkey Dinkey Parlez Vous." If a man must tremble in the early dawn, let him pretend that he is rocked with laughter.

But it is well that the quality and inspiration for this

mirth should always be sharply understood by all who hear its fearful cackle. I would have the men of the Mullins Marching Club take thought, now that their panicky jubilation has subsided. Eighteen years ago other undergraduates paraded through the Harvard yard gripped in the fervor of the coming war. They were perhaps a shade less larky than the present generation. To them there had been sold a last crusade which was to make all future conflict impossible.

Nor did they cry "We want cannon!" They knew full well that the munitions makers of the world strove night and day to fulfill all the requirements in this respect.

The goose step of today under the elms was an echo of the tramping feet of eighteen years ago. And each humorist set his boot down where one had marched before. The rains and snows have obliterated the marks of Harvard, 1917. And of that band many have not and will not walk again past the entries of Hollis and Holworthy.

And so the Mullins march wasn't really very funny, after all. Even through the din there must have been some whisper of compelling voices from far off saying, "Weep for us. We are your comrades. We are the Harvard dead who died for a lost illusion."